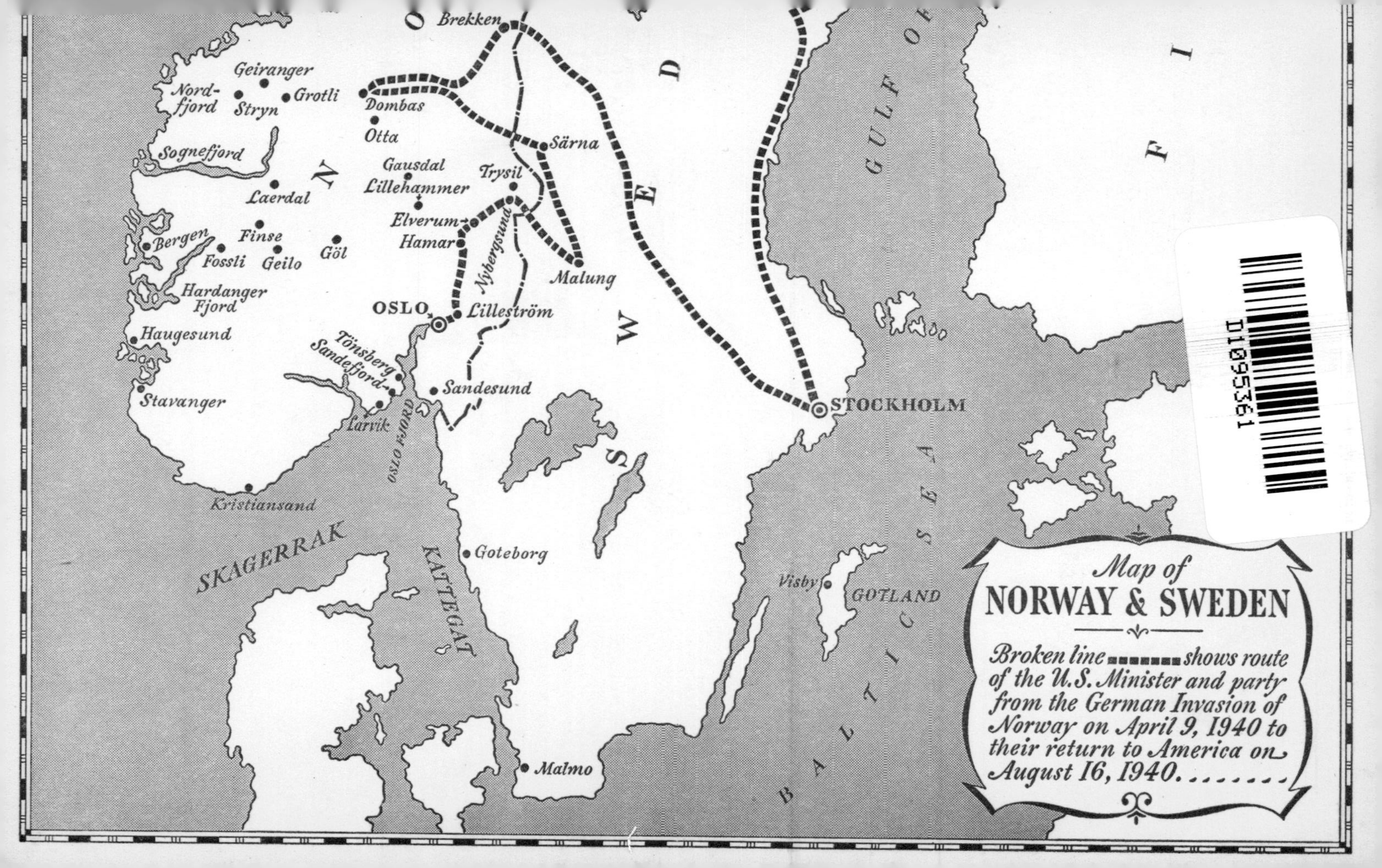

Map of
NORWAY & SWEDEN
Broken line shows route of the U.S. Minister and party from the German Invasion of Norway on April 9, 1940 to their return to America on August 16, 1940.
Brekken
Geiranger
Nord-fjord
Stryn
Grotli
Dombas
Otta
Sognefjord
Gausdal
Lillehammer
Trysil
Särna
Laerdal
Elverum
Hamar
Bergen
Finse
Fossli
Geilo
Göl
Nybergsund
Malung
Hardanger Fjord
OSLO
Lilleström
Haugesund
Tönsberg
Sandefjord
Sandesund
Stavanger
Larvik
OSLO FJORD
STOCKHOLM
Kristiansand
SKAGERRAK
KATTEGAT
Goteborg
Visby
GOTLAND
Malmo
BALTIC SEA
GULF OF
N
O
R
W
E
D
E
N
S
F
I

MISSION TO THE NORTH

FLORENCE JAFFRAY HARRIMAN

MISSION TO THE NORTH

BY

FLORENCE JAFFRAY HARRIMAN
Former U. S. Minister to Norway

17 ILLUSTRATIONS

J. B. LIPPINCOTT COMPANY
PHILADELPHIA NEW YORK

Second Printing

PRINTED IN THE UNITED STATES OF AMERICA

To those whose deepest faith is the future of free peoples,
To those who are pledged to preserve that future
and most particularly
to
Franklin Delano Roosevelt

CONTENTS

ILLUSTRATIONS

MISSION TO THE NORTH

CHAPTER I

The Pace Quickens

One volume of memoirs, I would have said myself, is enough for any woman. Certainly when "From Pinafores to Politics" was finished, I put the cork in the ink bottle firmly. That was that; no more writing for me; and indeed I expected there would be very little more to write about. The house and garden on F Street in Washington were my "permanent address." I had started the book at the request of *The Century Magazine* and had finished it for my grandchildren. Around me the world was speeding up. People whisked back and forth across the continent by plane for week-ends. How wise I had been to pack all the gist of the family papers and some account of my own public life into a little box like a book. The records themselves could be sent to the library, for what they were worth; the little things that gave color to my personal experience of a certain period in history had been set down. This pleasant sense of having cast up accounts and having my house in order to be an "old lady" went on for quite a while.

Perhaps I did not have the talent for being an "old lady," or perhaps I tired of the role. More things began to happen than had ever happened before. I sold the "permanent address" on F Street and moved to Uplands, on a hill overlooking all Washington. Nor have I settled down at Uplands. Who has been able to "settle down" this last decade? More has been crammed into the last four years than into any ten of my life before. My Mission to the North, my appointment as United States Minister to Norway, was utterly unexpected. I read of it in the newspapers and only found out that it was true by investigating the rumor. In Scandinavia I discovered the most charming, small royal court in Europe and ever fresh concepts of democracy, as if those children of the Vikings had remembered much that Americans of the frontier have, to their loss, forgotten.

Through the white summer nights of the north and whiter winters, I glimpsed every conflict in our modern life; the recrudescence of the pagan world; the counterthrust of more than one form of socialism. I learned more geography than I had ever learned at school, saw the world from a corner where what happens in the Baltic is as important to them as what happens in the Mediterranean or the Atlantic is to us. I lived through the Munich crisis in Paris. I visited the Soviet Union, not long enough to judge its future, but just long enough to know how close it lies to western Europe, to taste its food, to mark the tempo of its people in that strange new Moscow, not Mother Moscow any more, but Commissar to all the villages and new cities that dot the wastes across another continent to the Pacific.

Like most Americans in 1929, I rode with my reins clasped tightly in my hand, on an incredible merry-go-round, which we now know to have been the false whirl it was. Ten years of post-war world were already part of a quarter of a century of preparing for another. I could not know that I would hear of the German-Russian Pact soon after sailing up the Oslo Fjord, on one of the fifty thousand boats that make that fjord one of the fairy tales of the world; nor that I would take depositions from the Captain of the *City of Flint,* stand at the edge of the Finnish-Russian war, be bombed by Nazi planes in April, 1940. Nor could I have dreamed when I set forth on the S.S. *Washington* in June of Coronation year for my mission in the north, making my debut as diplomat under Bill Bullitt's auspices at a dinner party in the Paris Embassy, stopping in London, and relishing my talks with Maggie Greville, that I would return from a port I had never heard of—Petsamo, on the Arctic Ocean—with hundreds of refugees from Lithuania, Esthonia, and Scandinavia, and the Crown Princess of Norway and her children, alike seeking refuge in America from the confusion and horror of a second European war.

My three years in the North, with joy in my mission as representative of the United States, ended, or perhaps only halted, with the coming of the Nazi planes in April, 1940. Waiting in Stockholm for orders to return, and on the steamer *American Legion* sailing from Petsamo in August, I began to make notes on these years since "From Pinafores to Politics." I wish it were possible to call this second personal scrapbook "From Politics to Peace and Plenty." I write this second volume while I can and when my grandchild, now married, asks me gravely, "What sort of a life do you mean to live in Volume III?" I say, "I am trying to find out by going back over these last years to see if I can discover trends."

March 4, 1933, is a signal date. I count the great acceleration in my own life from that date. I joined the milling crowd on Capitol Hill and found my seat eagerly on one of the temporary grandstands—though inaugural ceremonies had long ceased to be a novelty to me. That day the skies were gray and a cold rain fell intermittently. It was the first occasion on which, as we later learned, the radio broadcast of the public event would so poignantly broaden the sense of national participation. I might have stayed at home and listened with other citizens, lumbermen in the northwest, farmers in Illinois, fishermen off Maine. Still, seeing the inaugural ceremony was tied up in memory with times past. I have never minded rain, and my heart beat fast as I took my seat. The sky was leaden, and so too the tense depression of the crowd gathered on the Hill. The past week had been marked by grim headlines: banks closing all over the country; able and trusted men committing suicide, thousands of wretched and lonely people whose deaths never got into the newspapers were also the victims of despair. I sometimes think that the 1933 Inaugural Speech was more like a sermon than a political address. We were human beings in trouble, our sense of insecurity was spiritual as well as material. We had a new President and turned to him, uncertain.

Suddenly the clear, strong voice of Franklin Roosevelt, penetrating every corner like a ray of light, came to us from the pillared portico of the Capitol. "There is nothing to fear but fear." With those words, it may not be literally true that the sun began to shine again, but standing there in the rain, we all felt it did. "We face our common difficulties." I found myself committing phrases to memory as we listened. "Confidence thrives only on honor . . . Our greatest primary task is to put people to work." Toward the end of his speech he said that he would ask Congress "for broad executive power to wage a war against the emergency."

The speech had been kept a secret. The half million people restlessly nervous, or standing silent in the Washington streets, had been hoping. They had also held their breaths fearfully, for the days preceding the taking over by the new party had been days of disunity. Abroad the world promised nothing but calamity. On March 2nd the Japanese had taken Jehol. The Congress and the State Legislatures were rushing through measures to stem disaster; but dikes are hard to build in flood season.

It was all this, perhaps, which made the end of the old administration and the inauguration of a new seem so tremendous a date. Nothing was gradual about the change. The new cabinet had been chosen, and the inclusion of Senator Walsh had been a portent of strength and integrity. His death two days before cast a shadow, darker than the rain. Many spoke of him as we left the Capitol at two o'clock. The cabinet had been sworn in. Party leaders had been summoned for a conference next day on policy. It was known that a special session of Congress would be called within the week. And so to the White House! Louis McHenry Howe (like a first Cecil), Marvin McIntyre, Raymond Moley and Rexford Tugwell, the Morgenthaus, the Wallaces, the entire family of Farleys, Robert Jackson—were all there—faces not yet familiar as belonging to the "New Deal." Twenty-five hundred people had sandwiches and tea at the White House, and seventy-five of the family stayed to dinner.

The next day, by proclamation, the banks were closed for

four days. And on the day after, the governors of the states met to confer on the crisis and to express their confidence in the President's leadership. The Exchanges were shut; the Scottsboro trials were postponed. From France came anxious dispatches about Hitler. On March 7th we had inklings of the new economy program, and people began to talk about economy not as saving but as expansion and social distribution of our resources. On March 8th came Secretary Hull's announcement of a world economic conference in London for the following summer. Two days later we learned that frightened gold hoarders had turned back thirty million dollars. Few weeks in history, and none in Washington that I have ever known, were so emotionally crowded. I am inclined to think that the fireside talks, which were at once like simple school lessons and personal messages from the air, had a great deal to do with the emotional recharging of the nation. Our engine had gone dead; and now something began to spark in us.

The first Sunday after March 4th, the largest supper I had ever given at Uplands overflowed the dining room. These suppers were no New Deal innovation; they had a tradition of ten years' standing, and though only private, informal parties, had indeed taken on a sort of institutional character. People came that evening as they might have to a Theater Guild first night, to get a glimpse of Raymond Moley, Mikadoan Pooh-Bah of the New Deal, who arrived with his sister. Also, they were curious to size up Frances Perkins, the first American woman ever to fill a cabinet post. I had known her for many years and treasured the remembrance of her helpfulness twenty years before, when my own appointment as the solitary woman member of

President Wilson's Federal Industrial Relations Commission had brought out a great deal of disparagement from a number of prominent social workers. Perhaps they were justified in their distress that the appointment had not gone to one of their group, but they need not have been so certain that I would not learn to speak their own language. It was Frances who, somehow, managed to establish diplomatic relations between us and I have never ceased to appreciate her generous sense of public service.

"This *is* a party," said someone who was amused at the gathering of Sunday nighters and as excited as I was. We felt, even the most reluctant to welcome it, that it was not merely the eve of a new administration but the morning of a new era. Mrs. Woodrow Wilson was there, gracious as always, and General MacArthur, the Chief of Staff of the Army; Messrs. Junius Morgan, John W. Davis, and Norman Davis were down from New York. There must have been fifty people, here a labor leader, there a Justice of the Supreme Court, a pinch of Senators and a dash of foreign diplomats. Frank Polk, who had been Undersecretary of State in the Wilson Administration, and his wife and daughter were stopping with me. I remember quite well his worried look of surprise when, after coffee, as was my custom, I pushed back my chair and asked Elliot Thurston, then of the *Philadelphia Record,* a leading question. Once in a while on Sunday evenings there was a sort of spontaneous combustion of argument springing from some foursome at table, but usually it was necessary for some one person to introduce a general provocative note before the conversation would become general.

That evening in 1933 people were brimming over with

news and opinions. The highlight of the party was the simple, straightforward explanation of the intricate economic adjustments before the country in which the new administration must take the lead. Parker Gilbert, who spoke to us, was one of those young men accounted a financial genius when he was appointed Undersecretary of the Treasury while still in his twenties, who was, as someone put it, an elder statesman even in his youth. As American member of the Reparations Commission, his modesty, perhaps his too great modesty, and his unrelenting hard work were noted far beyond his friends and countrymen. How often since his sudden death his counsel has been missed in the crisis.

There is no denying that social life in America has been changing since the last war. The rituals, the seasons, and high days of Society with a capital S, no matter how tenderly some of us remember them, seem to be not phenomena of thirty years ago, but of a hundred. Phrases like "the carriage trade" are comical in these days of airplane travel and Hollywood magnates, stars whirling over the continent, and thirty-three million automobiles taking us somewhere and often not back again. In a way my little Sunday night suppers, about which too much was amusingly written in the newspapers, were a part of the new gregariousness and came about naturally. It was an accident that this sort of Information Please fashion of spending an evening took place in my particular Washington drawing room. I started them when the Republicans were in power and well entrenched, as an agreeable meeting corner. Here Democrats still in office, progressive spirits in the party ranks, and journalists might gather and, in a leisurely spirit, plan the coming offensive.

When the Congressional Campaign of 1922 was over and there was no denying that Democratic fortunes were at an all-time low, the Sunday night suppers stopped too. Presently guests who seemed to have liked the habit began to ask when it could all start again. I gave in, but stipulated that the gatherings should be non-partisan. And that turned out to be an even more lively sort of party. At first I was shy of trying to open discussions myself, like some Mrs. Throttlebottom, and would ask Bill Hard or Senator Walsh or another friend to throw in the ball. Then one night I was left high and dry and suddenly discovered I could tap on a table and start people off myself. Once I learned, it was easy, except for one or two times when factionalism frightened the referee and only a hasty changing of the topic managed to save the evening. Once it was a clash between Secretary of War Hurley and a British diplomat, about the debts. Once Ogden Mills, Secretary of the Treasury, took umbrage at Charlie Michelson, the Democratic publicity director, who went in for satirical criticism of the Hoover Administration, just to keep himself in practice.

Seldom were there any prearranged subjects up for discussion and there was no list of guests. From week to week, I simply asked whomever I happened to be meeting. A few friends, especially among the Washington correspondents, took the evenings for granted and came on their own steam and kept things going. I remember Frank Simonds best of all. He was one of the most serious, and yet when he talked, rapidly and with a curious little twinkle in his eye, one often wondered if it were only talk for talk's sake.

His tone of voice was never that of a solemn prophet, but prophet he was. I think many of the Sunday nighters must remember now his reiterated statement that, sooner or later, the Polish Corridor would be the occasion of another European war.

Both abroad and at home, the problem to him was to reconcile a twentieth-century industrial world with eighteenth-century doctrine. I remember copying out of my day book a sentence that was provocative of thought. He wrote in his "Can Europe Keep the Peace?"—"The task is not to adjust life to a dogma but a dogma to life; not make the world safe for democracy but democracy safe for the world." And again he would say, "Isolation is not merely one, but perhaps the last, of the illusions of democracy." He knew that whatever came to Europe would rack us, too. Of all the correspondents who covered the first World War, none is more missed than he, for bringing knowledge and judgment to public opinion in the present crisis.

Richard Oulihan of *The New York Times* was another unique observer and a man of distinguished manners whose like we shall not see again. I remember him vividly the night the Washington correspondents gave a dinner to Sir Willmott Lewis of the London *Times* on the occasion of his knighthood. Dick, in a pink coat—an old English custom—was toastmaster. His gray hair and patrician features set off by his dashing costume, he seemed to have stepped from a gold frame on the walls of some Devon country house. No wonder people often repeated the comment, "Oh, no, Mr. Oulihan is not the correspondent of *The New York Times;* the ambassador of that journal, rather!" My own notion was that he might as easily have had a distinguished career in the church, for a certain gentle, spiritual quality was never absent from him.

One thing I must set down. We live in a strange world in which privacy is no longer the privilege of either rich or poor; and in days when misquotation and malicious rumor can do untold damage. I remember, therefore, with special gratitude, in all the years of those Sunday suppers, the smiling promises given and kept by journalists. Even those who made their fame and fortune out of gossip columns realized that what they heard at Uplands suppers was really off the record. That was why so many people did speak their minds, knowing there would be no consequences in stolen marches. I have run on about those Uplands suppers to show how little like a "salon" (the favorite designation for them in the newspapers) they were. Evenings of democratic civility, yes; just hit-or-miss enough, just formal enough, they afforded opportunities which might not have occurred in smaller and more partisan companies. Healthy home truths were exchanged between men who might have sworn at each other on the Hill. But there they put on amiable tones and listened to each other, over coffee, with attractive women smiling at the charges and rebuttals.

A great deal of my close-up of the summer of '33 was due to the fact that Frances Perkins shared Uplands with me. I had asked her at that first supper party where she intended to live and, when she said that she had had no time even to look for a place, I proposed Uplands, my reasons being selfish enough. I knew she would be getting breeze and quiet on one of the pleasantest hilltops in Washington, and that would count in July and August in the unforgivable climate of the Potomac basin. I would have the joy of her companionship, and the fun of watching the first woman cabinet officer play her part. Many things I learned that summer. If I had ever thought of myself as a truly busy woman, I learned better. My close-up of our Secretary of Labor disclosed a woman with a phenomenal capacity for hard work. "Horny-handed sons of toil" and kibitzing left-wing journalists often harped on her "bourgeois origin," and the woman's clubs claimed her as one of themselves who had made good. But the President had known quite well what he was about. No man could possibly have worked harder; nor accepted so simply the physical buffeting of long hours and continuous traveling. Many nights the office discussions of the day would be transferred to my terrace and would go on into the night, midnight, one, two or even three o'clock. I marvelled at the endurance and the patience of the Secretary of Labor who, after the burdens of the day, could graciously give her attention to visitor after visitor who came to consult her on suggested NRA codes. One time, when rather drab discussions were dragging on, a telephone call from the President made her laugh outright. "You should be happy tonight," he said, "I have just signed the code for brassières."

On one occasion Frances had made a speech in New York, and motored all night to get back in time to be at her desk in the morning. She had had interviews all day; and there had been late-staying guests for dinner, all wanting her advice. She went to bed at midnight, but at half past one my telephone rang violently. "I *must* speak to Miss Perkins," said a voice from New York. I hated to wake her but Mr. Alexander Sachs would not take no for an answer. For over an hour I heard the steady, patient voice of the Secretary of Labor, explaining, countering, quietly debating. There is no time clock for any cabinet officer but, at times, I thought that, for Frances, there was no clock at all. Nor did anyone think of time during "the Hundred Days." In that stretch of crisis, as in a war, people found new reserves of strength. Men of the most diverse opinions worked together like sailors in a storm at sea. The big bankers had flocked to the capital, many of them in a state bordering on panic. The Emergency Banking Bill had been passed, and not only the fresh minds of the new administration, but the counsel of such able Republicans as Messrs. Mills, Ballantine, Awalt and Meyer, were teamed to meet the threatened breakdown. With every concerted stroke, the country grew calmer, the storm seemed to abate, and we were aware chiefly that our common country was worth pulling for. I wish often nowadays, with new crises upon us, some of the bitter critics of the Administration would think of 1933, and keep the stroke again. Justice Brandeis called those early days "an emergency worse than war." We had not yet imagined the war that is being waged today.

There followed the season of the Great Experiments. AAA, NRA, FERA and all the rest. I admit that one evening, listening to a long discussion on currency, instead of finding it all clearer and clearer, I only grew confused. They seemed to speak a lingo of their own. "I'm not quite clear," I said, wishing to be honest, to Professor Sprague of Harvard who sat next to me.

"I haven't understood a word they've been saying for the last half hour myself!" he assured me.

I know now that volumes could be written on the legislative and administrative policies of those years. The whole world was in flux.

The Democratic Party had come back at the 1933 elections with a ground swell. Washington was full of new names and new faces, especially among the women. With Frances at Uplands and Mary Rumsey in and out of the house, I had the illusion of being at the heart of things. Mary moved from New York to Virginia and back again, fascinated by the Washington scene and beginning to take part in it. Actually I was more observer than doer.

Mary Rumsey in Washington was something new under the sun. Her sudden death in 1934 left people in many walks of life without a favorite comet and a devoted friend. Her energy played in all directions—with almost equal enthusiasm she had been for Roosevelt for President on the Democratic ticket and Colonel Donovan for Governor of New York on the Republican ticket. She came by her tumultuous energy straight from her father, E. H. Harriman, the titanic manipulator of railways. Mary had many enthusiasms to her father's one; if he was an arc light, she was a dazzling neon sign. Except for Dorothy Whitney Elmhirst, I have never known any woman so passionately anxious to serve other people. Her part in founding the Junior League and her indefatigable work for certain artists were only a few of her many achievements. She had a sense of the need for change, and a vision of what a tremendous future was possible. When she was named Chairman of the Consumer Division of the NRA, she brought a breeze into an organization already full of high wind. She discovered the coöperative movement as her father might a gold mine. The other day, reading some of AE's letters in a copy of *The Ireland American Review* Dick Tobin had so kindly sent me, suddenly I felt as if Mary were alive again. I could have laughed and cried at the same time. "My dear Dick," AE was writing, "I have received both your letters and also several imperative wires from Mary but as yet no letter from her making clear what it is she wishes me to do so that I can judge whether I am able to help in the way she desires if I go to the U.S.A. You see I have been completely out of touch with all economic efforts since I left the U.S.A. . . . I would not like to put dear Mary to the expense of bringing me over if I was too antiquated in my knowledge to be of any assistance to her. I am very much attached to Mary, a great woman, and would put myself to any inconvenience to please or help her if I could."

Someone showed this letter to Mary, and she explained quickly, "I was really not 'imperative,' only pleading."

How many fine opportunities, how much good, was done by her "pleading" and her generosity even her closest friends did not always know. She mixed the ways of the caliph with reform politics, and wherever she was, there was color. Frances, Mary, and Eleanor Roosevelt, all three were signs of the new times. Women were needed in politics and would, henceforth, probably always be part of the Washington scene, not merely to abet and counsel, but to propose and to dispose.

At the Women's National Democratic Club, I saw the new and younger women, with their new technique, come in. Some of the old suffrage leaders were glad enough to retire to the reviewing stand and watch the new women voters at work. Now and again one of the older Democratic women, whose loyalty and valiant support through the Harding, Hoover and Coolidge administrations had helped to keep the ideas of Jefferson and Jackson alive, would ask me, with just a murmur of doubt, whether everything was going well. I was such an active onlooker that I never noticed but once or twice that the triumphant members of the Roosevelt-before-the-Convention inner clique had a little gray mark against me. The President, I hoped, had understood my position. I had had lunch with him on New Year's Day in '32. I told him that, for years, I had been pledged to remain neutral at the Convention until it was plain that Newton D. Baker, who had been Secretary of War in the Wilson cabinet, would not get the nomination. Long, long before Franklin D. Roosevelt was Governor of New York, I had been interested in having someone with the Wilson perspective in the White House. That New Year's Day I told Governor Roosevelt that I would be neutral at Chicago, or wherever the Convention was to be held, but that, if he were nominated, he would have my vote, and my whole support in the campaign. But would-be neutrals can please neither side.

CHAPTER II

UNEXPECTED MISSION

THE WINTER OF 1934 spent in New York with my family, and another near Hollywood, did not prevent my keeping in touch, unofficially, with the whirling machinery of government. But the months that I spent away from Uplands only convinced me that Washington was my proper climate, and national politics the real center of my interest.

Even from a distance, it had become more and more fascinating to me to watch the patience and the skill with which the President could turn from one program which had not proved all that had been expected of it, to another which looked more promising. When he first took office he had announced he would do just that. His critics grew noisy, but one could note that none of them had a concrete counter-program, and the Congressional Elections of 1934 were ample proof that he still had the confidence of the country. The patient knew quite well that some of the medicine was patent, and so did the doctor. The economic depression was a world-wide epidemic, and at least our simpler American cures were not Nazi tonic.

Somewhere between the campaign of '32 and the autumn

of '36, trying to be "just an observer" in politics, I fancied that novel writing might be my forte. Egged on by well-meaning literary friends, I laid in a great supply of paper and launched forth on an ambitious production. Yes, I even finished it and, like ten thousand others, sent it hopefully to several publishing firms. Each time it was returned ever so politely; and finally came a letter from a conscientious editor who put it plainly but firmly. The book was well written, he said, but lacked the most essential quality for any novel. The characters must live. And none of mine did. I bided by his plain speaking and packed away my paper. I cannot now even remember the title, nor more than one character of my creation, but the whole business was an engrossing affair while it lasted. I recommend heartily trying to write a romance to anyone with too much leisure, or too much ego on his hands. One thing worth recording, before I burn that manuscript, is the rather comical effect novel-writing has on the would-be novelist's way of looking at his friends. I didn't, as the editor wrote me, ever bring any of my characters back alive, but as I looked about me, I suddenly saw nearly everybody as hero or heroine, or minor characters. Now, if I could just have set down the Washington Commissioner of Police, whom I first met one hot summer night in 1932, at a dinner party given by Mr. and Mrs. Noyes, in Virginia. Brigadier General Glassford, a new face in Washington, was six feet three, and looked like the ideal army man. As we were leaving the party, very late, someone with a delightfully old-fashioned point of view inquired whether it would be safe for me to drive myself home alone at that time of night. The General said quickly that I would be quite safe, as he would drive me himself. "He carries a six-shooter!" someone threw in. Absurd, of course, as he never carried a weapon of any kind while he was Superintendent of Police. Neither Washington, nor any other town, ever had a Chief of Police quite like him. There might have been two of him, he managed to be in so many places at once, so many drawing rooms, so many troubled alleys and traffic jams. His favorite form of locomotion was like Lawrence of Arabia's—a motorcycle, the fastest he could afford. One evening, a friend coming to dine with me, finding himself late, stepped on the gas with a fine disregard for the speed limit. Suddenly, he was conscious of a traffic cop hot on his trail. Arriving breathless, he was in the midst of explaining what a narrow escape he had had from arrest, when in through the drawing room door came the cop. "So it was you I was trying to pass," said General Glassford, as he caught up with his quarry.

In more ways than one, the General reminded me of Colonel Lawrence. He had a romantic sense of what was real in this world; he was that rare thing, a man of action, interested in other people's feelings and other people's reasons. The many dramatic and threatening marches of the unemployed that occurred during his term as Commissioner would, I have always thought, have been less of an open scandal if the authorities had left him alone to work matters out. He had his own theories as to how the Legion Veterans should be treated. Once he had an idea, he was always on the warpath. That made him a storm center, to be sure. But, more important still, he had the confidence of the men.

I drove out frequently to the Veterans' Camp in Anacostia, and though there were certainly some men who may "never have seen Europe," as some of the papers charged, I talked with many of the campers and found I knew the units they had served in "over there" and remembered well the time when they had been told that the country's helping hand would always be theirs to the end of their days!

It is a twice-told tale, but I believe no one who, with his own eyes, saw the charge of the soldiers down Pennsylvania Avenue as I did—troops ordered to drive the unemployed veterans, their women and their children, away from Anacostia, and to burn their camp—will ever forget it. The troops were anything but happy. Their orders were to evacuate their former comrades. Many times since, in Europe, I have remembered that circumstance. It was our infinitesimal sample of a world to come. The troops were silent and restrained. The casualties were few. The old order, which was not good enough nor inclusive, prevailed. Next morning, very sadly, many Washington men and women drove their motor cars to rescue the dispossessed along the roadside, giving lifts to old people, and women and children, trying to cross the Maryland border by noon. The warning had gone out that if they lingered in the District of Columbia after that hour, they would not be safe from prison. Why members of the Hoover Administration did not know what a sense of outrage would ensue, and what a boomerang to the Republicans the unimaginative, impatient, unkind handling of an exasperating situation would be—in a campaign year especially—I cannot see. Afterwards, General Glassford, casting aside all the conventions of the Police Commissionership, made speeches that I sometimes regretted—even though he spoke for the Democrats. But I knew what he had seen, and I knew that he felt there had been an offense committed against American ideals.

He was always one of the characters whom I wanted to describe, and now that I am doing it, I see that I do not quite know how. He painted very creditably; he had a certain musical gift. He was too active to serve these quiet muses alone. When hitch-hiking among those out of work became a widespread symptom of national disturbance, he was at once interested in trying to find a way out. At that time, driving down from New York to Washington, I would be stopped thirty or forty times by boys and girls desperately trying to "go somewhere" or "anywhere." It was natural that, when General Glassford was relieved of his post, he put his mind at once on the problem of our youth, how to save their health and morale in a shifting order. He formulated a plan, a concrete one, for establishing work camps all over the continent, in the national parks, to teach men to build and to tend the land. He hoped some of the great foundations might act in the matter, if individuals with private means, able to act quickly, did not take over the financing. My sister-in-law, Anne Vanderbilt, in her usual generous way, was interested at once. And so were many others, who saw both how heart-rending and how fundamentally threatening the situation was. General Glassford worked unceasingly, laying out his proposals. In the spring of '33, when the New Deal was proposed for the forgotten man, and a wave of hopefulness thrilled the country, though still no specific measures like camps for boys had been suggested, I went with General Glassford to discuss the subject with Frances Perkins. She listened attentively and volunteered to talk over the matter with others. Sometime later, when the CCC camps were proposed and established, and even the severest critics of the Administration found something to admire, I used to credit the General for an initial share in the idea and wish his vision could be used on other problems. But I dare say, somewhere in Arizona, he has found some equally important and stirring project to engross him.

The would-be novelist forgot her rejection slips, and the "retired old lady" forgot her age and retirement, as the 1936 campaign took shape. The convention had been cut but not dried. The depression was still world-wide, but the country was better off. Only, as usual, the Party out of office still found its out-of-office state hard to forgive. Would I caravan for the Democrats in New York State? Political caravaning is, in fact, the greatest kind of spree. When the route lies through the Empire State in the autumn, when the countryside is ablaze with color, even speaking from four to eight times daily is not work, so constantly refreshed is the campaigner with a sense of being alive, in a great and beautiful land. One's eyes are always opened to the kinds and varieties of fellow citizens who make up the democracy; and the quadrennial razzle-dazzle of campaigning, serious, and yet full of exaggeration, hysteria even, and always a lot of fun. And mixing is a social tonic. I like it.

I had been coached for my talks by a member of the Federal Reserve Board. He used not only to see that I was loaded with accurate and simple accounts of the Democratic financial policy, but threw in a little general economics for my own education and future. The finance planks were my bit on the platform. Another member of our troupe, whose special allotment was to boom Governor Lehman's candidacy to succeed himself, time after time, used to wind up her eulogy of her candidate by saying, "And his name is Landon." She *would* say Landon, to our embarrassment and horror. We would rebuke her; she would promise to remember; and then, the next time, she would carry her audience along with an account of Lehman's record, and then end again, "His name is Landon." The slight similarity in the two names seemed to hypnotize her.

We did each have a special subject and rather set speeches, and we did make our speeches all over again a great many times. But we were taken aback one morning when our chauffeur, a boy from the Middle West, poked his head out of the car window and said: "Well, girls, if any of you get stuck, just call on me. I know all your speeches by heart. Only Mrs. Harriman keeps me guessing—I never know whether she's going to begin in the middle, the end, or the beginning."

We had a loudspeaker in the trailer, and it gave out fine noises like a calliope. Over and over again "Happy Days Are Here Again" would roll out over the hamlets and villages as we passed through without stopping. When we went slowly through some little upstate town—this is a confession—I used to feel so like a circus parade that unconsciously I would inflate my chest and bow right and left, quite as if I were the Fat Lady in the Barnum and Bailey parade. I liked playing this game, but when I turned brightly to one of my fellow Democrats and asked her if she were the Bearded Lady, there was a very definite coldness in her "Certainly not."

I enjoyed every minute of that campaign. The result

seemed such a foregone conclusion, however, that I used to wonder what earthly reason there was for any of our speeches.

That Christmas I spent in California, returning for the Inauguration which was held, for the first time, in January instead of March. April found me in New York on a visit. One night the telephone rang at one-thirty. A reporter from *The New York Times* asked what statement I had to make on my appointment as Minister to Norway. I told him I had never heard of any such thing. Finally, he pressed so hard for some sort of interview that I did what I could. "Interesting, if true," I said, wondering what it was all about.

The news, it seems, had leaked out from Norway, where there had been some delay in granting the *agrément*—that is, their consent to my appointment. I fancy the idea of a woman Minister was not quite acceptable to Oslo at first and, also, a funny contretemps had arisen. My given name is Florence, but all my life I have been called Daisy, and most of my friends never knew me by anything else. The Norwegian Minister in Washington, asked by his government who "Florence Jaffray" Harriman was, replied that he had "never heard of her." When the State Department pressed him about "Daisy" Harriman, he said that was quite another matter.

The morning after my conversation with the *Times* reporter, there was the *Times* announcing my appointment; and on my way to the Washington train, there was the same news with more headlines in all the evening papers. When I arrived at Uplands, there were notes, cards and flowers from friends. "Interesting, if true," I kept repeating to people who telephoned, for there certainly was no letter or message from the State Department. Naturally, somewhere there had been a misunderstanding. I did take an interest in the matter, so I called my daughter in California on the long distance telephone. "If it's true," I asked, "what do you think?"

Ethel, sagely, thought at once. "Think it over for a long time before you decline," she said. "At your age, women are apt to find their interests growing narrower. Now here are you, with a chance to have an entirely new experience, and a real adventure."

"A real adventure"—until then my mind had been a whirligig of pros and cons. Had I the courage to go so far away, by myself, where I knew no one? Could I make good? At the same time, I was immensely heartened to think the President had considered me for such a responsible position. That is, if he had. . . . The next morning I went to the State Department, and laid my dilemma before an old friend, Sumner Welles. I couldn't, could I, go on considering myself a prospective Minister when no such job had ever been offered to me, I said. At which he laughed, "That *is* funny. Do you mean to tell me all the news you've had of this has been through the papers?" Then, he assured me that all the preliminary steps were over. I had only to say "Yes" or "No." Perhaps I should have said "Yes," at once, but instead, I went along to see various department heads to find out what I could about the Norwegian post. I was not a "first" in the Department's experience for, after all, Ruth Bryan Owen had broken the ice, four years before, when she had been sent as Minister to Denmark, and many things were easier for me because she had distinguished her office so well in Copenhagen. I knew, too, that Oslo had, from 1923 to 1930, except for one year, received Mme. Alexandra Kollontay as representative of the Soviet Union.

The President was away. On his return, his secretary wired me that the President would like me to have luncheon with him. We sat at his desk and talked, as we ate, and when he began explaining what, confidentially, my first task would be in Oslo, then, and only then, was I sure that I was really going north. It was his suggestion that I travel slowly to my post, taking ten days in Paris and ten in London to study the general European situation, especially through talks with our ambassadors in the two capitals. It was his suggestion, too, at that meeting that I convey an invitation to the Crown Prince and his Princess to visit America the next year.

From the State Department came the suggestion that I time my arrival in Oslo so that I could receive at the Garden Party at the Legation, a long-established Fourth of July custom. A hectic month lay ahead of me. I must have four weeks' instruction in the duties and intricacies of diplomacy at the State Department. Whatever furniture, silver and linen I wanted to take with me must be sorted and packed. There wasn't much time to think. Every moment was crammed with preparation.

I remembered many times what Ethel had said to me, "To few women of your years comes such a chance." My friends were very kind; a good many of them felt as Ethel did, and rejoiced in a sort of vicarious adventure. But there were others, naturally, who disapproved of innovations of all sorts, and the innovation, this time, was having a woman at the head of a Foreign Mission. I rather especially liked those who felt that way, and who told me frankly that they couldn't conscientiously congratulate me. I liked less well those who gushed a little to my face, and whose voices I overheard running on about "the absurd appointment."

I think I understand the Tory point of view very well; it is always a waste of time to argue with people who hold it; and in due course Tories do eat so many of their words, eat them all up pleasantly and neatly and never dream what they are swallowing. When, nearly forty years ago, we were busy organizing the Colony Club, the talk ran high about the new club as a move bound to disrupt the home and teach women all the naughty ways of men! And in the days of the suffrage movement the granting of the vote was going to bring down lava and destruction on a misguided republic. But we vote; and the tomes of outraged comment gather dust.

One ex-Ambassador, who disapproved heartily, could not have been kinder. On one side, there was he, endlessly helpful, going over his own experience, suggesting this or that, telling me how others had dealt with diplomatic episodes and contretemps. Quite the contrary was the wife of an ex-Ambassador who would look at me with a sort of grim melancholy and keep repeating, "You are a very brave woman." Then when I asked why, a little bewildered, she would only say, "Because you are," as if to leave me thinking a Foreign Mission was a mysterious cave of pitfalls. Oh, well—

Mildred Bliss, wife of one of our career diplomats, former Ambassador to the Argentine, may have held the Tory point of view, but this did not prevent her, also, having generous good wishes for the success of my mission. This took the form of her lending me a very handsome court train she had worn for her presentation at the Court of Sweden. I was no less grateful for the gesture, when I found out later that the Norwegian Court had, since the last war, abolished formal drawing rooms. I never had a chance to use it.

The month flew by; everything was done. The adventure contained but one dark hour, and that was at the State Department press conference, where a journalist, not one of the regulars—planted for the occasion, I am pretty sure—asked if I were going to take up the question of a Trade Agreement between the United States and Norway.

I answered, "The State Department is looking after that," meaning that all preliminary conversations on trade pacts were handled by the Department first. Fearing that I had pulled a bud open before it was ready to bloom, the cautious Mr. McDermot quickly interposed a line about there being no negotiations for such a treaty at present, etc. This was all headlined in the papers, as if I had made a serious blunder, and had been rebuked by the Chief of the Press Bureau. Naturally, it worried me deeply, but when the officials of the Department made little of it to me—one, by chance, having overheard the question and answer—I tried to reassure myself. I did my utmost not to let it make me uneasy and self-conscious about the responsibility of my foreign post. The newspapers continued to play it up as a "gaffe." But the incident was worth while as an experience (in a way, all such incidents are). A misadventure makes some friends rally; others seem to have a little relish in their will to believe the worst. I remember those who called up at once to commiserate with me, and at rather too great length. Mr. Farley, however, told me that he was always glad when a diplomat made some trivial break before starting for a post, "because it gives him a little, needed lesson in being more careful afterwards." So kind a man! In the years that I have been associated with him in politics, I found him always scrupulous and fair and a wizard at prophecy. But his wizardry is made up of a long memory, and almost a scientist's regard for details, of simple circumstances and ordinary men.

During the whole of my stay in Norway the Trade Treaty was "unfinished business," and seldom a day went by that the question of whale oil and the effect of the American excise tax on this product on the 40,000 Norwegians engaged in the business of the whaling fleet did not come to bother both sides of the dispute. Dispute may be too strong a word—"discussions" is better. The difficulty dates back to May, 1934, when the import tax of three cents a pound on whale oil laid on by the Revenue Act of 1934 became effective. This was a tax added to the already existing tariff of six cents per gallon in the Tariff Act of 1930. When I study the figures, the tax was perhaps, I am obliged to admit, prohibitive. The *ad valorem* equivalents of the six cent per gallon duty and of the combined duty and tax show 14.7 per cent in 1930, and 129.9 per cent in 1935.

In Europe whale oil is almost entirely used for food values. In Scandinavia and Germany it figures in the manufacture of margarine. In America it is bought primarily for the manufacture of soap, particularly by one of our chief Middle Western manufacturers. Whale oil does not come into competition with domestic edible oils at all, yet the legislation seems to have been forced by agricultural interests who did not realize that they were being manipulated by sellers of inedible fats, rendered from garbage of the great cities by garbage contractors who were part of our least scrupulous city political machines. The agricultural groups, who fell for a misrepresentation of facts, are responsible for the way the price of whale oil to American consumers rose one hundred per cent. And, as the American market dropped away, naturally the Norwegians sold to the German market. It is not too much to say that the Nazis are fed today by our unsettled dispute of yesterday.

My last days in America were hurly-burly from dawn to dusk. Some evenings we spent quietly on the terrace at Uplands. Little winds came up the Potomac from the sea. Early summer in Washington is never as depressing and still as August can become. Across the valley, there was the illuminated dome and the Washington Monument—symbols of the Republic. The great expanse of starry sky and the heavy scent of honeysuckle and tobacco plant in the quiet night closed us round. Harsh quarrels at home and abroad seemed far away.

The days had no such quiet. It is all very well in this modern world to take foreign posts and move swiftly over the face of the earth, but for a very long time our habits and customs have not been that of nomads and migrating birds. Few of us can travel without exhausting preparations: subletting houses, storing this and that, trying to imagine future needs, which books, which clothes. Jacquie Story, my attractive secretary, was as out of breath as I. I pride myself on the ease with which I have learned to travel in this changing world, but this time I was taking my departure very seriously. I felt, too, that if I made mistakes they would not be private ones, someone else would suffer; other women, perhaps, would be given opportunities more reluctantly, if all did not go smoothly on our journey. I remember nothing of the steamer trip but sleep.

Arrived in Paris, Bill Bullitt, good friend that he is, at once filled my little engagement book. I must dine with him that first night and, when I arrived, it was broken to me that I was to act as hostess. As Bill greeted each guest and presented me, he said in his enthusiastic way, "This is the American Minister to Norway, *not* the wife of the American Minister but *the* Minister in her own right." Everybody got it straight, and I was launched. There were many old friends in Paris I was glad to see again.

No host or hostess I have ever known is so good a *compère* as Bill. His custom is not to sit at the end of his table but at the side and, from there, toss the ball of conversation from one end to the other. What he manages to do, with thirty or forty guests, is something that only the most skilful hosts can accomplish with a dinner party of six or eight—preserve a witty and personal intimacy in general talk. And where someone else would only produce a scrambled company, he could whisk up a table with Messrs. Herriot, Blum and Daladier, mixed with members of the old regime like M. and Mme. Claudel and Mme. Jusserand, and have it turn out a perfect combination! None of our ambassadors to Paris has ever been a more fluent master of the French language, and not merely classic French but patois and argot. But then, of course, his forebear came from somewhere in Provence. Some ambassadors who were far less popular with the French have gained more favors, by giving more favors to the American Colony in Paris—often a *charming,* but a very miscellaneous, exacting set. Much as Bill likes to be liked, he conceived his job in Paris as of vital importance; his business was to forward the good relations between two *governments,* and to prevent misunderstandings. In this connection I want to set down for the record what an important member of the French Foreign Office told me not long ago: "Trouble makers have tried to make the public believe otherwise, but to us in the French Foreign Office never once did your Ambassador hide the truth. He begged us always to discount any notion that America *would* enter the war. Over and over again, knowing as he did the inner workings of American domestic politics, he held out no hope whatever of assistance to us French."

Our arrival in London was at the height of the season. The rosy afterglow of the Coronation lay over the great, gray and white city; the parks were still full of coronation blossoms. It seemed to me that every jewel in England had been unpacked for the gala summer. Such pearls and diamonds as we saw in Covent Garden, such pretty women!

Mr. Bingham, the Kentucky publisher who was our Envoy at the Court of St. James, gave me no such schooling as Bill Bullitt had done. I remember chiefly his remark that I would find diplomacy had longer hours than I imagined; he got up early in the morning and was dictating letters by seven. Well, opulent London was the center of the world. If I had to rise early in Norway, *tant pis.*

There was a ball at the Embassy for a debutante. All the younger crowd were there, with a scattering of officials, such as Mr. and Mrs. Alexander Weddell, now our representatives in Spain, but, at that time, on a visit from their Argentine post. The surface of life was imperial and prosperous. There were Rolls-Royces beyond counting; yet sometimes, even inside them, talking with English friends of many years' standing, I heard things which should have warned me. There was uneasy awareness that British foreign policy was making no headway. Things were looking ominous on the continent. Bill Bullitt had assured me that, if the Nazis so much as took a step in Czechoslovakia, France was engaged. There would be war. The British mentioned Danzig with some nervousness. They spoke with distrust of this one and that amongst their own leaders. They asked me a question I could not answer. What would America do in case of a war?

I enjoyed briefly a snatch of feeling that all was right and everlasting, when I was in the company of old friends. Maggie Greville, rosy, confident and urbane as ever, in her hospitable house in Charles Street, was one who gave a sense of stability. Among fine pictures and bibelots inherited from her father, she gathered poets and statesmen and ambassadors, M.P.s and Sitwells, and Americans. Maggie was full of plans for a dinner she was going to give the following week, in honor of King George and Queen Elizabeth. I was disappointed at having to decline, but the A B C of a diplomatic post is punctuality in meeting every engagement. I was due in Oslo forthwith. I had my written orders. I did want very much a closer view of this monarch who had accepted responsibility and was achieving so much in healing a breach in the hearts of his people. Even more, I wanted to meet his Scottish Queen, who, though shy and supposed to be a "home body," had developed a genius for doing the right thing with a lovable grace, through an arduous round of public occasions.

We embarked on the S.S. *Venus* at Newcastle, as planned. Over the North Sea lay Bergen, the ancient Hanseatic City of the North. My Mission had begun.

CHAPTER III

28 Nobelsgate

Thirty-six hours later, on the 29th of June, Jacquie and I were on deck. The Bergen fjord reminded us, at first, of the coast of Maine; the same small islands, we said to each other, the same gray-green shore. Hills we could see and valleys but, behind the old town, so bright and pretty in the sun, were far-off mountain peaks, a glorious scene. Our excitement mounted. Suddenly we saw two top-hatted, tail-coated officials waiting for us on the quay. We dragged our thoughts from the mountains, and came down to earth and our diplomatic honors.

We landed, were greeted, and whisked to our hotel. No sooner were we settled in our comfortable apartments there, with hardly five minutes for breathing, than, like a swarm of June bugs, reporters stormed our sitting room. So the old world was not so different from the new! Perhaps they hoped to trap me into what would seem like a second indiscretion. They asked such leading questions, one after another, that they quite upset our rather nervous and very conscientious consul. "You can't ask the Minister that," he would interrupt, trying to protect me. "No, no, that's not a proper question," he would put in, until both the reporters and I were bewildered. Many of the men I admire most, and count among my most valued friends, are journalists, but I admit that I would rather face a squad of invading soldiers than a group of, even friendly, interviewers. A single slip of the tongue can make an embarrassing stick in the newspapers. But the translations of that first consul-chaperoned interview could not have been more innocuous. And indeed, during my whole stay in Norway I had nothing but the most pleasant and coöperative relations with the many newspaper editors and reporters I came to know. For one thing, they all spoke English. Many of them had lived or visited in the United States or England, nearly all had studied the language in school, and read New York and London papers fairly regularly. It was my observation from experience later that the journalists of Norway were governed by a sense of social responsibility. They did not wish to make trouble out of slips, and valued as much as I did the clear understanding between our two countries. If I, on my part, had the slightest misgiving about the propriety of any statement, they were only too glad to protect me. I needed no consul.

At the end of our first Scandinavian day, we had a surprise. When we went to bed, instead of sheets and blankets for the beds, we found eiderdowns in linen bags. Though I later travelled much in Norway, I have never learned to cope with an eiderdown. So light, so pleasant, so warm; but even the June nights in the Land of the Midnight Sun are cool, and in the winter nights are frigid, and how often I have waked, chilled to the bone, the eiderdown slipped to the floor. Jacquie did no better with hers, the first night, but it was the only fault we found with the new, unexplored land, as we started off at an early hour on one of the loveliest railway journeys in the world, over mountain passes, down the rim of fjords, each wooden house shining in its meadow or clinging to its crag. Once we stepped out in the snow, at Finse, to pick lilacs, and all the way, pleased with each station, and the freshness of the air, I felt the Mission was pure adventure and pure poetry. Presently, two hours before we were to arrive in Oslo, there appeared in our compartment a woman journalist, triumphant because she was stealing a march on her Oslo colleagues and getting the first interview with "the new lady minister." I had to explain to her that I could make no statements until I had presented my credentials to the King, but she stayed on and talked with us. She was interested in the frock I was knitting, and suggested that since I was going to be in Norway, I should learn to weave. All sorts of handwork have always interested me, and a few months later, I followed the talk up by borrowing a loom from Hedwig Paus, one of my charming neighbors, and making cloth for a suit for my daughter, Ethel. Almost as many women weave as knit in Norway and there is, in doing so, a sort of substantial satisfaction like baking home-made bread.

When we reached Oslo station, many members of the Legation staff were there to meet us. One was the Legation messenger, Alex Wilse, who, with his white beard and ruddy complexion, carried his seventy-three years with such distinction that I took him at once for a Foreign Office official. In the months that followed I found that he was Santa Claus in character as well as looks. Whatever we wanted to have, whatever we wanted to know, he always tried to find for us. When last year, on his seventy-fifth birthday, it seemed only right that he should retire, we were all sad to tears. Past Ministers and secretaries joined with us in giving him a silver tankard engraved with the autographs of the many who had enjoyed his long and faithful service to his adopted country. He was born a Norwegian but had fought in the Spanish-American War and now has been awarded a pension from the U. S. Government.

Jefferson Patterson, the Secretary of the Legation, introduced us to the Norwegian officials and to the Legation staff. His presence made us feel at home at once, as he was an old acquaintance from Washington. Would we come for dinner if our luggage materialized in time? We would be delighted. Then I turned over the papers for the two dogs we had brought from America, and who were in quarantine, kenneled in red tape. At the station already was my own Ford car, sent on ahead of us from Washington. I got in. My first glimpse was of a rather unexceptional city, but blithe with window boxes. Then we drove up Karl Johansgate, with the dignified palace showing at the top of the sloping hill. I leaned out of the car window and said, "I like this town," but I never dreamed how, later, everything in Norway would captivate my affections.

To this day, I am not sure of the whole history of our Legation building at 28 Nobelsgate. It is the best and most suitable Legation house in Oslo, though the British Legation site, picked out by King Edward VII at the time his daughter, Princess Maud, became Queen of Norway, has a finer view. 28 Nobelsgate is comfortable and commodious, a replica, the story goes, of a Russian Palace, much admired by the brother of Alfred Nobel, who built the house in 1912

The American-Scandinavian Foundation

THE PALACE AND KARL JOHANSGATE, OSLO

as a present for his daughter. The garden must have been lovely twenty years ago, for it extended to Bygdö Allee, one of the main thoroughfares of Oslo, and on either side there was land enough to protect the Legation from the curious. There were tennis courts, too, but best of all an uninterrupted sweep of the Oslo Fjord, a radiant vista in winter and in summer alike.

There are those, of course, more social perhaps and less romantic about scenery, who have no regrets for the modern and model apartments that now cluster around the Legation grounds, so close that everything that went on in our garden, from dog-fights to skiing lessons, echoed through the town. I confess that often, seeing nothing but lawn and brick apartments, I wished the housing problem had been settled in some other direction. Only from my bathroom window was the beauty beyond discernible. From there to the west I could catch a glimpse of distant mountains. Often I would steal up to enjoy the colors at sunset; and later, when the Northern Lights began to play in the sky, the same window was the best stand to watch from. While I am at the bathroom window, I may as well go on. I seem to remember that the hot water system at 28 Nobelsgate was a really serious problem. My love of antiques stops short of outmoded plumbing. Only one person could have a hot bath at a time and "the perfect hostess" very often had to go without. Minor inconveniences like these were all adjusted the next winter when the Department of State despatched to us a very clever young architect, Leland King, to undertake "all necessary renovations including redecorating" as part of his mission. Several of the rooms we transformed entirely, notably the largest living room. Where there had been a fake fireplace, an elusive flue was discovered, and now a comforting wood fire burns all through the long dark winter days. We tore off the cheap buff paper and experimented with a delectable paint that shows robin's-egg blue in daylight and a pleasant green at night, toning in well, at all hours, with the red damask curtains. We went to no end of trouble searching for that color, but it was Mme. Lodi Fe, wife of the Italian Minister, who helped us by producing a book of colored reproductions of primitives, in which we found a woman's cloak of just the tone we had been unable to describe. We retired to the attic a too impressive chandelier, and mounted two graceful appliques on the panels either side of the chimney. All in all, the room became one of the most grateful I have ever tried my hand at, and I still love to think of it, the scene of such varied and such happy times.

But all this runs ahead of those first days. I spent them, when not in my office, surrounded by packing cases, just dealing with the problem of where to place this or that. Tony Biddle, before going as Ambassador to Poland, had been my predecessor as Minister to Norway, and Margaret Biddle, his wife, had shown me the most thoughtful courtesy imaginable. She sent me, in America before I left, two sets of photographs of each room in the Legation; first, as they were arranged with only the government property and furniture, and then, as she had arranged them, with the addition of her personal *bibelots* and *meubles*. It was of great help, in choosing what, and what not, to take with me. Margaret's rare executive ability and her kindness did not stop here. I doubt if many Ambassadors' and Ministers' wives were as thoughtful of their successors as she was of me. She had remembered everything—even to classified card catalogues of everyone she and her husband knew in Norway, and I think there were very few they did not know. Best of all were copies of her dinner lists, telling me how best to group my guests. Old and new divorces, ancient political disagreements rippled the waters in civilized Oslo, as elsewhere. No one will ever realize, perhaps she, herself, least of all, how she oiled the machinery and made the American Minister's first social duties easier. She set me right on court etiquette, whom to send in with the Court Chamberlain, etc., etc. She made me notes on people's ages, and sometimes bits about the origin of their names or titles. She helped in another way, too. Perhaps if I had realized how immensely popular Ambassador and Mrs. Biddle were in their post, I would have hesitated to succeed them. They were not there more than eighteen months, but they left countless devoted friends in their wake.

Arriving as I did at the end of June, just after schools had closed, I found social and political Oslo away with the children in the mountains and by the fjords. This made things much easier. There were fewer Norwegian calls to make and receive, and my first days were taken up with formalities within the diplomatic corps. As a newcomer, it was necessary, from my side, that appointments should be made by telephone. Then Jefferson Patterson and I would call at the appointed hour. According to protocol, that seasoned code distilled from a thousand years (or so it seemed to me) of mutable and immutable diplomatic relations, the Minister we called upon must and did, within a day or two, return the call, followed by a second visit accompanied by his wife, if he had one, and if she were in town. I found all my colleagues agreeable—this also is according to protocol—and soon began to make real friends among them.

Perhaps I was lucky; perhaps a corps diplomatique is not always as interesting and diversified a lot as we were in Norway. From the beginning Sir Cecil and Lady Mary Dormer, in their "little bit of England," were more than kind to me as colleagues and neighbors. She was a famous gardener, and worked hard, bending, clipping, weeding, coaxing things into bloom with as much energy as the gardeners who worked for her. Sir Cecil always kept an eye out for me in my first days, and I cannot be grateful enough for his thoughtfulness in my last days at my post when we were both dodging the Nazis together. Because the Queen was English-born, the British Minister and his entourage were always much more in touch with the Norwegian Court than the other missions, except of course the Swedish, which had much the same sort of personal tie because the Crown Princess was Swedish-born. Britishers attached to Sir Cecil's staff came and went often during the last year of my stay, always full of equanimity, and drawing our admiration for the way they bore the increasing difficulties.

The French Envoy was changed three times during my stay, and it was the third incumbent, Comte de Dampierre, whom I knew best, for we were refugees together after the invasion.

One of my colleagues who shall be nameless was a frequent source of entertainment. He had made up his mind to speak English and did so constantly. Fluent he was, but prone to mistakes, and once he had made a mistake he clung to his own precedent with tenacity. His disputes with his secretaries were famous, and his secretaries succeeded one another briskly. There was nothing he liked better than airing his troubles to a group of acquaintances.

"Ah, this new one," the Minister would exclaim of his latest secretary, "he is a phenomenos, I tell you, a phenomenos."

"You mean a phenomenon," someone would murmur.

"No, no, no, I tell you a *phenomenos!*" and on he would run.

He often telephoned me to find out what I, as the Minister of the Greatest Republic, was about to do. He was determined not to deviate. Once when special envoys were being appointed on the occasion of a state funeral, he rang up in great agitation.

"Are you going to represent the body of your President, or your country? Me, I do not wish to represent the body of my President, I wish to represent my country."

I replied as best I could: "As I am appointed by the President, I am his representative and *he* represents the country." I thought I had chosen words carefully.

"No, no, no," he wailed into the phone, "I will not represent the body of my President." He came to the funeral of course, but in precisely what role, I never did find out.

He was always being thrown into excitement about the manners of his colleagues, and the chips on his shoulder were continually tumbling off. I met him one afternoon.

"Did that Turk and that Egyptian throw their cards at you?" he demanded.

"I didn't feel it if they did," I consoled, wondering what it was all about.

"I will not have them throw their cards at me. I shall throw them back at them. They will see," he barked.

Only when I got back to Nobelsgate and found that the Turkish and Egyptian diplomats had had their cards sent round but had not called in person, did I really gather what the little cyclone was about. Every week there was some such colorful little rumpus, but we all found our colleague's foibles and troubles positively endearing, and spice to our formality.

Our doyen of corps when I first arrived was Mr. Höjer, the Swedish Minister, who had been in Oslo time out of mind. He died when I had been only four months in residence and was succeeded by Mr. Gunther; but during my whole stay I heard and saw so much of the exceptional Mme. Höjer that I felt I had known them both for years. Mr. Gunther was himself shortly succeeded by Baron and Baroness Beck-Friis, whom I had known in Washington, and whom I was to know much better during the invasion.

Mr. and Mrs. Ullens de Schooten, he the Belgian Chargé, were the youngest of the corps. Their zest for Oslo ways was enormous; they fitted in like natives. Our anxiety about them after the invasion was enormous too, for though the Nazis promised to transport them and their young children to Switzerland, and deployed a special plane to take them, the promise was broken and they were transported instead to Berlin and held there as prisoners for weeks, presumably because they had seen too much of the invasion.

My most important visit, of course, was made on the first day. Dr. Halvdan Koht, the Foreign Minister, was truly cordial, and his candor and kindness put me instantly at ease, and in the troubled days that followed my admiration for him grew steadily. His country was "neutral" and he strained every nerve to keep a balance that was constantly harassed from both sides. He was veritably Norwegian in his sense of single standard. He wanted to know what was right and then to do it. To rationalize evil was, to him, to double the evil. One way of putting it is that, as a nation, the Norwegians are a people of few ulterior motives—as all democratic peoples should be. Confronted with nations or individuals hypocritical in protesting friendship, they are lost—they simply do not understand. Dealing with Dr. Koht was always a straightforward matter. When asked for information on a question, he would give it to you quite frankly, or, as frankly, say that the matter was a secret that could not be divulged. He never gave worrying, evasive or equivocal replies. Dr. Koht, for many years professor of history at Oslo University, had been named Foreign Minister upon the nomination of the largest single party in Norway, the Labor party. His piercing brown eyes, his inky-black eyebrows like a brownie's, his gray hair and gray mustache, made him seem southerner as well as northerner.

The Foreign Office, near the palace grounds, was one of the most old-fashioned buildings in Oslo, as informal as a country manse. Dr. Koht and his wife might have lived in the residence provided for them in Oslo—they did do their most formal entertaining there—but they both preferred to live in their own country house near Lysaker, where their children had been brought up. I remember that the first time I dined there, the guests were shown into Minister Koht's library where not only were the walls lined with old and new volumes, but there were so many piled on the floor that we picked our way as we might in a garden maze.

Every one of the twenty-five thousand volumes was precious and familiar to him and to Mme. Koht. The good professor's wife is a motherly and scholarly woman beloved by old and young alike, radiating in all directions like a placid Eleanor Roosevelt. How especially she must be grieved at the amount of disarrangement the Nazis are making in the Lysaker books.

"The Nazis in Norway." I cannot be sure whether this idea ever occurred to Koht as a concrete possibility in the days before they did come. There were plenty of people who, in memoir fashion, could repeat the remarks of German officers who would say, "The mistake of the last war was that the High Command did not take Norway at once and use it as a base to break the blockade." The Norwegian policy did not start with that in mind. Government after government looked to the League of Nations, to the slow federation of European states into an entity called Europe and a part in the world at peace. Some used to say the Norwegians' fault, if one can call it a fault, was to put their trust in the integrity of the Great Nations. The four northern countries—Norway, Sweden, Denmark and Finland—in the Scandinavian Block, which I shall try to describe later, did try, as I think no nations have ever tried, to practise their policy first at home. In every direction they experimented with domestic schemes of social betterment and equality for all citizens. Peace with the world, and peace between all classes—that was their endeavor. The spirit of that endeavor was in every interview I ever had with any member of the Norwegian Government.

The first call on the Foreign Minister, however, was not devoted to discussion of policies, but to simpler and more immediate matters of form—the presentation of my credentials to the King, for I was not really official until this took place. Dr. Koht told me the King was about to make a journey to the north and it might be a week or so before I could go to the Palace. But the next day a message came from His Majesty, who had himself remembered that it was the American custom to give a Fourth of July reception at the Legation for friends and citizens of the United States, that he would receive me within the next twenty-four hours and my official status would be put in order. This was my first taste of that graciousness of temperament which is one of King Haakon's many distinguished characteristics.

The Protocol Department of the Foreign Office sent word about my costume. For such occasions, the men of the diplomatic corps, all except a few who represent some of the republics, appear resplendent in ceremonial gold lace, cocked hats and swords, and crusted with orders. In anticipation of being part of such a scene I had ordered a lovely confection in Paris which had followed me to Oslo. The Protocol Department had sent word to wear a dark frock with long skirt and long sleeves. My new frock would have been just right, only it did not fit! It did not fit at all and there was no time for alterations.

Out came a rather ancient tie silk from Chanel, and a hat whose chief recommendation, when I bought it, had been that it was cheap. The whole effect was decorous but unexciting.

CHAPTER IV

Digging In

In a landau drawn by horses, two men on the box, in top boots and breeches, Colonel Brock, the impressive "Introducteur," in uniform, drew up at the Legation door. Norwegian punctuality, I had been warned, was famous. I was ready and waiting. Colonel Brock greeted me in French, and continued to speak in that language throughout the drive to the Palace. Like many Norwegians, he spoke both French and English well. English is compulsory now in the schools, and it is not unusual to find Norwegians who speak four, five, or even six languages.

Our drive was not long. Before the Palace, troops were drawn up and presented arms as we passed. This, for some reason, gave me an absurd palpitation. I did so want to do and say precisely the right thing on my job and I had not expected troops! I felt more and more like an actress, fearful of forgetting her lines, as we mounted the great staircase. On every landing, and all through the long upper hall, we met soldiers presenting arms. I moved along, my heart thumping to a new fear. Now, suppose I not only could not say the right thing, but even lost the voice for saying anything at all? As we neared the end of the hall, I was handed over to the Court Chamberlain, Mr. Wedel-Jarlsberg, and escorted to the King's reception room. The door was thrown open and I was presented. I saw a tall, slight, handsome man, not looking his sixty-odd years, in a dark blue uniform, with a sympathetic expression and a manner so natural and cheerful that, far from losing my voice, I may have talked too much. I give you a guess as to what we talked about: that fine old subject, prohibition. He questioned me and we compared our two countries' experiences. Whenever anything amused him he would throw back his head, slap his thigh, and peals of laughter would follow. He thought prohibition very bad for the police. The weather being so cold, the police were always having trouble refusing kindly meant drinks. He gave me, too, a surprising new notion of European geography—if Norway were turned right around, he said, from Christiansand, it would stretch as far south as Rome! I had wondered how I would know when it was time to leave but, after twenty minutes, with a slight indicative gesture, I was given my congé.

An army could have presented arms as I came away and I would have taken it calmly, I was so rejoiced at the prospect before me. Things were bound to go well. I was aware that, in any walk of life, the man I had just left would have distinguished himself. His simple graciousness, his dignity, his candid charm were evident even in that first quarter of an hour. As the Sailor Prince Charles of Denmark, he had visited his aunt, the beautiful Queen Alexandra, in England and had fallen in love with her daughter, the Princess Maud.

Their marriage followed—and one of the happiest marriages in all Europe it was. When their son was three years old, Prince Charles of Denmark became King Haakon of Norway. From the day of his accession he has merited the respect, admiration and deep affection of his subjects. Months later, after hearing farmers and fishermen speak of him with special warmth, I said to him, "I think you must be far and away the most popular man in the country." At which he laughed that characteristic warm, chuckling laugh and, slapping his thigh once more, said quizzically, "I work all the time at it, don't I?" In a way that is, I believe, what he does—not in the ordinary sense of seeking personal popularity, but in being the Man of Good Will toward all classes, the constant reminder of their national unity, the first respecter of the rights and social aspirations of the Norwegian democracy. Monarchy becomes in him no longer an anachronism, but a dedicated way of life.

It was the custom of Queen Maud always to spend several months, both spring and autumn, in her girlhood home, England. When she traveled, her horses always accompanied her. She was a perfect horsewoman, and hardly a day passed, except in the winter—and even then, if she were not at Holmenkollen skiing—that she did not ride. Beautifully turned out, she was one of the last to ride sidesaddle in Oslo —she and I and one other. Next to horses, I think she loved flowers. The Palace garden always made me think of her. In summer, when the King is out of residence, the Palace grounds are left open. The lovely perennial borders, rich with all the blossoms that grow on English soil and live in English poetry, are there, for whoever wants to take the shortcut down the hill to the heart of the city.

I did not meet the Queen until winter, at the great annual

banquet and ball given by the Foreningen—a society such as our Patriarchs' Balls used to be—at the Freemasons' Lodge. After dinner, the diplomats went to a room set aside for them, and Her Majesty was gracious enough to send for me. I was presented.

"How does it feel," was her first question, "to be a Minister, when you are a woman?"

"Very nice, indeed," I answered, "when I remember that I *am* a Minister."

I had, by this time, all but lost my self-consciousness about being a diplomatic representative. In that marvelous climate, and amongst friendly people of all classes, the business of being a Minister was, except for the desk work, just the business of a usual, rich, out-of-doors and in, everyday life. I hesitate to use the word "classes," in reference to Norway, because, although there is stratification in economic life there as elsewhere, the culture of the country is so universal, so rich, and the aspiration of democracy so real, that one is only aware of "Norwegians."

The ball was an annual event, proclaiming the opening of the winter season. By squinting a little I could imagine myself back at old 26th Street Delmonico's in New York—something about the way the rooms, especially the ballroom, were arranged. Delmonico's, even when I knew it first, was old-fashioned. So was this building where the Foreningen was held. Commercial developments swept away the former; I hope the war does not destroy its Norwegian counterpart. The evening's gaiety reached its climax when everyone, including their Majesties, took part in what you might call a square dance—a curious mixture of a quadrille and our own Virginia reel.

I was happy to have met Queen Maud; happier still in recalling the evening, for from that moment until her death she showed me much kindness. I had been told by several people that she had been opposed to the idea of women Ministers. She was a small, dark, fragile woman, more reserved than King Haakon, yet she spoke often of intimate things, oftenest of all of her father, King Edward VII, and his many American friends. On one occasion she asked me especially to take a message to Mrs. Theodore Roosevelt, saying, "Tell her how, through all that spring, when my father died, there was only one bright memory, her visit here with the Colonel, on his way back from Africa, and from visiting in Germany." I understood what she meant. I know of no American alive today who is a greater personal symbol of the heat and light and terrific energy of America than "T. R." was.

To Queen Maud I have a debt of which I was always aware. She was devoted to dancing, and that made it possible for me, as an older woman, to indulge my own love of dancing. Early in my stay in Oslo, a woman—American born—sitting with several others, bent forward and ever so sweetly, too sweetly, in fact, remarked, "There has been great discussion since *you* came as to what age women should give up going out." I replied, also very sweetly, that fortunately I didn't have to take any thought on the matter, as going to parties was part of my job. It was the dancing that made parties one of the pleasantest parts of my job, too; and how the Norwegians do dance! There were not many balls, or full orchestras, but Northern houses are spacious and, after dinner parties, out comes the gramophone and you have your choice. The bridge players settle down, but always there are old and young who prance until the small

HER MAJESTY, QUEEN MAUD

HIS MAJESTY, KING HAAKON

Courtesy of Norwegian Travel Information Office

hours. I soon learned, too, that a dinner party in Norway was no affair of dining and going on or leaving promptly at ten-thirty. Your guests mean to put in a good five or six hours' enjoyment. I hope I contributed my share by teaching the Palais Glide and the Lambeth Walk to more than one retired ship-owner, and I learned many new, energetic steps.

In memory one makes a sort of album of those one will always recall with affection and delight. So many people contributed to make my Norwegian interlude a happy as well as a profitable time. Colonel Reidar Waaler and his wife used to come often to the Legation. He had been in the American army during the first World War and had won the Congressional medal for conspicuous bravery under fire, and his beautiful American wife was the secret envy of us all, for radiant youth had never left her lovely face. I think often of Jan and Marcia Janson, and good times in their hospitable house where she had introduced so many of the customs of her native Kentucky, which kept our hearts twice warm. And I think of Leif Hoegh the successful young ship-owner, whose wife aroused our constant admiration by the way she worked for every worth-while undertaking, and the buoyant grace with which she faced all crises. When gasoline became scarce, she gave up her car without a word, and could be seen riding on her bicycle at all times of night and day, graceful and indefatigable. There was Johan Collett, who looked like a story-book grand duke, and was an adept at all sports—he is in my album; and the Grand Old Lady of Norway is there, Betsy Kjelsberg, who has for years led every movement for helping women and children, and whose government sent her as a delegate to Geneva;

and Dr. Tove Mohr, handsome, and a famous woman physician—and, oh, so many more.

It may be of interest to some people to know what constitutes the official day of a Minister—at least, my day while in Norway. The Chancery in Oslo was in a building about thirty yards from the house. The Secretaries of Legation and clerks arrived there at 9 A.M. If there was anything of immediate importance in the early mail or by cable, they would consult with me by telephone, or come over to see me in the upstairs sitting room. There I opened my letters and saw my personal secretary for about half an hour, unless an early caller made it necessary to be in the Minister's office sooner, which is on the ground floor of the Legation. After that, on a normal morning, all routine work was taken up first.

Average routine work consisted of going over appointments for the day, dictating answers to official letters, reading the local newspapers, and conferences with members of the staff. Of course, when there was a diplomatic pouch going out to Washington, there was a despatch to be worked on and written. The arrival of a pouch from the U. S. brought many matters to be studied and correspondence that required replies.

My correspondence would usually include numerous requests for intercession in business matters, appeals for help from stranded Americans, as well as miscellaneous matters too numerous to mention. The mornings when the pouch arrived always carried with them an aura of excitement, for not only letters but magazines and newspapers arrived in abundance—each with a flavor that gave us zest. It would bring me also the instructions on cases and questions which

I had referred to Washington, and a résumé of important diplomatic events in other parts of the world. This is regularly furnished to the Department by its representatives abroad. Thus I could know accurately what was happening in China, Japan, or the Balkans, just as a résumé of my reports would be sent to other missions for their information. Occasionally, confidential communications to the Minister of Foreign Affairs would come and these I would deliver to him personally. Then, when the war began, the periodicals came later and later and sometimes not at all. Often the long way around, over China and Siberia, letters would arrive three months late. Though we would exclaim over the delays, how we valued every tie with the United States, of whatever brand of opinion. And, as the war continued, official communication with Washington was of necessity almost always by cable.

Visits to the Foreign Office were generally made in the morning and by appointment. I always enjoyed these, as I learned much from the Foreign Minister on any subject under discussion. Also, I often found several of my colleagues awaiting their turn to be received and it was an opportunity to get their views on pending questions. A drawback for a woman Minister is that she cannot go to the clubs, and there gather the news as the male diplomats do.

Occasionally I was asked by one of our consuls to see a bureau chief on some trade question that he had not succeeded in ironing out. This is not a usual duty of a Minister, but I was always glad to respond when told that I was the court of last resort—all other efforts having failed. It was only during the last few months that a Commercial Secretary was attached to the Legation, and after that matters relating to trade fell to him.

There was one question that caused trouble during all the time that I was en poste in Oslo. The quota allotment for importation of a certain brand of American shoes never seemed adequate and a request was always made for an additional amount, which in the end was generally granted. However, it necessitated numerous pourparlers, and the poor Foreign Office official, who had these matters in hand, became as weary of them as we did. I had an amusing experience the last time that I saw him. I brought all the last arguments to bear and then said:

"I wear these particular shoes myself now, as they are the only ones I can find in Oslo that are comfortable."

The official had been extremely courteous always, but that morning I felt a certain tenseness in the air. He studied his notes, interrogated me further to help refresh his memory, then very quietly said:

"As I understand it, these shoes are really only suitable for crippled and deformed feet."

Instinctively, I lifted my foot and looked at it, puzzled. I could only murmur, "So?"

"The matter can only be finally decided by the Minister of Commerce, but I'll do what I can," he continued.

"I know him," I said. "Can't I go to see him?"

"Oh, no; all requests must go through the Foreign Office."

I left not quite sure whether the issue was the shoe quota or the quality of my own feet, nor could I stop wondering when I heard the official racing after me down the corridor, and his half apologetic last word—

"But if you should see the Minister of Commerce at dinner, there is . . . no objection."

I resolved with new fervor that American shoes should be sold in Oslo!

A diplomat's office hours for the most part contain the same sundries. There are always the tourists who may find themselves in trouble; the business men who knit up the web of international trade and who call at the Legation to give and get information about local conditions; there are always requests from colleagues for appointments to discuss things, for diplomatic visas and the like.

Luncheon at the Legation was a rather informal and a very movable feast. We allowed an hour or an hour and a half, and the meals had to be elastic as so often unexpected arrivals in Oslo were asked to drop in at the last moment. The butler and cook took these extras as a matter of course. Nothing makes a household run more smoothly than when the staff makes a rule of always expecting some "unexpected guest." Of these guests, the traveling journalists going east, coming north, were the most wished for, and we listened greedily to their opinions and experiences. Mr. Callendar of *The New York Times* Bureau in London, Mr. Tolischus from *The New York Times* in Berlin, were to us also what a spell of favorable weather is to farmers. They came; they went; and we knew that trouble was brewing somewhere. Now it was Callendar hurrying in from Sweden and Finland because the iron ore squabble at Narvik was growing furious.

Leland Stowe came twice in 1940, representing *The Chicago Daily News;* and Mr. Stephens of *The Christian Science Monitor*. Leland Stowe was so very clever and so fast with his news, that his stories became one of the news beats of the war, but I cannot help regretting that he mistook the stunned and shell-shocked attitude of the Norwegian people in the early days of the blitzkreig for acquiescence in invasion. Journalists have to be fast, of course, but their misjudgments often require atonement; and I understand perfectly the resentment of the Norwegian people at the rumors spread by wire around the world. For, when they realized that invasion had come, they fought with grandeur, and against all odds.

Local guests were no less welcome than foreigners. A very clever professor of Modern History at the University, Professor Worm-Müller, lived across the street from the Legation. It was always a red-letter day when he could be induced to spare the time to come and shed light on the many complex questions at home and abroad. When I arrived in Oslo, the Professor was on a trip around the world, so that it was not until I had been in residence for a number of months that I met him. He was the first person I ever heard prognosticate the immediate future correctly. He kept repeating, as early as 1937, that Germany's real objective was the disintegration of the British Empire. Few people took that to heart then. He was one of the few Norwegians I talked to who, from the Anschluss on—and probably before—appreciated the depth of Hitler's sinister and brutal plans. Another friend whose opinions I valued was Professor Keilhau. He was a member of the Nobel Prize Committee and a great admirer of Secretary of State Hull's efforts for peace through his trade treaties.

The afternoons were ordinarily passed in clearing off my desk and, as a usual thing, I did not get out before four-thirty or five o'clock. Then I would take the dogs for an hour's walk, generally in Frogner Park. This was very invigorating and inspiring in the winter, because though it was dark, or nearly so, and the ground covered with ice and snow, the lights in the sky were beautiful and the air crisp and life-giving. Even at that hour, the children and young people would be still coasting and skiing on the hills. Of course, there were some afternoons when it was possible to get out earlier to go shopping or skiing.

After six, there was time for rest before dressing to dine out, or for a party at home. The evenings that were free, I either sat by the fire with my embroidery and the radio, or I had a lesson in Norwegian. This latter was made possible because among the numerous American women married to Norwegians was one who had a genius for languages. She was the wife of Colle Morgenstierne, and her maiden name was Florence Day Adams. She spoke and knew thoroughly six languages. (Because of her knowledge of German, she was able, at different times after the invasion, to motor Americans, among them Leland Stowe, through the Nazi lines and across the border into Sweden. She would get out of the car, look at the officers with her handsome brown eyes and explain her errand fluently in their own language; and always they would allow her to go on.) My lessons were necessarily too intermittent to get me very far, but they made it possible for me to read the newspapers and to speak enough to do simple shopping.

Twice a year, at the opening and closing of Parliament, the whole diplomatic corps—in uniforms if they had them—took part in one gala Court occasion. At high noon, the King and the Crown Prince would drive in an open barouche behind four horses with postillions to the Parliament Building. Karl Johansgate would be lined with troops nearly up to the Palace grounds. Our seats at the ceremony were carefully assigned by protocol. When I first arrived in Oslo I was seated far down the line, for I was only fifteenth in rank, as far away as that from the Doyen, but as time went on and death thinned our ranks and transfers changed our status, I became the fourth. My place the last time I attended this ceremonial of democracy, after England had declared war on Germany, was between the heads of the British and the German Missions, and I am afraid I held myself a little stiffly, feeling like a buffer state, and finding a face of strict neutrality very hard to assume.

How right Ethel had been. It was wonderful to find myself in a new place and one so full of love of life, of movement, of ideas and of health. The life was both slower and faster than ours—more patterned, with more awareness of social relations. I found charming the old custom of shaking hands with the hostess after each meal and saying, *"Takk for maten,"*—"Thanks for the food"; and even more I liked the custom which prevails whereby the first time after a party when you meet your host or hostess, you say, *"Takk for sisst,"*—"Thanks for last time," which makes going about a continued story, full of little memories. Our American way of taking everything for granted, of eating and running, avid always for What Next, seemed less civilized to me, after half a year in Norway. Life in Oslo was lively, and yet was still leisurely and old-world enough for gratitude and politeness to bloom gently. I was, I admit, more fortunate than many others. I gathered that there was another side of the picture. There were those who felt a lack of warmth toward foreigners. Members of Legations could be in residence for months and months and never meet anybody outside the Diplomatic Corps, unless they themselves made the advances. Once I discussed this with a Norwegian friend who said, "I know what you mean. But there are reasons. We are a small country. It is not precisely that we have an inferiority complex. Rather, we are shy, we like our own ways and we are not prepared to be overborne by cosmopolitan manners. Yes, we are rather more contented than most nations with our own way of life. We do not take much interest in foreigners unless one of them interests us as an individual."

For some newcomers, whatever the cause, life in Norway has seemed chilling and difficult. The American Minister, in the trail of the popular Biddles, with an appetite for outdoor sports, and for seeing how people lived in town and country, loved every minute of her stay. I keep wanting to run on about the climate, too. It agreed with me so well that I find myself advising a winter in Norway, a summer, an autumn or spring, as cure for every ill of mind or body. I want to go back.

CHAPTER V

WHITE NIGHTS

THE FOURTH OF JULY garden party was just a sea of strange faces and one recurring question—"Are you going to hear Kirsten Flagstad tomorrow night, at the Frogner stadium?" If I had been in Norway more than one very busy week, the fact that Oslo's native daughter was to sing in the open air, before ten thousand people, would never have escaped me. I joined the throng next evening that came from all quarters to Frogner. I, too, was happily expectant, but not quite prepared for the thrill that was in store for us.

Frogner Park is almost more "the heart of Oslo" than the Palace or Karl Johansgate. Cheerful in summer, with glimpses of the mountains to make it perfect, it is the point at which all interests converge . . . here are talkers, dreamers, walkers; here the whole town skates in winter. Nearby the great Wigeland fountain is being placed—but that is another story.

That evening in July, I saw a great homecoming. Flagstad had been acclaimed in New York as the greatest of all Brünnhildes and Isoldes, and many of those who were out to welcome their famous daughter felt not only pride, but deep affection, for "Kirsten, who grew up here."

As the rich, glorious notes of Brünnhilde's battle cry reached to the farthest corners of that vast field, it was not difficult to imagine that one of the Valkyries had come down to the plains to lure others to her mountain fastness.

Flagstad, by her superb renditions, has brought about a renaissance of Wagner in America. She is no longer as slim as many of her Norwegian sisters, but the carriage and regal poise of her head are there. To visitors and natives alike that night she seemed the embodiment of the "Volsunga Saga." She is, I think, the archetype of her countrywomen who so often combine beauty of body, developed through an almost religious physical culture, with a deep and solitary poetic spirit which expresses itself both in artistic creation and appreciation.

As I listened I had a foretaste of all that I would find in Norway. The land is steeped in mysticism (things felt but not seen); the ancient folklore lingers in the country places, in the dark pine forests, the valley farms and the fisher villages that hug the shores of still and narrow fjords. The cool magnificence of the Norwegian scenery has for centuries fed the imagination of a people living close to the earth. The Vikings, eleven hundred years ago, had their bards—or skalds, as they called them—who celebrated their adventures or wove great, imaginative tales on the themes of birth and death, war and love, men and gods. The Edda, their collection of sagas, appeals alike to poets and students of history, to men of letters and of science. It is a great source book of human experience. Not all remember that we owe Wagner's Ring to its finest story, the "Volsunga Saga." The son of Odin is the great-great-grandfather of Siegfried, the favorite hero of the North. One of the loveliest chapters in this saga describes Siegfried when, after tasting the blood of the slain dragon, he finds himself able to understand the songs of the birds. How many times in New York we have listened to that most fanciful and loveliest motif in all the Wagnerian Ring, sprung from an old Norwegian story.

Those who enter Norway by the Bergen gateway are welcomed there by a statue of Ole Bull—in spirit a direct descendant of Siegfried. As a violinist, his only instructors were the songs of the birds, the music of the waterfalls and the woodland streams. It was through Bull's influence that Grieg, another son of Bergen, entered the Leipzig Conservatory. Grieg wrote his first pieces at the age of nine. Always the gifts of his native land were with him—the white nights and the dark days, the amazing contrasts of her seasons. Whether in the musical setting for Peer Gynt, or in his best-known song, "Jeg elsker dig," the coloring is Norwegian. There is the great common heritage of a poetic view of life—a heritage not exploited but continually refreshed by new weavers of the tapestry. There is deep popular respect for the artist, as one whose fate it is to replenish the people. It is not surprising, therefore, that it is a race of many artists in many fields.

The whole country is proud of Kaja Eide Norena, prima donna of the Paris Opera. She comes from the village of Horten and has gone far—she has sung "Traviata" at the Metropolitan. Oslo has no grand opera now, but I enjoyed listening to its citizens who, connoisseurs of opera music, loved especially to talk of Borghild Langaard. She still lived in Oslo, and taught, but she was almost legendary. "There was no other voice like hers," someone would say; "she was not merely a great singer but a great artist. She drew from her listeners all they had to give. She gave them more than they had ever dreamed." And when I came to know her and her Italian husband, I felt this too. Her husband had never heard her sing, yet he, too, was in love with the singer, as well as the woman. Nothing she ever had been was lost. There was no decline in her personality.

For most Americans, the Norwegian artist best known, I imagine, is Sonja Henie, the Oslo girl who raised skating to the level of the ballet. Yet in Norway, Sonja Henie was supreme but not unique, for every Norwegian makes an art of the use of his body. Not since the Greeks has there been a people who cared so much for a sound mind in a sound body. Indeed, in the summer time, along the beaches, as I looked at the beautiful forms of both men and women, saw them in their boats, or diving, or walking, or running, I used to look and look again, for it was like some fantasy of a Greek temple frieze coming to life.

Sonja Henie's skating, so close to ballet, delighted me; so did the national sport of skiing, which came to its perfection in Norway. Skiing, daring and hazardous, is as free and joyous as the dance, and happy the nation which finds skis in its very cradle. There is more poetry in skiing than in half the poets of the world; and to sit half-way up the Holmenkollen and watch the jumping contests is a glorious experience. The skiers take off and fly through the air like swooping, giant birds; they accelerate their speed, lengthen the distance of their landing and keep their balance by using their arms like wings. Even when they fall, it is with an amazing freedom and grace.

Heroes and goddesses on skates, or skis, or plunging into

the summer seas—that is how the Norwegians seem. One wonders whether the fame of the strength and physical perfection of the Valkyries, as they bore their dead heroes to Valhalla, was a true picture of the daughters of Scandinavia in prehistoric times. Or did the early mothers and fathers so saturate their thoughts with legends that they ended by breeding this magnificent race?

Flagstad's Brünnhilde, her splendid heroic cries, seemed to me that night in the stadium to be the voice of a whole people, insisting on courage, celebrating an undying tradition of bold enterprise beyond known horizons. Perhaps some echo of the spirit of her song remained with me and stirred me to accept an invitation, the very next day after the concert. A friend had arrived from England in a private plane and asked me to fly with him over one of the largest and most perilous of the glaciers and the Jotunheim Mountains, famous in legend as the home of the gods.

I must admit that I only fully realized the risks we would be running once we were in the air. We had no pontoons. There were then only two fields in Norway where land planes could ground. The country is honeycombed with grim mountains and lakes and rivers, and the terrain over which we flew was many miles from those two army fields.

We soared until the highest peaks looked no more imposing than the hills of Nebraska, without their green, while the valleys appeared to be what the ancients thought them—paths made by the gods' huge footprints. And, in this mood, it was possible to believe, as did the ancients, that the rivers were created by the tears of the goddesses as they witnessed the destruction wrought by their mates.

Suddenly I was awakened from my reverie, as we began

to descend. We straightened and swung over the glacier. We seemed to be looking down on ocean rollers frozen in mid-air. It is a magnificently terrifying experience to look down from a great height on such an expanse of imperceptibly moving ice. But we could not linger too long to gaze and wonder. Even in that farthest north in July there does come an hour or so of darkness. Slowly we turned about to make our way home.

I twisted in my seat and looked back. On one side rose a wall of solid, inky black clouds, while on the other, the sky was as scarlet and gold as if the oriflammes of heaven had been unfurled to form a backdrop. My friend and I looked at each other; I could only murmur "Valhalla!" It was easy to imagine that Odin stood there with his infallible spear, having commanded us to fly and bring him news of the world. We had become one of the ravens who sat on Odin's shoulders—Hugin (thought) and Munin (memory). It was Munin, as most prized by Odin, that I hoped we were. Then, from the black mountains on our left, there seemed to come distinctly the cry of Brünnhilde, drowning out the hum of the motors. Was she riding her galloping steed into the sunset flames or was it only a subconscious echo of last night? Time stood still, and I had a sense of disembodiment as we glided on between earth and sky.

Even after a perfectly prosaic landing, it was difficult to shake off the feeling of having been in another world. I forgot to give thanks for our safe return—I forgot everything except that I must know more of that magic country, the home of the gods, from which we had just come, for in it lay all the romance and the cold charm of Norway.

For this adventure I was indebted to Mr. Walter Case of

New York, whose sudden arrival had disrupted the usual routine of our days. Cables from mutual friends had heralded his approach, but we were unprepared for his dynamic personality and unique point of view. He was always unpredictable and unexpected. In looking through my files a short time ago, I found notes that I had made as he talked—suggestions, many of them, of what I might do to make my Mission outstanding. He assured me that a more extensive market for fats was essential, and he suggested a way to open up a demand for whale oil in India. The first step would have to be to convince the natives that a whale is not a mammal but belongs to the fish family! He wore the bright mark of those who give color to the world and, as well, he was Mr. Case, the clever business man. Though I knew that his health was precarious, it was a shock to hear the next winter of his death.

For my next most interesting experience of that first summer, I was also indebted to Mr. Case. He knew that I had long been full of curiosity about Norway's great whaling industry. So, a few days after his departure, an Englishman—a friend of his—telephoned me from Tönsberg asking if he and his brother-in-law might pay me a visit on their next trip to Oslo. When they came for luncheon, it turned out that the brother-in-law was Mr. Ronald Bugge, the head of one of the big whaling companies. Before they left it was arranged that my daughter, who was visiting me, and I should go down by motor the next week and meet the leaders of the whaling business.

Not yet used to the very narrow and crooked roads, we were terrified by the speed with which the skilful chauffeur, sent to fetch us, dashed us towards our destination. At one point we found a limousine, with an Oslo tag, completely turned over with its wheels in the air. The occupants, more shocked than hurt, were extricating themselves. We offered help and were asked just to leave word with the nearest garage. But the accident increased our alarm, and we screwed up courage to beg the chauffeur to take warning. Whereupon he explained to the friend who was acting as guide that, as he had once driven the King at that pace, he thought, surely, the American Minister would want to make as good time. Not many weeks later, even on circuitous roads, I began driving my own car at the same good clip.

At Sandefjord, what they showed us first was the whaling museum. I love my history, when I see it in things—not just in the record—and I tingled as we studied the little models of boats and the changing instruments with which men from prehistoric times have hunted whales in all the seven seas. The museum was built by Mr. Lars Christensen, the explorer, in memory of his father, and it recalled his father's life as no cold tomb could ever have done. From the museum, we went along for lunch with Mr. Christensen at his summer home. It was not one summer home, but a sort of village, a series of fishermen's cottages put end to end and sprawling along the sand dunes of the North Sea. I have seldom been in a more enchanting place. "Skaals" were drunk and stories told while we dawdled over the delicious sea food, until it was time to go along to see the real object of our visit. By launch we went to Sandefjord, where the fleet lay in gala array. The flag dressing was in honor of "the American Minister." I made a note then always to remember, at such times, that it is only one's office that counts, and to keep down any childish personal gratification. Not everybody does.

What astonished us most in the whaling factory was the lack of odor of any kind, the extreme cleanliness of every inch of it, the hundreds of steps to go down, and the immensity of it. A floating factory is really a mother ship of 20,000 to 30,000 tons, which has attached to it a group of smaller whaling boats, or killers, from which the whale is harpooned. After this the enormous blue whale is hauled on board the factory, is cut up and the oil is extracted by boiling the body. In modern whaling, stations on land are no longer necessary. Everything is done on the mother ship. Our hosts explained that there was no oily smell on the factory because, directly after the oil is secured in the great tanks and all the waste parts thrown overboard, the great mopping up begins. "Plenty of time, you know, on the long trek from the Antarctic to make things spick and span."

I took endless notes of everything. After climbing up from the bowels of the ship, we were glad enough to sit down in the skipper's room and have tea. There they told us about the whaling industry, and its increasing pitfalls—penalties, now, for killing females with young, and those under age and a given size; and still worse, the hunted animal itself is becoming scarcer and scarcer. The glamour that used to surround our own New Bedford whaling fleet, they told us, has gone a-glimmering. All is mechanized and modernized. Factory ships have every modern convenience on board, even newspapers and movies. The men need distraction, since from December to March and often longer, they never set foot on land, nor often see any.

This bright, red-letter day wound up with a swim off an

island—one of the myriad islands, or rocks, off the coast near Tönsberg where the charming Bugges spend the mild months. Then dinner and to bed.

To bed and to sleep! And sleep was not easy those first months in Norway. For well on into August, the sun never seemed to set, and quite willingly one stayed awake to enjoy the loveliness of those unending days. Only those who know the northern summer, can quite know what I mean. In the morning, I waked as stiff as I was when I had climbed down into the Grand Canyon. We must have inspected miles of whaling factory, up and down.

That first summer in Norway shines especially because my daughter and her Phyllis and Howland came to have a look at my northern Mission. For six weeks, every day, at the end of my office hours, like most of Norway's population, we made merry at the beaches, or sailed on the fjords. It was the season, too, of tourists—tourists for a day or a week. They came on their way, to play or study, looping up from Germany and Holland, on to Stockholm, and Helsinki, perhaps en route to take the Trans-Siberian. We never lacked for tourists and their calls at the Legation; and every day my own work became more absorbing.

My first week-end at my post is heart-warming to recall. Sir Thomas and Lady Fearnley asked me to lovely Toresplassen, fifty kilometres out of Oslo. They were friends of friends, and wasted no time in making me welcome. Sir Thomas is a Norwegian, one of her great ship-owners, and, as well a citizen of the world, at home in many capitals, and for many years a constant traveller. The title he enjoys is a knighthood, seldom conferred abroad, for his services to British shipping during the last war. His grandfather was a famous artist and I enjoyed seeing not only Toresplassen, but pictures of old Norway that were family treasures. The spacious house of old Norwegian design is set high on a hill three miles from the main road, with a lawn sloping to a lake. I was to know Lady Fearnley as friend and perfect hostess many times. I loved going there in summer. In fact, there was nothing to choose among the seasons. In autumn, with gun in hand, we tramped the forest and seldom got a hare. In the wintertime we took the slopes on skis, the only shadow on my enjoyment being that I remained in the duffer class, and being a duffer on skis, while comical, is not nearly as bearable as being a duffer at golf. After delicious dinners—Lady Fearnley was famous for them—everything would center round the great fire in the hall, and every time I would go up to bed I would find myself echoing an old French friend who used to say, "I have had a very seldom evening," meaning, I suppose, "special." For those many "seldom evenings" when I was a stranger in a strange and lovely land I shall always be grateful.

Suddenly September arrived and everything happened at once. My children left for France en route to America. And Jacquie, finally deciding that being a private secretary was not so congenial as an office job, sailed for home, too. The waterside restaurants and bathing beaches that had made up so much of the summer scene closed. Altogether I felt lonely and very far from the Bowery. I had never seen Stockholm, perhaps this was the moment to go there. A little trip, a change of scene, would interest me and bridge over the first days of family separation which are always the most difficult.

The same experience happens to me over and over again.

When I finally see something very beautiful, I always wonder why I have never believed or been at all prepared for the wonder. I can't at all tell anyone else about Stockholm. It so has to be seen to be believed; and each time I returned to it, I would say to myself that something was wrong with my memory. It was always astonishing, had always grown more impressive. I began to find it, and find it still, as a whole, the most beautiful city in the world. I was prepared to like its people, too, and have not been disappointed. And the Town Hall is a work of architectural perfection. Enjoying Stockholm always made one remember that ancient Greece, too, was an archipelago of lovely islands.

One unexpected feature of Stockholm that delighted me was the abundance of the flowers. Beautiful urns and great shapely cement tubs in groups of threes or fours adorned so many street corners and all the open squares. Nowhere but in California have I seen greater variety or more gorgeous blossoms. In Norway, most of our flowers came from Holland or Belgium, but in Sweden a whole nation of cultivators was at work adorning the town. I was told that in the bright nights of the north, flowers cannot be expected to have the rich perfume of the gardens of England and France and the United States, but they make up in sheer color. I do know that the lilacs have fainter fragrance, much less rich, than they have along the Hudson, but, oh, how beautiful they are and how beloved by the people of the north.

At that time, Mr. Fred Deering was our Minister to Sweden. He and his beautiful wife did innumerable things to make my visit a happy mixture of learning about the north at work, and enjoying Stockholm's many amusements. In the morning, we would set off for a round of co-operative enterprises—flats, mills, bakeries and food shops. They are models of aesthetic arrangement as well as a determined experiment in lowering prices and making for stable distribution of goods. It was early in the season, and many of the pleasant people Mrs. Deering assembled for lunches and dinners had just returned from summer shores and woods. I always love the first gathering at the beginning of an autumn season for that out-door look that people bring back to town.

I was enjoying myself vastly in Stockholm when our Secretary of Legation sent me a telegram. He said that the President of the International Chamber of Commerce, Mr. Thomas J. Watson, was arriving shortly in Oslo and that meeting him would be of interest to numbers of Norwegian business men and government people. Had I any suggestions as to his entertainment? This was simple. I telegraphed that the occasion called for a dinner party, would he begin arranging it? Capable official that he is, Jeff Patterson made the list, kept me posted, did everything, while I stayed on in Stockholm. As it turned out—and this at first distressed me—my first dinner party was going to clash with a Lawrence Tibbett concert. But all's well that ends as well as in the case of that initial dinner. After the concert, Mr. and Mrs. Tibbett and several members of the audience came on to the Legation for supper. We were all longing to hear him sing, but always a hostess hesitates to make such a request of a great artist. Everyone was enchanted when, quite simply, he offered, and sang "The Road to Mandalay" and "Going Home." Never was he in better voice, and never was an audience more quick to show its pleasure. My first dinner party had turned into a reception. We looked at the spirited faces of that Norwegian, American and English gathering and Mr. Watson remarked, "How much this resembles a group in New York."

CHAPTER VI

Northern Winters

I had lived through a great many winters before I came to Oslo, but in the north I learned about Winter. The days are short, as short as the summer days are long, and one would imagine the many hours of darkness might make the winter gloomy, but, no—in the north they keep warm and they glory in the snow and ice; and parties, an endless chain of them, make the long evenings pass in music and talk and eating and dancing. I remember once suddenly feeling tired, and saying something about it to my secretary. At which she smiled and said, "Only a little tired? Did you know you had been out for dinner parties seventeen nights running?" I had indeed, but the foregatherings had all been fun and refreshing. And so many all at once was an exception. The new Minister was being made welcome. At them I had learned so much about Norway and Norwegians that the first sixteen had hardly tired me at all.

My first diplomatic dinner at the Palace had started me off at an enjoyable pace. I had a debutante's expectancy about it that might have been a little ridiculous, but other people, even old-timers in Oslo, had the same feeling. An

Englishwoman who arrived with a large feather fan, not at all a match for her gown, had much the same zest. It was an occasion, and since the feather fan had been carried by her grandmother to a Court at Buckingham Palace, she felt she owed it to the family heirloom to bring it.

The dining room at the Palace was made for great entertainments. It was an immense room with a Minstrel Gallery at one end. The table was in horseshoe shape, like that used for state occasions in the White House. I was seated between the Minister from Portugal and the representative of the Soviet Union. The Russian spoke not a word of any language known to western Europe, but his spirit was effervescent and coöperative, and I am told that our signs and grimaces convinced the other diners that we were enjoying ourselves immensely and "spoke each other's language."

"Skaal" is the great word of the north; the key word of all dinners. At the dinner before the Foreningen Ball, the King, as usual on such occasions, skaals each head of Mission. He lifts his glass, and the diplomat stands, sweeps a deep bow, and drinks. My turn was bound to come. The King lifted his glass, I started to rise, but he motioned me to be seated. I compromised by bending my knees which got me half way back in my chair but not quite. At the Palace dinner, I did the same, not quite up, not quite down. The Finnish Minister, who had a sort of anti-talent for diplomatic remarks, gave one look at me, and called across the table to the Queen and to his colleagues that it was ridiculous for me to be treated differently from the rest. Was she a Minister or was she not? If she was, she should stand up, etc., etc., etc. He spoke in Finnish, and my amiable Portuguese neighbor had to translate for me. I had a moment of embarrassment, but their Majesties, by their tact and kindness, tempered it later. It was explained to me that, of course, the King would not let a woman stand without standing himself; that if he stood for the American Minister he would have had to stand for all. It seems I had "played ball" in just the right way after all. When the meal was over, we went into the ballroom and His Majesty came to me, and addressed the "Minister," "Are you ready for your cigar?" and then laughed that hearty, characteristic laugh when the "Woman" managed to say, "Not yet, thanks!"

After coffee, Her Majesty took her place, standing in the middle of the room, and an equerry moved about designating those who were invited to come and speak to her. I was pleased to be included. I remember I had my first conversation with the Crown Princess that night, and that she was a lovely vision in her pale blue frock. She has an air of great distinction, even of a worldly kind, but when you speak with her you see her gentle sweetness and her deep devotion to home and family. So I saw her when I first met her, and the impression remains valid. To which, during these years of war, has been added a revelation of great gallantry. Princess Märtha is the daughter of Prince Carl of Sweden and Princess Ingeborg, sister to two kings, the King of Norway and the King of Denmark. Her sister was the beloved Queen Astrid of Belgium, and the third sister, also tall and dark and with an exquisite figure, is the Princess Marghareta of Denmark.

Every dinner party that first winter was like another and yet different—the same warp of pleasant drawing rooms and laden tables, and warm social conversation; and bright threads of new people, intimate talks, opening up vistas of

Norwegian Travel Information Office

CROWN PRINCE OLAV AND HIS FAMILY, 1937

other parts of Norway where this one had been born, or which some other deemed the most beautiful spot in the world.

Seated next to the Prime Minister one evening at dinner, I made a vow to myself to travel all over the country as soon as my work at the Legation permitted. We had been talking about his old home in the country north of Trondheim. I realized that an Ambassador or Minister sent to Washington might feel that to gather knowledge of the whole United States would take a lifetime. The U. S. A. was too vast to travel in; and entailed too much cost. I would play my job as if I were not only accredited to the court and government in Oslo, but to all the Norwegian people, as indeed I was. I liked to imagine that I had a mandate to make contacts with the mountain valleys, with Finnmark where the Lapps lived, and with the people who lived along remote fjords. I soon found out that the "small country" to which I was accredited covered 125,000 square miles, and had twelve thousand miles of shore land, but my fantasy of "knowing Norway," product of the will to see, encouraged at Oslo dinner parties, came to make the next years some of the richest of my life. And I was always eager to find out where each new Norwegian personality came from, what valley, and what travels made the man.

The career of Mr. Johan Nygaardsvold, the Labor Prime Minister, fascinated me and helped me to understand his country. I could have claimed him as a Norwegian-American, almost; for his father had died when he was still a boy, he had gone to work when other boys were still at school, and as a young man had emigrated to the New World. I thought I knew a little about Montana, but he knew vastly more, for he had worked on the railroad in that state for eight years. It was in Montana that he amplified his education, studying history and many languages at night so that when he returned to Norway and bought a farm in his native valley, where he married and raised a family, he brought with him a knowledge of the past and of the common problems of working men and women the whole world over. He was already a farmer-statesman when his valley sent him to the Störting.

The tale runs—the King told me this himself—that on one occasion when His Majesty was traveling in the north, he observed a giant of a man carrying some planks on his shoulder, and when he asked who the fellow was, he was told prophetically, "Your future Prime Minister, no doubt." Sure enough, when the Labor Party came to power in 1935, Nygaardsvold became Prime Minister, and was the more kindly received because the King had for a long time been following the career of the scholar who could bear so much weight on his shoulders. His rugged form, his face, on which is engraved so much of his experience, his hard outdoor labor, and constant search for truth and learning, gave to visitors what it gave to his own people, a sense of stable values. It is not unusual today, this winter of 1941, for the Prime Minister, along with other members of the Labor Party, to be held blameworthy for the unarmed state of the country at the time of the German invasion. Someone has to be the scapegoat, it seems. Yet the spirit of the country was united, and in spirit it is still indomitable. Time may tell a different story and credit be given where blame now seems to tarnish.

Mr. J. L. Mowinckel, head of the Liberal Party, father of

the Oslo Convention, three times himself Prime Minister of Norway, is another—now made a scapegoat by the big armament advocates—of the men I made acquaintance with that first winter of discovery in the north. He was a native of Bergen. His fortune had been made in shipping, as is true of most fortunes in Norway. I happened to be sitting next to him at dinner on an evening of a day when the Storting had been debating naval appropriations. He talked to me about the Norwegian position in the last war, about how important it was to protect the entrances to the fjords; for the Norwegians to escape involvement, the belligerents seeking refuge must be kept out of neutral waters. He spoke at some length, advocating a destroyer program, and I was, therefore, much surprised the next day to discover he had voted against the Naval Appropriations Bill. Dining a few nights later, however, I heard an explanation of his attitude, and more intricacies of the naval bill than had at first been apparent. He showed me how the bill had been written to include the building of capital ships, not worth the cost to a non-aggressive power, and likely, because of the huge demands on the budget, to mean the curtailment of social legislation—which was also a defense measure working for the strength and unity of the population. That he has since been made to bear the blame for Norway's meagre armament has interested but not upset me. I have only to remember that most of the little, vociferous circle of critics did not work very hard for armament, nor could they possibly have dissented from his stand for social expenditures which made for a united nation. As President Roosevelt has said in his message to Congress— "As men do not live by bread alone, they do not fight by armaments alone. Those who man our defenses and those behind them who build our defenses must have the stamina and the courage which come from unshakeable belief in the manner of life which they are defending. The mighty action that we are calling for cannot be based on a disregard for all the things worth fighting for. . . . Certainly this is no time for any of us to stop thinking about the social and economic problems which are the root cause of the social revolution which is today a supreme factor in the world."

In discussing Norwegian neutrality, I was interested to hear that, in the late autumn of 1915, a royal decree had been issued forbidding belligerent submarines from coming into neutral waters. The Germans brought such strong pressure to bear against this that Norway, at one time, was on the verge of war with them. In the end Germany gave in.

Norway's small population and geographical situation always made neutrality a necessity for her. Therefore, Norway has always adhered rigidly to international law, and thus preserved neutrality as long as international law was taken seriously—in spite of such strains on diplomacy as the submarine episode just referred to.

In 1939, Norway made every effort to follow this same strict neutrality. Their policy in the *City of Flint* case, which was versus the German claim, and in the *Altmark* incident, which was critical of the procedure of the British, proved that they were again following the strictly neutral lines laid down from 1915 to 1918.

The President of the Storting I met at dinner, too—the second man in the kingdom, for the President of the Storting ranks above the Prime Minister. Mr. Carl Hambro is versatile, a statesman of international reputation. He was always the man of Europe and of the world as well as of Norway, a worker for the League of Nations, aware of religious developments throughout the world, for a time a pillar of the Buchman Movement, since he saw in it a way of orientation to modern living. He wrote enormously, translated many foreign works into Norwegian, carried on correspondence with other statesmen and politicians all over the world, knew America and England, and was inexhaustibly energetic. But then, nearly everybody in the north seemed to me blessed with energy and staying powers. It was, perhaps, I finally decided, the climate; for, in spite of that lapse after the seventeen dinner parties running, when I complained of being tired, I myself often felt that I was growing younger, not older. I decided that whatever weariness I felt was due to my being, as it were, both the Minister and his wife. The social side of diplomatic life is considerably lightened for men in the corps by their wives. A bachelor Ambassador or Minister can always call on the wife of his Counsellor or First Secretary, but a woman Minister remains her own hostess.

My first winter was the gayest. The second was full of quiet warmth and a great sense of being at home in Oslo. But the untimely death of the Queen cast a pall on all our spirits, and we feared—as we now know—that another European war was slowly ripening.

The Queen's death was a tragic blow for His Majesty, and the whole country grieved for their own loss and his. There was a note of sadness in everything.

Someone from the Foreign Office called me early one Sunday morning to give me the news. We knew that, after arriving in England, Her Majesty had undergone an operation by her old surgeon, but we so wanted her recovery that we counted on it. The Legations had the news at once and then, as I walked along to church in the snowy morning, the tidings were broken to the people. The slow firing of twenty-one guns made a doleful sound in the frosty air. At first people did not understand; several stopped me on the street to ask what the wordless message was, and their faces when they understood the news, became stricken. And the universal expression of sadness at the loss was to be seen and heard everywhere long after the state funeral at the great cathedral had taken place. The ritual of that occasion was enormously impressive, yet the feeling was personal, too. The great wreaths from all countries, the tributes of state, the personal expressions from royalties and chief executives and the profusion of giant pink carnations that we in Oslo knew to be the Queen's favorite flower, made it both a formal and an intimate occasion. Our hearts were full of sympathy for the King and for the husband who had lost so beloved a wife.

My granddaughter, Phyllis, was spending the winter with me. I had had an unhappy experience as I journeyed down to Paris, over Antwerp, to meet her. I sailed in a fog and, in the fjord, we had struck a schooner amidships. She sank in fifteen minutes. It is true that the crew were rescued and taken aboard; but the sight of a ship foundering, going down bow first, was horrifying. Our own ship, the *Bretagne,* being unharmed, we had proceeded on our way to the Belgian port, but it was so sudden and so horrible that I found myself thinking more and more about war. I thought of it in connection with going to fetch Phyllis. I hated even thinking about having her with me in the midst of warring Europe. But I knew she would be so gay and delighted to be abroad I indulged in a little carefree wishful thinking. Not for long.

To have been in Paris during the Munich negotiations was to have had a foretaste of disaster. People in Paris the 26th of September, 1938, from hour to hour became more silent and stunned by the news they found in half-hourly editions.

All night in our hotel off the Champs Elysées we could hear the steady rumble of all kinds of cars and trucks carrying people into the country. People off to Brittany and to Normandy. People afraid and uncertain. In the parks, men were busy digging trenches. I could not be sure why. Was it for practical purposes, or for demonstration that war could be the implement of foreign policy on two sides of a frontier? Shops told their employees to go. Peace-time buying and frivolity were over.

My coiffeur took it more calmly than most, but even he launched into memoirs about the last war, and how his class would be called soon. He seemed about to rush off before he had put in my combs.

Some of my friends began systematically moving their household goods to the country. Everyone was having bags of sand put on the roof. The street lights dimmed at night made me think of 1917. 1917 all over again! The steamship offices and Morgan's bank were jammed with Americans. One wondered if anyone had stayed at home that September of 1938.

At the American Embassy, where the crush was so great it was difficult to enter, I was greeted with "Good Heavens! What are you doing here? You must fly to England at once. Antwerp will be the first port to be closed." I explained that

I must wait for my child, and I did. The boat train arrived very late at night, and while I sat in the station waiting for Phyllis, I saw hundreds and hundreds of people patiently waiting their turn to be off for some safer refuge.

Phyllis bounded off the train, as buoyant and gay as usual, no matter what, her ship having weathered the great hurricane as she left New York. There were no porters, all had been mobilized. The station was shrill as always. Somehow we assembled the luggage, somehow got it on a cab.

The next day the fever and confusion mounted; strangers spoke to us in the streets, asking if we had any news of the conference at Munich. Everyone was tense yet still hopeful. Evacuation continued. We heard that the *Europa* had been called back to Germany from Cherbourg and many friends had dolefully to return to the base in France they had left so thankfully. The Morgan bank in the Place Vendôme told us that more than two hundred of their clients were being thrown back on them, and lodgings were difficult to find.

Phyllis and I dined with my friend Henry May the crucial night at the Cambon side of the Ritz. After a pleasant dinner, as we walked through to the Place Vendôme side, Olivier, the famous maître d'hôtel, rushed up to us saying almost passionately, "Peace has been agreed upon, there will be no war!"

"How do you know?" we said in one breath. "There are no 'extras' out."

"I assure you I am right." He pointed out the Minister of Finance. "He has just come from the Ministry," said Olivier, "he has talked by telephone with Munich."

We rushed into the street, deciding to go to our Embassy. On the Rue de Rivoli a charming old gentleman, running out of the Automobile Club on his way to a taxi, bumped into us, took off his hat and said excitedly in French to me, "Peace has been signed. I have just been talking to the Ministry."

We replied as excitedly as he that we had already heard it from Olivier and that we were on our way to our Embassy for confirmation. It was now ten-thirty. The Embassy was closed up tight. We rang and rang and at last got a response at a side door. The watchman eyed us dubiously and shook his head. Everyone had gone home. I showed him my passport and begged to be let in to telephone. I called a member of the Embassy staff, and was distressed to find that I had waked him. He, like others, had been without sleep for nights, owing to the great stress of work of evacuating our Nationals. With the worst over, he was trying to catch up.

"No," he said, "there is no news. The Foreign Office has promised to let me know the moment anything comes through."

I told him what we had heard. He did not seem impressed. We went back past the Automobile Club again, looking for a taxi. Our old gentleman was just alighting from one and this we commandeered. We exchanged bulletins. His was a reiteration of the one he had given us before. Next morning at seven-thirty my Embassy colleague called me, and said that he had heard from the Quai d'Orsay at 1:30 A.M., but had not liked to disturb me.

Then I called Henry May and said, "You see, if anyone

wants the latest on affairs of state, they should always ask Olivier. He was like that in the last war, always a jump ahead of the Government."

The days after the Munich crisis were strange, half-hopeful, half-distracted days. There was enormous hope. People said they had not been afraid. But we really knew we had been grazed by disaster. Phyllis, who had been so gay, was laid low by flu. People argued. Always in the immense relief—but there was a rather artificial gaiety in the relief—there were those, like Poe's raven, who predicted the worst. Munich, they said, was only a postponement of the evil day. Chamberlain and his fellows had brought a false peace for less than "our time."

However, the times called for some sort of celebration. Phyllis being up again, we decided to detour via London. She should have both London and Paris at once. We had seen them both bombed in our anxious dreams, and we wanted to be relieved.

Back in Oslo, I found out how settled and in love with the north I was, now that I had a grandchild to discover it too; and through her eyes I could see it as if for the first time all over again. Our return was less happy because our first news was of Jeff Patterson's transfer to Berlin. Later I had news that Ray Cox was coming in February to take Jeff Patterson's place. I remembered him from some twenty years before when he had been stationed in the Department in Washington. I had liked him and I looked forward to meeting his wife whom I had not known before. Meanwhile, however, I would have to run the Legation, with no perfect Secretary of Legation, indeed with no Secretary at all, for three months.

An American woman's club was organized in Oslo by the wife of Consul General Bevan a few years before I arrived. During the winter it held business meetings once a month, but every week there were days for bridge; and they had a very excellent library from which members could borrow all the latest American and English publications. I was very much interested in the venture and attended the meetings whenever my official duties would allow. Several times they asked me to speak—once it was to explain the New Deal, another time on my trip to Russia and again about the Lofoten fisheries. The last time the acting President, in introducing me, said, "The Minister is so kind that she comes to us whenever we have failed in finding another speaker! We turn to her as a last resort!" I didn't dare look at the other members as I knew that we would laugh. It was not a very heart-warming introduction to receive but I knew that, though it sounded maladroit, she had meant to be complimentary, and I never held it against her.

The most unforgettable picture of all my three northern winters is that of the Sundays in Oslo—

"... and now a wood
Comes toward Dunsinane."

A veritable forest of skis used to move through the streets, like upright masts in a crowded harbor, like a wood coming toward you. The whole town used to go into the country to slide and to ski—rosy cheeks, rosy mittens, tassels on their caps. The motors in winter are fixed with racks to hold the skis. The tram cars are all arranged with slots on the outsides, and with hundreds of skis aboard they look like yellow porcupines.

Oslo was a rather sober town during the week, not many crowds of people on the streets. But Sunday brought everybody out like so many jacks-in-boxes: children with skis no longer than your arm, grandfathers who had been leaping down the mountains for threescore years. They did not always leap in safety. There were, as winter wore on, almost as many crutches as skis. I exaggerate, of course, but I never ceased to be astonished at the way breakage of bones was taken as a matter of course. Splints and slings at parties, blistering sunburns, were all taken in the stride of a people who valued winter. "Other people don't *use* winter really," a Norwegian once said to me, "but we have so much of it we have to get a lot out of it."

CHAPTER VII

Third Fleet of the World

I AM ALWAYS finding new reasons why it was so easy to feel at home in Norway. Not for nothing had I grown up amongst boats, listening to the talk of ships and yachts. For two hundred years my mother's family had been British Navy people. My father had run the blockade from Bermuda during the Civil War and for twenty-five years had been in trans-Atlantic shipping business. The past was often with me in Oslo. My first link with Norway goes back a long, long way. When I was about eight years old, Chris, a young Norwegian sailor on Grandfather's yacht, made me a pair of oars for my birthday. Then he taught me to row. He was a great favorite with all of us children, and every now and again through later years I ran across him in the yachting world. One of the first things I did after arriving at my post was to try to trace my old instructor and friend who had retired at a ripe old age to spend his last days in the homeland. Alas, he had died in a hospital just two years previously.

Fifty thousand craft spin and chug and float on the Oslo Fjord. If every other subject should fail, there isn't a child or an octogenarian in Norway who couldn't be drawn into argument or story about boats.

The most important single factor in modern Norwegian life is that the country has the largest merchant marine in the world, excepting only the United States and Great Britain. There have been years when Japan ran close behind; and she is now their chief competitor in the Orient. But the fleet grows so constantly and is such a part of the life even of the farmers in the farthest valleys, that there is truth as well as glamor in the Norwegian toast—"The Vikings are come again!"

From pre-history down through all historic time, the peoples of the north have lived and grown by fishing and by shipping. I never had a Norwegian dinner party without two or three ship-owners, and almost all the owners had been seamen and captains in their day. Traveling through the country, I was always hearing of a son who had been away for years working on some ship, owned in Norway but plying perhaps between Australia and the China Coast; some uncle, captain of a boat running to Juneau from Seattle; a sister married to a husband overseeing Norwegian contracts being executed in Italian yards.

The whole history of Norway is the story of the sea. There is evidence that, in prehistoric times, from 5000 to 2000 B.C., some sort of intercourse was established between what is now Norway and other coasts. Communication was by sea alone—there could have been no other, for even today, between some of the mountain valleys, there are no roads at all and all traffic is by water. The earliest boats were rafts and hollowed tree trunks. Little Norwegian fisher boys try to navigate this same way today. When the use of metals was learned by these early men, the new technique improved the ships at once. This improvement we can trace from the rock carvings dating from the Bronze Age—from about 1000 B.C.—which show boats made of planks which could carry fifty men and must have been shaped with metal tools. In these open boats, long before the Christian Era, there was commerce over the North Sea.

The thrilling days of the Vikings date from the ninth century. When one sees now in the Museum at Bygdö those still resplendent relics of old ships, the same sense of the great creative past is evoked that one gets at Chartres or Canterbury; the same sense of mankind as forever building. Who can be dismal about the human race who remembers what was done by the Vikings in their open ships, how their voyages embraced many oceans, and stretched the minds of men ever toward new sights, a greater world. Their intrepid excursions on the old trade routes, their fearless steering through unknown waters, their bold founding of colonies on remote shores, some to become permanent outposts of civilization, some to rest in poetry among the lost ventures of history—whenever I read of them, or come upon some monument which tells their story, I am given a new sense of hope and pride. It was always a mystery to me at Norwegian banquets that no one ever overdid this sense of Viking past; I do believe I had far less restraint than the Norwegians. So much of it was new to me, and I was always excited at finding another old book with stories of the new states organized so long ago. There were once Norwegian Dominions overseas, including a large part of Ireland, the Orkneys, the Shetlands, the Isle of Man, the Faroes, Iceland, Greenland and a substantial part of the Kola Peninsula in the White

Sea. The Vikings, like the Phoenicians and the later Carthaginians in the Middle Sea, were masters. And the pride of mastery is still there. The small Democracy seems to me to have all the good points of Imperial enterprise and none of the ruthlessness or decadence of empire.

The past was more warlike, of course. In one expedition along the west coast of Ireland in the year 812, there were one hundred and twenty Viking ships. And in an attack on England described as having taken place in the year 892, there were two fleets, one of two hundred and fifty-nine and one of eighty vessels. Those sallies were certainly for plunder, but the aftermath is a civilized record of regular trading expeditions, and we know that the first trade agreement England ever signed was with Norway, in the thirteenth century.

How many times I used to go to Bygdö and take my guests there. It was a constant pleasure to read between times, then go and further awaken my imagination and fill my eyes with the graceful lines of those old ships, and to study the carvings on their bows. All my visitors—Captain Gainard, General Reilly, and Mrs. Emmett—used to linger over the Oseberg ship, famous especially for its interlacing carving of animal heads. Near Tönsberg, on my visit to the whaling fleet, we had been shown an immense mound, the place out of which this ship had been dug in the summer of 1904. The year before, a farmer digging in a barrow there had struck some woodwork. He went at once to Christiania—now Oslo—to make his discovery known to Professor Gustafson, at that time director of the University collection of antiquities. Professor Gustafson returned with him and made a trial excavation. Convinced that they were discovering a treasure, the long and difficult task was begun which resulted in a real romance.

The barrow lay close to an ancient river bed, five kilometers from the sea. In the Viking age, the river must still have been navigable for a vessel of the size of the Oseberg ship. The barrow, composed of huge masses of peat, formed a complete airtight covering over the whole of the interior. Behind the ship's mast was a sepulchral chamber in which lay the dead—two women, the Oseberg queen and her bondwoman, surrounded by coverlets, pillows and clothes. With them, too, were many personal possessions. There was a fine oak chest containing both fruit and grain, and two other chests. In the forepart of the ship there were a number of oars, booms and gaffs for spreading sails, anchors and anchor stocks and other relics of ship's gear.

There was a four-wheeled wagon made of oak, intricately and beautifully carved. Four sledges, also with richly carved bodies, three beds, a chair and endless articles of furniture were found. There were the remains of fifteen horses, four dogs, and an ox. In the forepart of the ship, oars had been stuck out through openings in the vessel's sides ready for the voyage. Just as in her lifetime, the Queen was to be able to use the ship. The Oseberg was no sea-going craft like the Gokstad ship which was excavated in 1890. It was the Queen's yacht for summer cruises along the coast and in the sheltered waters of the fjords.

Even more than by the ship, I was moved by the story of the Queen Asa who died at the early age of thirty in the ninth century. I always wanted to hear more of her. She was married against her will to King Godröd. Her son was King Halvdan the Black and her grandson King Harald the Fair-haired. The year after Halvdan was born, she had her husband killed in revenge for his murder of her father and brothers. A remarkable woman, she was both loved and feared. She spent her life bringing up her son, Halvdan the Black, and gave him lofty ideas about his vocation as King and Viking.

Many times in the summer of '39, my visits to Bygdö were a way of escape from too much talk of imminent war on land and sea in the twentieth century. For everybody knew that, if war came, the existence of the "Third Fleet" would impose great strains on Norway. In a war on the sea, with tactics of blockade, the fleet was bound to be a coveted prize and pawn by all belligerents.

A merely agrarian country could huddle in the mountains, but the Norwegian flag was everywhere in the Baltic, the North Atlantic, the Pacific. And, except for Poland, the first period of the war was fought upon the sea. And, as Germany and Britain fought for supplies and trade routes in the North Sea and the Baltic, the victims were more often the ships of the neutrals than of the belligerents. The Norwegian Government, with desperate restraint, followed a completely neutral line in its foreign policy. Its relations with Great Britain have always been particularly good. So many ships for a thousand years have traded between their shores, the very strains of the people are mixed. I have asked many questions again lately about the shipping picture since the war. My Norwegian friend emphasized the good terms existing between Britain and Norway. "Our foreign policy," he said, "was strictly neutral. The *Altmark* case made for strain, and the British mining of Norwegian waters just before the invasion alarmed us. In both cases our Government protested and would have swept the mines with Norwegian vessels if the British had not given in.

"In shipping, the British have always been our chief competitors, but by and large, it has been a friendly competition, and considerable Norwegian tonnage has been running for British charterers. With the outbreak of the war, naturally the British wanted an agreement to secure a supply of Norwegian tonnage, and in October and November, 1939, such an agreement was carried out between the Norwegian Shipowners' Association—not the Norwegian Government at all—and the British authorities. The agreement promised only that the same amount of Norwegian tonnage should continue on charter with British charterers as had been usual in the years preceding the war, at the hires prevailing in the world freight market. The marine insurance on this trade was carried by Norwegian companies, which, as usual, often reinsured in London. The special war risk insurance was handled through the Norwegian War Risk Club, a mutual insurance association, which had been started during the Spanish Civil War and which worked completely free from any foreign interests."

Since the German invasion of Norway, the whole Norwegian mercantile marine has been requisitioned by orders in council of April 22nd and May 18th by the Norwegian Government. Their insurance has now been effected in London on the pound sterling valuation in the London market. Part of the Norwegian fleet, of course, which at the time of the invasion consisted of 4,900,000 gross tons, was captured by the Germans in Danish, German and Norwegian harbors, and many vessels are still bottled up in Swedish harbors. More than three quarters of the fleet, however, is active and sailing the seven seas under the management of the Norwegian Shipping and Trade Mission, and under the Norwegian flag. People ought to know these figures, for American newspapers have reported that Norwegian vessels have been sold to British interests or have been transferred to British registry. More ships, to be sure, have been chartered by the British Ministry of Shipping since the invasion, and more than half the available Norwegian tonnage is sailing for British charterers, or in lines running to Britain. Most of the trans-oceanic steamers continue to run as usual, and for neutral charterers all over the world. Inspired stories in the press have it that Norwegian vessels laid up in American ports in the winter of 1940-41 have been looked at with "a covetous eye" by the British, but this Norwegian ship-owners deny. The freight rates collected by Norwegian ships chartered to the British Ministry of Shipping are under the prevailing market rates and are paid in sterling currency.

The capital of Free Norway—except the gold supply, which was rescued from falling into German hands and transported to the United States and Canada—consists almost exclusively of the mercantile marine, now under the management of the Norwegian Shipping and Trade Mission, stationed in New York, and a part of the Norwegian Government in exile. The income from the carrying trade of these vessels has been available for the Norwegian Government in exile according to the Provisional Orders in Council. All over the world, men discuss the extent to which the Norwegian Government after the war will be able to return the incomes of the various ships to their pre-war owners. The war expenses of the Government are great, and payment will be due on government bonds held by persons and institutions in neutral and allied countries. Even now, while the struggle is still on, the Norwegian Government has assumed responsibility and paid interest and made down-payments on the foreign-currency debts of some Norwegian municipalities and all government-guaranteed banks.

I never tired, during my stay in Norway, of hearing stories of the great shipping firms, the men who had founded them, and dealt so imaginatively with world trade. A great part of the wool cargoes of the world are carried in Norwegian bottoms, and why? Because long ago a Norwegian shipper studied the wool trade, and planned his fleet to serve it.

The most interesting and the largest shipping concern in Norway is the firm of Wilhelmsen, founded in 1861. Today the firm is not only the largest in Norway, but is the largest private ship concern in the world. The late Halfdan Wilhelmsen, who made the firm outstanding, was a genius. When he was twenty years old he went to his father and said that he would like to be made head of the firm and, as such, be given carte blanche to do all that he thought necessary to expand the business. The elder Wilhelmsen, recognizing in his son exceptional talents, retired and handed him the reins. From then on, the enterprise grew and grew until today it leads all others of its kind. No other Norwegian firm comes near to it. But Westfal-Larsen and Company, A/S, Bergen, founded only a quarter of a century ago, and the Knut-Knutsen O.A.S. line of Haugesund, the Fearnley and Eger Line, founded in 1869, Fred Olsen and Company of Oslo, founded in 1881, A/S Mowinckels Rederi of Bergen, and the Norwegian America Line of Oslo, founded in 1910, all have magnificent histories. Even the school children know the names and exploits in seamanship and the carrying trade that attach to dozens more of the shipping names of the north. Besides which, there are literally hundreds of smaller, independent boats owned by their own captains and thousands of sailors who have sailed "on shares."

Norwegian shipping, more than that of any other country, is forced to compete in the international freight market. Its fleet is many times too large to be dependent on the trade of its own small and relatively poor land. Good seamanship, an untarnished reputation attaching to all its nationals for fair and honest dealing, have helped the Norwegian merchant fleet to make its living even in competition with heavily subsidized foreign shipping. There has been no Norwegian subsidy, no "other people's money" easy to come by. The Government has dealt gently with the shipping interests on taxes (and this is always mildly an issue with the landsmen) but this gentle dealing must have played a part in the continual growth of the industry.

The international carrying trade remains a strenuous game. The Norwegians play it superbly. The problem of ship-building is one of Norway's constant problems. Wages are high in Norway. It is not profitable, except under certain conditions, to construct at home. The modern fast-running ships which Norwegian owners mostly build are expensive, and the Norwegian money market has not always been available for the necessary loans to finance the growing fleet. The Court of Arbitration appointed by the Norwegian Government in 1920, after the last war, to settle the matter of wages in the shipyards, set wages so high that, for a time, it was impossible to modernize and rebuild the fleet at the rate the operating companies desired. Smaller ships continued to be built in local yards, but owners let many contracts in foreign yards, oftenest where the trade between two countries, especially in the case of the Italian-Norwegian trade, solved economic problems at both ends of the bargain. Today, however, and for the last four or five years, the Norwegian yards have been building large, modern ships—magnificent engineering projects, beautiful in their new design and as distinctive as the Viking ships were in theirs. Often in the Legation at Oslo, I have had American guests who sang the praises of the Norwegian cargo ships they had traveled on.

"It was like a little yacht," said someone of the little *Bagdad* of the Olsen Line, describing a journey from New York to London River that had cost ninety dollars, "and I mean to travel always on such little boats. A new one every year. You have no idea, Mrs. Harriman," the enthusiast said, "how you can make faces at the *Europa* and the *Aquitania* from the *Bagdad's* snowy decks." I was tempted to travel down to Jaffa on one of the orange and lemon trips.

The Norwegian carrying trade had made a kind of cooperative peace with British sea power. With the challenging Germans, it was not always so easy. The Norwegians, great critics of seamanship, admired sailors of the German mercantile marine as very able seamen, but the attitude toward the German navy could not but grow bitter. Even when Norway was neutral, and trading in neutral ports, Norwegian ships were often sunk without warning by German U-boats and bombed by German planes, and Norwegian crews on rafts and lifeboats were machine-gunned.

These outrages were not without repercussions. One dramatic, yet pathetic, story is that of the Captain of a Norwegian torpedo boat, the *Sleipner,* whose wife was killed by a bomb in Bergen and whose two sons were killed in the war. After the navy went to join the English fleet, he took to free-booting with his six-year-old son on board—all that was left of his family. He continued in Norwegian waters, molesting German shipping. The people along the coast all know him, and at night he runs into the fjords and they supply him with food and other necessities.

Norwegians smile when someone asks them whether the German dream of a new Hanseatic League is possible and quote the German business and shipping journals which write about Hamburg as the great port of the world for German *"Grossraumwirthschaft."* And when paragraphs assert that industry and shipping are not suitable occupations for the Norwegians, who are a people suited better to produce raw materials, it is no wonder that the members of the third fleet of the world, sons of the Vikings, are apt to say, at the mildest, that Germany is having a pipe dream.

CHAPTER VIII

To the North Cape

In the spring of '38, I made a short trip back to America. While there, I discovered that Laura Wood had been harboring a wish as old as mine. I cannot remember when the North Cape first began to fascinate me—to take a cruise to the top of the world. She promised to visit me at Oslo in the summer, and once the Fourth of July garden party and the first wave of tourists were over, we would take a West Coast holiday. She arrived the middle of July with her two handsome boys and her daughter, whose exquisite form always reminds me of a Tanagra figure. We sped the young people off on a walking trip, half envying them. Whether it is speed-boating, or walking, or climbing, or swaying along on narrow roads in old-fashioned droshkies, everything there is to do in Norway in summer beckons at once. However, their mother and I were booked.

We motored up to Bergen and boarded the *Meteor*. She was a ship built by Kaiser Wilhelm about 1910 to take his naval officers for summer cruises through the Norwegian fjords. Her lines were those of a yacht and, though long since passed to Norwegian ownership, she is still spoken of as the "Kaiser's yacht." One can but speculate now about the *Meteor's* early history, and the number of German cruise ships seen year after year in Norwegian waters. Certainly the officers of the naval vessels that crashed the various fjords on April 9, 1940, showed studied familiarity with the geography of the country.

The British, on the contrary, were the butt of many absurd but affectionate stories. There were members of the British Cabinet, some of the newspapers reported, who thought Narvik was the capital of the country. Others thought Narvik could be easily reached from Trondheim, by rail, whereas, as is so often the case in Norway, there is not even a road connecting the two places. The newspapers said that the late Mr. Neville Chamberlain, who was then Prime Minister, went so far as to correct a member of the House of Commons who was talking about "Narvik," by telling him that he must mean "Larvik," with an L. Now, Narvik is the seaport that leads to the iron ore mines in Sweden, so vital in this war, and since 1914-1918 a disturbing factor between Great Britain and Germany. Larvik is only a small whaling centre, situated away south near the mouth of the Oslo Fjord. Many Englishmen, for countless years, have rented rights to salmon rivers in Norway. One humorist had it that the British Cabinet called in some of those sporting gentlemen and inquired where their familiar rivers were located. The Laerdal is generally considered to give the best sport, and it seems to be true that some of the British transports sailed through the Sognefjord to the town of Laerdal, without any special objective for the troops once they were landed.

Our journey by motor to Bergen was rapturous, as always. We first ascended the beautiful Numedal Valley, a lively stream always by our side, tumbling over itself in sudden rapids and waterfalls and then, for a little space, running so quietly that it mirrored mountains and sky. From the Numedal we turned into the Opdal Valley and finally into the gaunt Ustedal.

At Geilo, where we spent the night, we were warned that the road was rough and narrow for some miles westward. Such warnings in Norway are no idle words. We were obliged to creep slowly along for miles before we reached a good road, one of those made with great skill, but at nearly prohibitive cost, across this difficult country. We now followed over the Hardanger Vidda—a high plateau which the guide book describes as "entirely Arctic in character." It is open for only two months of the year. Though it was mid-July, we drove through several cuttings in the frozen snow which lay in white patches in all directions. We began to descend and arrived for lunch at the famous Fossli Hotel, built in a wild gorge just above a gorgeous waterfall. The waterfall at Fossli was one of the most magnificent either of us had ever seen, although, being so tumultuous, it lacked the lovely lacework effect of more gentle falls. We hated so to leave that we lingered too long and had barely time to catch our ferry across the Hardanger Fjord.

The hotel proprietor took care to telephone down to ask the ferry to wait for us. The road is not one safe to make haste on; literally cut out of the rock, it twists and makes hair-pin turns. Only a few yards ahead are visible at any time; at most places it is too narrow for two cars to pass, and nowhere is it wide enough to pass at more than a snail's pace, with five or six inches to spare.

I suppose I give these details of the road because, through all these ups and downs, I was driving the car myself, and I want to record that I had overcome my early fear of Norwegian roads! We caught the ferry. They had been good enough to wait fully forty minutes for us, and we enjoyed our hour's sailing across the fjord. On the far side we found such beautiful and changing views that even after a day of grandeur, we could still enjoy every moment, and the setting sun gilded the last hour for us.

The next day the *Meteor* was just about to raise anchor at Bergen when the Captain received orders to hold the steamer for some arrivals from England, due in from Newcastle, a Mr. and Mrs. Harrison and their daughter. So we waited. Passengers were not allowed back in the town, and there were those who were all for having the *Meteor* start off and the devil take the Harrisons. But there were others who amiably loitered along the rail, full of curiosity about the important strangers for whom boats were held and who were to be of our company going north. The English boat was late by several hours. We made it up to ourselves by whetting the appetite for these tremendous Harrisons for whom the *Meteor* stood still. The boat from England docked. One motor after another departed from it. Motors stopped. None disgorged our Harrisons. The rain was coming down in floods—it always does in Bergen. The wind and wet drove us from the deck and still people loitered for a first sight of the Harrisons. Finally, the Captain sent the Purser ashore for the elusive notables. The Purser returned. The English boat had had no passengers at all by any such name! With an impatient toss of his head, up to the bridge went the Captain three steps at a time.

The Harrisons became a *cause célèbre* for the rest of the cruise. The imaginative invented gory detective stories to account for their non-appearance; and when, at the fancy-dress ball given the night before we reached the North Cape, two groups of British tourists appeared as "The Family Harrison," each one was the "Life of the Party." One passenger presented himself at the ball made up as Hitler—stare, mustache and all—and was taken so seriously by several other passengers, who found his disguise unpleasant, that they protested to the Captain that his getup was an "anti-Semitic demonstration." People danced all night.

My memories of the cruise on the *Meteor* lie heaped like a pile of colored jackstraws. It is no easy task to choose those that most merit description.

There was the magnificent Svartisen Glacier, whose ice is unbelievably beautiful and a strange, deep green-blue. We were now in Lapp country. Herds of reindeer, guarded by men in square caps and long blouses, were part of the scenery. The Lapps are a most picturesque people, but those we saw were filthy dirty—the only things, or people, in Norway not scrupulously clean and scrubbed. All the same, I liked them. The babies are carried in what they call "cradles," but much as Indian papooses are carried. At one place I saw a mother nursing her baby without removing any of the straps with which he was confined. After they grow up, nearly all Lapps' legs are very crooked and jelly-like. I suspect this way of hampering the movements of their limbs in infancy may account for the lack of muscle later. An unusual number of Lapps are natural artists, making, without any lessons, colored sketches of themselves surprisingly full of movement and life. They are one of the most talented of all primitive races.

The North Cape, the end of our journey, was in one way a disappointment. A thick, moist fogginess all but obliterated any trace of the midnight sun. My traveling companion, Laura Wood, now that we had arrived at our destination, was of two minds as to whether she wanted to wear herself out climbing the mountain. By the time she was sure she had rather rest aboard, all other tourists were gone ashore. But I climbed in the boat which was to take the stewards who wanted to make the ascent. They all stopped at the first hut to buy postcards, but I thought I had better jog on and let them catch up with me, lest I turn out to be the tag end, lame duck of the climb. Presently they did catch up, and very kind they were, helping me over the rough places as they swapped yarns about where they came from, and their experiences aboard ship.

One of the older stewards amused me by saying earnestly, "My family have not all been sailors, not at all. No, indeed, my grandfather, now, was a Scotsman, and a very clever inventor he was."

"And what did he invent?" I asked, for I am good at taking cues.

"Many a thing did he invent, but the best one I ever heard of was a fine invention of reversible trousers."

"And what may a reversible trouser be?"

"You fashion them so," said the steward, "that one day you wear them one way and the next the other way round, to make the seat last longer."

"What a splendid idea," I said, trying to imagine the

THE MIDNIGHT SUN AS WE SAW IT

"The jagged, black islands, looking like the Inferno, were on either side and between them the sun gradually slanted down." (Page 121)

Norwegian Travel Information Office

HARDANGER FJORD

"In May the skilled skiers can swoop down miles from the frozen summit to where the apple blossoms are in bloom on the Hardanger Fjord." (Page 158)

cut. "Did he make money out of them?" I asked, trying hard to recall if I had ever seen such serviceables in use.

"Ah, no," said the steward, "though I heard that he did, but no money of his has ever come down in the family. But what a clever inventor he was, that I have heard many times. It's God's truth I come from a clever stock."

The climb to the Cape's summit was unexpectedly difficult. Half way up I felt that I could go no further and would have to swell the numbers who had dropped by the wayside. Luckily I am one of those born not with second sight but second wind. It is not the steepness which is so hard to contend with; the ground is very rough and there are numberless treacherous, loose stones. I breathed deep and made the grade. Going down was harder than going up, and a terrible strain on the knees.

Another day and we found something more exciting than the North Cape itself. We anchored the next night in a bay among the Lofoten Islands and, this time, really saw the Midnight Sun. The jagged, black islands, looking like the Inferno, were on either side and, between them, the sun gradually slanted down and then, at what looked like a bare six feet of the horizon, turned to slant up again on the other side. As we gazed, I felt it to be one of the strangest and most solemn events of my life, entirely indescribable. From the reverent attitude of all the other passengers, I felt that they were moved in the same way. We were all completely awed and silent.

In the morning, the cruise carried us for a day's sailing through extremely narrow passages between the mainland and the islands. The colors of those shores were like no other beauties I have been blessed enough to see. The hills, one moment, are deep purple, melting into a tender mauve, then they change to pinks of every conceivable tone. Add the colors of the Dolomites to a Turner picture; remember the soft tones along the banks of the Nile at sunset. But no—that shore is more, and different.

I had one official act to carry out during the trip. Admiral Byrd had been writing to me over some months about the Congressional Medal for a Captain Eilefsen. Eilefsen, skipper on a fishing boat, had never been able to come to Oslo to receive it. My visit to Tromsö, his home port, would make the presentation possible. Unfortunately, he was at sea and out of reach, but he had left a note with the British Consul. I had finally to leave the medal with the Governor of the Province, one of seven such governors of provinces in Norway representing the King. I left the medal and the copy of the Act of Congress that went with the medal, which reads, in part: "Presented to the deserving personnel of the Second Byrd Expedition that spent the winter night at Little America or who commanded either one of the ships throughout the expedition, to express the high admiration in which the Congress and the American people hold their heroic and undaunted accomplishments for science, unequaled in the history of Polar exploration."

Tromsö is a flourishing town; it is where King Haakon and the Norwegian Government fled from Molde in April, 1940, and remained until the withdrawal of the British Expeditionary Force necessitated their evacuation to England. Still farther north is Hammerfest which is the most northerly town in the world, there being little or no vegetation.

It was on that trip, returning south, that I saw Trondheim for the first time. It was the Viking capital of Norway and her kings are still crowned there, including His Majesty, King Haakon. The wooden palace, built about 1750, is a treasure. The lines are lovely and simple, and the door trim is very like our own colonial New England. Parts of the cathedral, extraordinarily grand for that part of the world, were started in the eleventh century. The archbishop, who came from England in the fourteenth century, influenced the style, which reminds one of the Lincolnshire cathedral. Afterwards, he became Pope Adrian. That was in the days when Norway was Catholic.

The atmosphere on the *Meteor* was perfect, so happy and carefree. I felt as if I were in my teens again and sailing up the coast of Maine on Grandfather's yacht. The personality of Captain Weltz had a great deal to do with the success of that cruise. He was devoted to his job, charming to everyone, played no favorites, and knew every rock and cranny of his fjords.

The motor met us at Geiranger; and after climbing a tortuously steep and twisting road in a thick fog, we arrived on the heights to find the sun. Several hours of driving brought us down again to where the panorama of the Gudbrandsdal Valley lay below us. Great, lush fields, greener than the Emerald Isle, and rich farming lands lay on either side of us. The sudden transition from the wild and rugged mountains of the north made it seem all the more a land of milk and honey. I came later to know that valley well. It is one of Norway's few main thoroughfares. In winter we traversed it in trains en route to skiing centers. In summer it was the highway by which we motored to salmon rivers and West Coast spas. It was a path to every pleasure.

We talked that July morning of the pilgrims of the

Middle Ages who, coming from all parts of Europe, trooped up this valley on their way to the Shrine of St. Olaf and the capital of the Vikings. How little we dreamed that, barely two years after, those green pastures beside still waters would be one of the principal battlegrounds of these peaceful farmers against a devastating invading army.

As we came to Gausdal, our native chauffeur pointed out that here had been the home farm of Norway's national poet, Björnstjerne Björnson. His son, Erling, runs the farms on the same progressive lines laid down by his father. I remembered a story, apocryphal, maybe, about Björnson's son. Once on a steamer, he had resented the rather cavalier treatment he had received. In complaining of it, he said, "You seem not to remember that I am the son of Norway's first citizen."

"Oh, Mr. Ibsen," was the retort, "we didn't recognize you!"

On the *Meteor* journey, I had reread Sigrid Undset's "Kristin Lavransdatter," so that I was interested when, at Lillehammer, I saw her home. Later, in Sweden, I met and talked with her often, after she was driven from her home by the German advance, and forced to make a perilous escape by sea and land. To my long-standing appreciation for her genius as an author is now coupled my admiration for her Spartan-like character. Her eldest son was killed in the early days of the war. She learned of it only after her arrival in Stockholm, but she carried on with heroic composure. Her other son, a boy of seventeen, was missing for many days. How we all rejoiced when he was found!

Besides the home of Sigrid Undset, which we only looked at from the outside, we paid a visit to the Folk Museum. It was, I thought, even bigger and more comprehensive than the one I liked so much at Bygdö. Scandinavia has many such museums—the one at Skansen, in Sweden, is famous, and the Finns have one on the islands off Helsinki. The idea is to preserve from the past, not only the old, grand things, but the simple ways of country life, the old techniques, the ancient arts. I never used to go to Bygdö without hoping that, some day, in a thousand counties of the United States, some such altars to culture could be maintained as part of the public schools or the Agricultural Extension Service. We need these things to keep our racial memories alive, to hold our aesthetic tradition, to teach our children what the line of development is. At Lillehammer have been brought together, often moved stone by stone, many treasures, to re-create a community of the past. In one farm group, there is a most lovely little private chapel, built in 1600, full of exquisite carvings. In other houses there are kept fine examples of the old tapestries and the ancient silver, and, oh, what handsome silver, what magnificent drinking mugs the ancient Vikings had! What use men made of wood! How beautiful were the marriage chests; the old beds; and the cradles handed down for generations!

In Gudbrandsdal Valley we talked of the history and the poetry that had been made and first spoken there. Ibsen's Peer Gynt, they say, was a son of that valley. So is Knut Hamsun, whose "The Growth of the Soil" brought him the Nobel Prize for literature and the recognition of thousands of American readers.

We returned to Oslo as if we had been a thousand miles away in space and a thousand years in time. We found the native Oslo people in the full swing of departure. The first summer I had been taken aback to discover that summer vacations were both a sacred and legal custom. I had hardly settled in the Legation before the cook and the butler asked when they could be off to the mountains. As it was the height of the tourist season, I had expected my household to stand like a rock and do no shifting. But I soon learned that, by law, every clerk, every charwoman, was to have two weeks' vacation. This basking in the sun was part of the Norwegian birthright, and I am glad that it is so. I learned to be delighted when I saw the staff off; but, as finding substitutes was not all an easy matter, how even gladder I was to see them all returning, sunburned and gay, a long procession back from mountain and shore.

CHAPTER IX

Pulling Together

Silver foxes were once silver foxes to me, and nothing more, but in Norway they became one more symbol of the way in which the northern countries solve their problems, by helping their people to help one another. For this industry, jointly owned by the Farmers' Coöperatives, who enjoy carefully regulated Government credit, has been a mainstay of the depression years, and made stable the economy of many a remote farmstead. One of the fishing pools on the salmon river we rented was called the Fox Farm Pool. It was not my favorite reach of the River Stryn, for half the time the breeze carried far too acrid a reminder of the animals for whom the pool was named. But waiting for the fish to strike, I learned a great deal that should interest small farmers in America. There was so much more to a study on the farms than watching the beautiful creatures pacing their runs, and speculating a little sadly on how I might well be seeing these very skins again, hugging the throat of a pretty girl on Park Avenue.

On some of the farms the silver foxes are such beautiful and winning creatures that they take the place of dogs as pets. A veterinarian I know who went to call on a farmer friend found the whole household upset, for the particularly fine vixen was about to cub, and, as everyone knows how high the death rate is among foxes at such times, there was reason enough for the anxiety and unhappiness.

"We shall lose her, I know we shall lose her," said the farmer dolefully.

The vet handled her tenderly, then said, "Give me the kitchen table, and plenty of hot water. I will save her."

Within the hour six fine young cubs were delivered by the first Caesarian operation ever performed on a fox in Norway. Since then, it is as common a feat among veterinarians as in maternity hospitals.

The story of the platinum foxes which astonished the world a few years ago was another bit of "fox talk" in Oslo. A farmer had an albino fox which was such a rarity that he made a business of showing it at all the country fairs. At the final showing one autumn, another fox breeder offered to buy the animal at many times the normal price. The fox changed hands, and the new breeder set to work to see what the abnormal strain could bring. The six little cubs of this experiment of crossing with a silver fox were the first platinum foxes. One was bought by the Duke of Windsor for $6,000, two went to Bonwit Teller's in New York and were sold in their Fifth Avenue shop.

The next year, there were twenty platinum foxes, no longer priceless as rare diamonds, but still rarities. Now they are rarities, but not front page news, unless, like so many other things, they become casualties of this war. For food in Norway is every day more scarce for animals as well as human beings. Already many foxes have been killed because, otherwise, they might starve to death.

There are 20,000 fox farms in Norway, owning 500,000 animals. They yield in foreign trade about $10,000,000 a year. One astonishing thing about the fox industry was explained to me by a farmer who was showing me his runs. Their feeding has become an important factor in regulating meat production, and keeping the price of fish stable. The statistics he gave me were that Norwegian fox farms account for 60,000,000 pounds of fish and meat annually, including whale meat, in addition to 14,000,000 pounds of entrails of animals slaughtered in the abattoirs and elsewhere.

"How these people pull together," I used to think. "They look toward a future in which all parts of society realize their mutuality and coördinated functions." Perhaps it is easier for small and settled countries to do this than for larger, more heterogeneous continental states. And the fact remains that always for small European countries, until after the last war, emigration to America was a solution for ambitious, restless, individualistic, dissident natures. The home country became more homogeneous as America became more heterogeneous.

It was possible in a nation like Norway for problems of economics and culture to be considered the problems of all the people. I felt this when, on invitation from one of my friends, I went to see an abattoir. I shrank from the excursion. A visit long ago to a meat-packing plant in Chicago had given me goose flesh. Perhaps one's first visit to such an industry always does. But I know I would gladly have gone to a bull fight in preference to any second sight of the stockyards. At least there is a glamour and a sporting element which distracts one from natural nausea at the blood. Still, it had been put to me that surveying the Oslo Abattoir, which is really a municipal laboratory coöperating with the Farmers' Coöperatives, was part of my mission to the north. I screwed up my courage. I think the guide knew how reluctantly I had come, for the explanation of the humane, at least more humane methods than I had ever heard of, were described to me at once. The pigs are made unconscious by electricity before they are killed. I was assured that whatever squealing I heard was from fright, not pain. (Though fright, I believe, is still a kind of pain.) Clamps are fastened loosely about the pigs' necks, and through these are conveyed forty-five volts of electricity which make the pig unconscious. A moment later the butcher's knife enters the neck. All this makes the butcher's trade less terrible. It had, of course, been a long time since I visited the yards at Chicago; perhaps my sense of advanced method which I accept as Norwegian progress is a coal to Newcastle. But I think not, for hardly a month passed in Oslo without the visit of some delegation arrived to study the abattoirs, not only for their technical procedure, but for their form of farmer ownership, and for their system of marketing. They came from all over Europe, and were composed of all sorts of people—farmers, retail dealers, butchers, government officials.

The cattle and pig producers had a coöperative pool and three-quarters of the 125,000 farmers who raised meat and pork for the general market were members of it. Some farmers, of course, produced and sold only for the local markets of their home valleys. There was a time, not long ago, when Norway imported considerable meat, but so well has the coöperative farmers' association studied the needs of the national market that, in 1939, Norway was not only able to supply itself but had become an exporter of meat. As I write, the story of those little valley farms is wrapped in darkness. Since April 9th so many have been burned; so many cattle slaughtered. One knows that the fodder shortage produces starving cattle as well as starving human beings and an endless vicious circle is begun, where only yesterday an aspiring spiral toward plenty was under way. And the ever-widening field of export is at a standstill. What the Nazis take, they steal with unfair bargains.

I wonder what has become of all the people and places I used to visit while I was studying the economic life of the country. I remember the bacon factory at Stavanger where the meat and pork pool sent their surplus to be made into bacon for England. Norway had a place on the bacon quota. And on the lamb and mutton import quota in France. Something that happened to me in Norway is, I am told, happening to everybody in the modern world. It is part of our times. We begin again to see the world in pictures and not in figures. We begin to see where all business and all manufacture and trade transactions touch our daily lives. Maybe only as sources dry up and wars cut trade routes do we really learn where the things we consume come from. Certain it is that laymen everywhere who once toured cathedral towns now go on cruises to study bread and steel, and who does what about the price of milk.

I remember once in one of the most northern valleys of Norway coming upon a cluster of enchanting children in a farm dooryard, and stopping to talk with them. Norway has the most beautiful children in the world, and these were no exception. With their golden heads, their apple cheeks, and husky little bodies, more than one visitor had an itch to wholesale kidnapping. They seem to grow out of the earth. They have such charming and simple dignity with strangers. They do their chores about the farm so joyously. I wish more people in America would read the books by Marie Hamsun about children on a Norwegian farm, written about her own, and long regarded as classics all over Germany and Scandinavia. I forget what the children were telling me that morning when their mother joined us, and the talk turned to the coöperative marketing of milk—a field in which Norway, together with Denmark, leads every other nation. There is an exchange of experts, even from Finland and Sweden, who used to come to study the system. Oh, those little commissions of experts and ordinary people that one was always meeting in the north, those peaceful spyers-out of better and kinder ways of doing things, of how to feed the people, how to keep families on the farm, to avoid mortgages, and tenant farming. The northern countries and, of course, Norway for me most of all, always made one feel that by pulling together, by pooling information, almost any good deed was possible. When Mrs. Larsen showed me her rows of shining milk cans and I asked if she belonged to the coöperative milk pools, I really knew the answer beforehand.

"Indeed, yes," and in another moment she was off on the story of the chaos in the Norwegian milk market before the pools had been created. The price of milk had dropped year by year. The same cows, the same farms and mountain meadows, but the price of the product getting lower and

Norwegian Travel Information Office

SKI TRAIN LEAVING FOR THE COUNTRY

"The whole town used to go into the country to slide and to ski—rosy cheeks, rosy mittens, tassels on their caps." (Page 101)

Norwegian Travel Information Office

PEACEFUL NORWEGIAN FARM SCENE

"As I write, the story of those little valley farms is wrapped in darkness." (Page 131)

lower. The price of butter went down. The price of cheese, too.

"And then," she said, "we began to see how each on his little farm, dealing alone with the private merchants, was cutting his neighbor's throat."

I looked at her rosy, well-fed children.

"And then," she went on, "the farmers of southeastern Norway began to organize, and to pool all their knowledge, not only of the market but of the control and betterment of herds. We had grown poor apart. We would grow rich together."

She regretted that her husband was away from home. He would have had so many details to tell me of what had been done about fodder, and what had happened to prices from year to year. But it struck me, as it had so often before, that wherever coöperation prospers, the women seem always to be in partnership with their men. They begin to talk as if the work they do is not just "business" but as if all economies were part of one integrated pattern of living. They talk as if the customers were people like themselves; and they expect the townsfolk to think and care about the welfare of farmers and their children. When I congratulated her on the bloom on the cheeks of her boys and girls and how radiantly healthy they looked, she smiled, and went on talking about the little things that were helping Norwegian farms to have such crops of youngsters. The coöperative dairy pool had eased things up. Their household could now have not only all the dairy products they needed, but could buy surplus pork, which was being salted and sold at minimum prices to people of small means, who under any other system would have had less wholesome food. I then asked questions about the pigs, and Thor was summoned. He left his post where he was watching his brother milk and was told to skip and find out if a nearby neighbor would welcome a visitor. Mr. Christensen would, so I followed Thor up the hill, and as I looked back at the little family group in that hospitable dooryard, I thought how fine it was that the people of the north do so love red. In the fields in summer, and on the skiing slopes in winter, there is a touch of scarlet on nearly every costume, to make a warm spot in the landscape, and tingle the heart of the beholder.

Farmer Christensen told me the story of the pig marketing.

"The trouble used to be," he said, "that one year the price for pigs would be good. Then suddenly everybody would take to raising pigs. There would be such a scramble and so many pigs that the price would fall. Pigs would fetch hardly enough to pay for the feeding of them. None of us knew when to stop, or what would happen next. We had to get together, and to find out that what hurt one hurt all, and that only in coöperation could we move toward stable expansion."

His real interest was not in pigs, but in poultry. The eight Egg Centrals of Norway he spoke of with the pride in his voice one might have heard in a boy talking about a crack regiment which had won many banners.

"Time was, not many years ago, when Norway had to import eggs." And so he talked along about what has happened since the coming of the Egg Centrals. Norway now exports eggs. There were fewer egg producers than members of other pools. The Egg Centrals, while they stabilized city prices, are no great factor in country markets, where eggs are used as barter with other farmers and in the local stores. I think Mr. Christensen could have told me vastly more, but my Norwegian can be put in a pint cup, a very simple vocabulary, indeed, and besides, as was so often the case, he did not speak the Norwegian known to Oslo, but a vernacular peculiar to his own valley; not even my chauffeur could understand all of his words. Mrs. Larsen, on the other hand, spoke English fluently. She had learned it at school, or on a visit to America or England. Mr. Christensen's fund of facts gushed forth; his enthusiasm I understood; his figures not always. It was a long saga, for he had much to say about coöperative ventures in timber, in wool, in fruit, in vegetables, and especially in berries.

Berries! Not even people who come from Cape Cod, or Berrien County, Michigan, have any idea of what berries there are in this world, how delicious, and in what varieties. Blue, black, red, orange and yellow—Norwegian berries are as marvelous as the fruits of the tropics, and how Norwegians love them!

As commercial crop, in the last five years, the gathering had been so much improved in technique, that now an export trade was being developed. "*Was*"—over and over, I realize that the war has stopped all the social experiments we were watching in Oslo, as one watches a child grow and develop. Most of the export berries were going to Great Britain. Norwegian blueberries had long been famous with English sportsmen who fished the streams and fjords. Motoring through the valleys in the month of August, we found that blueberrying time was like a family holiday, or like the hop picking in Kent. From every farm and from the cities, someone was gone to the woods "for the berries." Sometimes whole families would go away berrying by the week. When their tubs were full, one or two members would carry or haul to the nearest sorting places where usually some coöperative association graded and packed. The choicest berries, in standard baskets, went by special refrigeration compartments to Covent Garden. Beside blueberries, also loganberries, cranberries, raspberries and strawberries went to the fruit canners. A farmer named Fossum once told me that he made up to three or four hundred dollars in cash from berries and was able to keep his own larder stocked with jams and juices the whole year round. By mid-summer my own cook always became immersed in glass jars, sugar and spices, and her ardor and concentration made it plain that she regarded "the canning" as a solemn high spot of the year. What she put up really *was* better than jars and bottles from the delicatessen; and there was a sort of wine growers' mummery in the constant sampling of juices and shrubs that goes on round the Norwegian summer.

As we came away from the Christensen farm Thor Larsen came rushing and stumbling toward us with his arms full. He was fetching us a good-will gift from his mother, a block of *gjetost,* the brown cheese that is a staple on every Norwegian table, eaten by the poorest peasants, relished by the richest ship-owner.

I think the almost passionate fondness of all Norwegians for this cheese is somehow tied up with the way it is made, and with memories of the mountain farms, called *seters,* that are part of every Norwegian's holidays. In the summer, the cattle are driven into the mountains to these little farms to get pasturage, while the grass in the valleys is made into hay. In the clean air of the mountains, with the pure water and rich grass, cowherds young and old and the cattle flourish all together in the mountain meadows. The farmers get nearly half of their annual milk production during the summers when the cattle are on the seters; and many are the Norwegian tales that begin with high summer in these mountain pastures.

Many kinds of cheese are made on the seters. How often I have seen the great round cheeses, and the square high brown ones standing in rows, drying in the open air. The gjetost (the brown sweet acrid ones) are still made in the mountains just as they used to be a hundred years ago and more. The farmers' wives mix the rich summer milk of the cows with goats' milk in huge caldrons. They stir and stir with wooden paddles while they add the "secret" which divides the foamy milk into whey and cheese. Gjetost is made in dairies, too, of course, but still every little farm makes some of its own and gjetost is a password to Norwegians the world over—school children's breakfast, fisherman's picnic, soldier's ration.

Less than in Sweden and Finland, but still spreading a noticeable network over the whole country from the polar sea to the farthest south, consumer coöperative stores have been a feature of Norwegian life. All Norwegian legislation has to be based on the peculiar geography of the country. Climate and the mountains tend to isolate many valleys for sometimes more than half the year. Something has to be done to preserve communication, and stimulate distribution. Under a devil-take-the-hindmost policy, some places would be abandoned and left out of the national progress. But with such different circumstances and needs prevailing in the cities, and in the mountain valleys, fusion of societies has been difficult. There are about one thousand coöperative shops in Norway, some with a great quantity and variety of goods, some selling only small things and necessities. Private industrial chain store and multiple shops are forbidden by Norwegian commercial law. The principle seems to be that it is to the interest of the whole people that as many persons as possible shall make a living in trade, but that any backing from the whole country to unprofitable remote corners must be balanced by a system profiting from the whole custom of the country.

I heard a great deal of discussion of the clause in the law which forbade a local merchant from having branches in a neighboring municipality. By this means, every effort at concentration of control was blocked. This, said many consumers, was often a loss to those who might have benefited, for a talented man in the coöperative field could never bring his talent to a growing market. The coöperatives were taxed for their property and the presumed income from their property; but the income from their trade turnover was exempt. And in Norway, as elsewhere, private business kept up a constant propaganda against "non-tax-paying coöperatives" as unfair competition. The final form of consumer coöperation in Norway was certainly not resolved; but the principle was established, and not only in labor and socialist circles but in the public schools, the history of coöperative experiment is part of the history of the country. I was always on the lookout to find what people thought about the subject. In the sixties and seventies there had been a widespread coöperative movement in Norway. But most people spoke of the modern movement as dating from 1890.

One evening I set out for dinner with a friend, with the express purpose of meeting an authority on the subject and had, as I started, an amusing little contretemps with private business. My own motor refused to start and, as the hour grew later, the butler called for a public taxi without telling the driver the identity of the passenger. It was arctic weather, and my host lived half-way up Holmenkollen where the roads were a glare of ice. Almost as we started off the chauffeur pushed the front window back and announced in English:

"I've lived in New York."

"How nice to know that," I replied.

"Yes, and I take a great interest in the American Legation . . ." I started to say yes to that, too, rather pleased, when he went on.

"And I tell you they made an awful mistake when they let Mr. Biddle go and got in this new Minister."

"Oh, yes?" I murmured, more curious than depressed.

"I should say they did! Why, we used to get calls as many as ten times a day when Biddle was there. Why, now nobody calls but once or twice in a week."

The road was getting steeper and steeper, and glassier and glassier, and the wheels were skating in little tentative skids. I looked forward at the road. He divided his attention between the road and me. I murmured that the new household was much smaller than Mr. Biddle's but this, so simple a reason, did not appease him. Now I was uneasy, for he turned still further around, almost glaring at me, and the wheels of the car turned around, too, as he reached the climax of his disapproval.

"We gave Minister Biddle a bouquet of flowers when he left and he made us a speech. This new one will never get that or anything else from us."

At that we slid to the side of the road and hung for a moment on the ragged edge of a steep incline. I held tight and assured him I thought he was very right, that the change in Ministers had been a great mistake, but would he please go more carefully. He lapsed into stony silence. I thought of announcing myself as "the new Minister" but thought better of it, for a shock might have taken us both over an embankment. Anyway, he was a Norwegian. I knew it could not have been malice, just "private business," anywhere self-centered about the loss of a customer.

My host had assembled a very agreeable party. They were already there when I escaped from my detractor. There was an expert to answer my many questions and to tell me how one Ole Dehli, on a visit to England in 1890, had become an enthusiast of the consumer coöperative movement in Manchester, and the Rochdale principles, and had returned to lecture all over his native land. The direct result was the founding of the Christiania Coöperative Society. (Oslo was then called Christiania.) Mr. Dehli, a prominent barrister, was its leader and the movement excited interest all over the country. But Mr. Dehli found his task no easy one, for to travel all over Norway is arduous and often impossible work. One wants to repeat all the time that everything in Norway is determined by the geography of the country. The mountains and fjords divide the country into regions separate and peculiar by nature, each with certain customs, long established and undisturbed, and neither roads nor printed matter made communication easy. But faith and persistence water all good ideas and, in 1905, the Journal "Kooperativen" was founded, and the NKL, the Norges Kooperative Landsforening, both came into being. No one can imagine Norwegian life without them. Or could, until the Nazis came.

For many reasons, the fishermen along the coast were among those who held out against coöperative development. Why, it is not certain. The followers of the sea, perhaps, accept with a certain amount of fatality the speculation in their occupation. But slowly, along the coast, Mr. Dehli sowed the seed of his idea, each for all and all for each.

CHAPTER X

Ahead of Us All

When I was appointed to Norway, the first thing Justice Brandeis said to me, and he said it in a voice of smiling envy, was, "Those Scandinavian countries are twenty-five years ahead of us all." Mrs. Brandeis had translated a very popular Danish book on education and the Justice had always had the wish to go to Scandinavia. Americans are used to traveling to see the past; I knew my luck in going to meet the future.

When I repeated Justice Brandeis' remark to a man in Oslo, I wanted to smile when the patriot puffed back, "One hundred years, you mean."

I said to him, "The New Deal has speeded up necessary change so much that I hope we shall catch up in ten."

For Justice Brandeis was right—in certain matters of social and political democracy, it is plain that the small countries of the north, less concerned with power politics and vast industrial expansions, have made patterns for us all. Norway, Finland, Sweden and Denmark, each has a certain homogeneity, and it is certainly easier to deal with housing, wage rates, agricultural planning, if you are not trying to cope with enormously varying elements. The regional compactness of the small countries—and, of course, the Scandinavian countries are not so very small at that—produces a sort of common knowledge. The great countries and the empires have too many elements strange to each other to make one rule of thumb for east and west that fits. Brutal repressions, and costly delays, have made them last, not first, as models of peaceful democratic life in which ordinary men may feel secure about the future and full of zest for the present.

Elsewhere in the world, I had taken beggars and slums as part of the enduring phenomena of city life. Not so in Norway. I understood what many Norwegians have told me they felt when they visited the great capitals of the world—such shock at the misery complacently exposed, that they were always glad to leave for home. Comments such as these came not from one class in Norway, but from everyone, for as a nation, the Norwegians have a social conscience. No one ever apologizes for serious uplift talk as we do even in America in many circles—there is never any slight irony in "social significance," for politics in Norway is primarily the contest of parties for the task of raising the standard of living.

Almost the first inquiry from citizens in America that reached me at Nobelsgate was a request for more information on the Oslo Breakfast, as if it were something special. And from then on, letters and visitors were constantly turning up about that famous meal.

The Oslo Breakfast is not only a symbol of all Norwegian aspirations for the future, the wish for a "noble breed of men," strong, intelligent and handsome, but one of the most carefully developed scientific experiments in the world today, the life work of the late Dr. Carl Schiötz, Professor of Hygiene at the University of Oslo. One can walk out any morning and into any school house in Oslo and find the school children having breakfast together, before their studies begin. It will be the Oslo Breakfast, free, as teaching is free, a scientific diet, worked out over many years of laboratory testing and weighing, so as to promote uniform normal growth in the children of the nation, to inculcate correct diet habits, to insure a sort of fellowship and an even break for the next generation.

I wish I could write about it in such a way that the Oslo Breakfast could become a plank in our defense program. School lunches are part of many American Board of Education programs, of course. The Oslo way, by laboratory tests, brings more returns. The first half hour of school is devoted to it, and more than one-third of the school children of Oslo arrive for it or have the same diet at home. Not only the poor children—"the underprivileged," as we say in America, and I cannot help, after Norway, disliking the very word—but great numbers of the spoiled darlings of rich Norwegian households, whose tantrums and sulks may need to be cured, sit down at table before school. But first there is a washing of hands and faces, and then, where it is necessary, a skilful little ABC lesson in table manners. It is a lovely sight, so many children all starting the day even. The total expense of the breakfast is borne by the Oslo Municipality. No questions are asked—all who want to may come in time for food. One of my friends, whose child ate with his school fellows, said to me:

"He has gained eight pounds since he began taking the

school breakfast. He enjoys meeting the other children this way. No more talk about 'eating it all up.'"

The menu is simple—one third of a liter of milk, one hard whole wheat biscuit, or a piece of whole wheat rye bread, vitamized margarine and rich cream whey cheese. Then the child can have as much as he likes of ordinary whole wheat bread with whey cheese or cod liver paste. A raw carrot. Or a raw apple! No, I know, for an adult it isn't a good southern company breakfast, but it does contain just the right vitamins and minerals for growing boys and girls. A physician visits the schools regularly, to study special cases which do not respond in weight and zest; and for these, open air schools, which I visited, are provided, in beautiful and healthy surroundings. Do you wonder that the health of the people is improving and that the good conscience of Norway is a national asset? There is a dental clinic in every public school. Arguments such as we have in America about whether the compulsory teaching of hygiene is an infringement on individual liberty, seem nonsense.

The average length of life—and a good life, too—in Norway is sixty years. The care given to children, and the almost universal insurance—everybody with an income under $1500 has compulsory insurance—make a health economy above the average.

In 1937, just before I arrived, the Storting had initiated a new scheme of unemployment insurance, to be administered by the sickness insurance authorities, by which 600,000 men and women in factories, shops and offices were protected against the starts and stops of the complicated modern industrial set-up. State, municipality, employee and employer share in the premium. A chain is no stronger than its weakest link. The chain itself was taking care of all the links. What made the social climate of Norway so pleasant was that all this weighing of individual and common responsibility, this endeavor to equalize burdens and opportunities, was taken for granted. No talk of dictatorships! No fear of the Have-nots, because everybody had something, and the line of development was always up and up, inch by inch. It is good to live among people who put their ideas in practice, and believe in the dignity of one another.

I was interested in the Norwegian laws regarding illegitimate children. They are, I believe, the most advanced in the world. The child born out of wedlock shares equally with the legitimate children in all matters of inheritance, irrespective of the wishes and will of the father, his wife and his lawful children. Illegitimacy is no social drawback to any honorable career in society, for the child; but the same cannot yet be said for the child's mother. A father, by law, must support an illegitimate child until he is sixteen and in some degree its mother, also.

It seemed to me that everywhere I turned I found Norwegians meeting what were rancorous problems of social life elsewhere with an acceptance of reality and a common sense worth copying.

A doctor once talking to me about a friend of his who was an arbitrator in the settling of labor disputes, said:

"You see, we are both physicians, my friend and I. He is sent for when a factory has pains. I am called in when an individual is sick."

There are strikes in Norway, many of them, but they seldom last long. Bitter battles between the employers and employees' unions are part of the history of this century in Norway too, but it is plain that, in the public interest, a humane code for industry is slowly being ground out.

The present united strength of the Norwegian labor movement owes more to Mr. Martin Tranmael, the editor of *Arbeiderbladet,* the leading labor daily and second largest paper in Norway, than to anyone else. The Norwegian labor movement is the most radical in Scandinavia, but Mr. Tranmael succeeded in keeping his party away from Moscow affiliations. He leads once warring factions in a strong, united party. He is the most remarkable labor leader in Europe.

Alliance between the Labor Party and the Farmers' Party was responsible for the government during my whole stay in Oslo.

The main reason why Norway's three million citizens have been able to create and maintain a democratic life so rich in general security, and adventurous in social experiment, is the profound respect all Norwegians have for education. And by education they mean not merely free public schools, but far more. School teaching in Norway is one of the exalted professions. Everywhere teachers are in the counsels of economic and political life. They feel themselves responsible for turning the whole country into a nation of readers—not alone of newspapers, but of serious books, books of all languages. I have had interesting conversations about Hemingway and Huxley and Sherwood Anderson with store keepers in the mountains, with stewards on Norwegian boats, with mechanics at the garage. Reading circles cover every trade and part of the country. You will even hear of electric light rates kept as low as possible because it is indisputably good that the poorest families should be able to read through the long winter nights. I liked this; and the fact that nearly everyone I knew was busy studying something. People seemed to grow like trees, adding fresh rings of growth every year.

"The world is so full of a number of things," sighed a Norwegian woman, "there is hardly time in life to find out about them and learn to do them."

When I began to study weaving at past sixty, it astonished no one in Oslo; and if I had, instead, suddenly attended classes in astronomy, or begun to learn Finnish or Russian, it would have been taken for granted merely that I was educating myself and orienting myself in the world I lived in.

It was part of the educational theory that you taught people by having them do things; you made people feel alike by letting them all participate in the same enterprise. That was it. The sense of participation was what made Norway so ebullient. Take so simple a matter as the forestry program. It might have been cheaper to set out trees by some small commercial tree-planting unit. Cheaper in money. But every year Norwegian school children plant three million trees; and in the process, they become owners, patrons, builders of their country. I was reminded over and over again of my grandfather when I was talking to Norwegian children and their teachers. My grandfather never went anywhere in the world without noting the trees. He was always buying new ones to be set out at "Willow Brook," and watching trees grow was a way of studying time as well as nature. Many a Norwegian, home from years abroad, will go to look at what he planted in the national forests when he was a boy. "There I planted trees" is a way of saying, "there is my country."

"The better world" we all talk about was really taking shape in Norway. There were fewer vested interests than elsewhere. The state owned the railways, and the business of the railways was not to pay dividends, but within a framework of the budget, to see what the institution of railways could do to make the citizens feel free, know the whole country, and move goods to market to the joint benefit of consumer and producer. Publicly owned utilities and municipally owned cinema-houses were taken for granted.

The curtain is now down on that evolution toward equality. The Invader with his theory of master races, and brute force, for the moment controls railways and ports, aerodromes and telegraph wires, newspapers and police. But he deals with a nation so strong in its inner life, so rich in experience of all but military force, that it cannot be bought or beaten. There is this about democracy—its leaders are everywhere, and its slogans call to the hearts of the humble. There are only three million people in Norway, but each one of them counts. If, before the invasion, they were ahead of us all in the democratic way of life, in a measure we owe it to them to carry on their experiments here; and to trust them to develop powers of resistance until the elements of democracy the world over are reunited and prevail. Theirs is a story that must be continued.

CHAPTER XI

HIGH DAYS AND HOLIDAYS

TRAVELING ABOUT THE world, the places you really get to know are those where you have kept the holidays. No matter how cosmopolitan the set you move in, at Christmas and at New Year's, you feel the local and the universal heart of the life around you. Through your friends, through the Court, through your servants, you find yourself participating in old and hallowed customs. And so it was in Norway. All the fête days were voyages of discovery into the enduring past. The bonfires on Midsummer Eve, the festive exchange of presents on birthdays and holidays, the Thanksgiving Day at harvest time, the Independence Day—not on the 4th of July, but on the 17th of May, celebrating the occasion of the Norwegian Constitution, proclaimed at Eidsvold on May 17, 1814, when Norway declared its independence from union with Denmark—were occasions for understanding.

I will, in a way, regret forever that I spent my first Norwegian Christmas away from Oslo, on the Riviera. It was reasonable to go away and to join old friends, but I delayed by twelve months the joy of the northern Christmas, on the heels of the winter solstice. To me, Christmas Day, besides its sacred significance in the Christian calendar, has always been the loveliest day in all the year. It is a time when people feel they can come out from behind their polite defenses and say to each other, without being shy about it, all the nice things they have thought during the year.

Christmas is not a "day" in Norway but a season that rises in December. The shops—there are many that deal in wooden things alone—are full of wooden toys, unpainted and painted animals of all sorts, and blocks that can be built into motor cars. From all over the country, even as far north as Finnmark, the peasant farms and village workshops have sent their products. And on the street corners, the peasants set up little forest clumps of Christmas trees, forty and fifty in a load. The climax of the festival is Christmas Eve, not Christmas Day as with us. It is then the rice with lucky almond is eaten. The whole family assembles to go to the four o'clock service at the churches. At Easter, like as not the whole family will be in the mountains skiing and lost to prayers, but Christmas is sacred to the church. The churches, practically all Lutheran, are crowded, and the carols sung by old and young stir the hearts of all.

Then home again for the tree and the present-giving. On the twenty-fourth the family dines at their own table, on the twenty-fifth with the parents of the wife, and on the twenty-sixth with the parents of the husband, or vice versa. The whole of Christmas is an exaltation of family life, and of loving-kindness. One sort of celebration and another lasts almost until Epiphany.

My first Scandinavian Christmas was one of the happiest days of my life. I had my grandchild, Phyllis, with me, and that made the church bells ring with a special joy. We were to make an American Christmas in the midst of this Norwegian cheer—all the Legations fell back on adding their homeland customs to the folkways of Oslo. From just around the corner we had got a beautiful tree—green, fragrant, straight enough to be a mast for a sail boat on the fjord, and all the Legation and Consulate children and those of several Norwegian-Americans were invited in for sweets and presents at five o'clock. And between thirty or forty grown-ups came to dinner. I made only one gaffe in the preparations. I had hung a Christmas wreath of green on the Legation door, as I might have in New York or Washington, but a few minutes later one of the Norwegian servants came to me in distress, for a green wreath on the door, in Norway, means but one thing. It is the old peasant custom when someone has died in the house, and wreaths are only taken to the cemetery on Christmas Day. A touching practice, and one I loved carrying out, was that of hanging large bunches of oats on the tree branches for the birds on Christmas Eve.

I had determined to have some Christmas carols and, in the ten days preceding the holiday, had asked everywhere and even eyed the little boys on the nearby hill playing in the snow and wondered if they could be lured in to sing. Then my butler suggested that, perhaps, the boys from St. Olav's were what I wanted. St. Olav's was a singing school for boys, a famous one in Northern Europe, supported by private subscription. The Director offered to call upon me, and, yes, he would send us not "a few boys" but fifty-five. Moreover, he managed to make me feel as if I were doing the school a favor instead of quite the other way around, and he would hear of no payment except chocolates from the tree for each young singer. I had singers. I must have an organ! I must have a Hammond organ, an American electric organ invented by Jack Hammond, son of my old friend, John Hays Hammond. How I did want just that, to hide behind some greenery for a surprise. It was all to be a great surprise! No one knew about it but Phyllis and me, and the secret was well kept. Not even the painter, who heard me ask for the organ and who told me that a woman who worked in the government-owned radio station might help me find one, suspected. The radio people did have an organ, two in fact, and were very glad to smuggle one into the Legation for a few days as a Christmas gift.

What a lovely dinner that was! Half way through our American menu—everyone's appearance enhanced by candle-light, and warm and gay—the doors into the drawing room were flung open and the boys filed in and around the tables. Their celestial singing was just that. Their blond heads shone, and in the piercing sweetness of the soprano voices, "O Holy Night" brought tears to many eyes.

Afterwards we danced, of course, in the large hall, and ended up with the Virginia Reel, which is in Virginia and Michigan a roisterous athletic fling, and can be turned into something even livelier by Norwegian Christmas revellers.

Next to Christmas the greatest fete of the north is Mid-summer Night. Christianity has tamed the celebration of the winter solstice to a sacred day for the family and for peace; but the coming of the summer solstice, June 23, in the white nights is still a pagan revel. It is the great outdoor festivity and the whole population goes out to the fjords, or the mountain tops, drives along the fjord or watches the bonfires and fireworks from boats. The marvelous madness of the "all night sun" runs in the veins, and bursts into singing and dancing.

Still my best Midsummer Eve was at an indoor dinner at Sylvia Salvesen's. Sylvia, one of the most sympathetic friends I made in Norway, was giving a party in honor of the King and Queen, and I was delighted to attend what proved one of the most informal and unusual evenings of my whole stay. Two refectory tables were laid; at one the Queen sat, and at the other the King. My place was just across the table from His Majesty, and it was great fun to see what a good time he and the Queen were having. Sylvia has a knack for verse, neat, comical doggerel, to be exact, and she had prepared little couplets and stanzas for each guest. She had piled all her little verses under her plate, and whenever her attention would be diverted, His Majesty and others would filch a few and hide them in their pockets. Then Sylvia would discover her loss, and we would all look everywhere, dive under the table and make a game of finding them, amid whoops of silly midsummer laughter. I enjoyed every minute of it except when my own verse was read and I had to respond to the toast, in prose, to be sure. I lost my reputation for impromptu speaking entirely, but everybody laughed at my halting.

Sylvia somehow reminded me always of eighteenth-century France; she seemed more Latin than Nordic. Her many social and artistic gifts would surely have made her famous in the Paris of long ago; her sunny temper, her endless energy, her piquant face, and her impulsive generosity gave continual delight. Before I met her, I was told that she was a leading Buchmanite and was warned that she would certainly try to proselytize me, or else take no interest in me at all. But, on the contrary, through all the many times I saw her, she never for a moment trespassed on my inner self, beyond now and then telling me of some good work she was interested in.

Almost as gay as Midsummer Night were the high spots of the summer on the Oslo Fjord, the visits of battleships and school ships from the other nations of Europe—sometimes bent on visits designed to make a political impression, and sometimes just fiesta for the young cadets, who must have been impressed by the beauty of the fjord and the fifty thousand speed boats, dories and lovely sailboats that skimmed the waters. In August, 1938, there were several semi-official Italian visits. Once the whole town was en fete for three days in their honor. Relations were particularly good between the Italian shipbuilders and the Norwegian merchant marine. One evening the Italian Minister gave a dance for the Italian officers. The next evening the Italian Consul General, Mr. Olsen, entertained at Valstrand, down the fjord less than an hour from Oslo. It was a still, brilliant night. The shore was gay with colored lanterns, hung out against the negligible hour when the white light grows dim. The dinner was served in the big pavilion where the cadets were to dance later with the pretty, blonde girls of Oslo. The host had gathered a select group of friends to dine with him and his handsome daughter, Mrs. Huitfeldt, in a little summer house on the hillside. The Italian Admiral was guest of honor. The Italian Minister somehow lost his way coming out from the capital and the dinner was delayed an hour.

The Minister was far too garrulous for a diplomat. He had risen, popped into the diplomatic service, someone said, from the ranks of journalism, and he remained a journalist at heart. I remember him at a dinner given by the Danish Legation on the date of the Anschluss. While we were having coffee the Italian was called to the telephone. He rushed back into the room with no sangfroid at all and shouted that the Nazis had occupied Vienna.

We all set down our coffee cups and flowed around the radio. As the news came over, I watched the expressions on the different faces. Many looked utterly bewildered, yet we were supposed to be those who should know most about the changing map of Europe. The German Minister, Herr Sahm, grew more and more grim. He soon excused himself and went home. The Italian, on the contrary, could scarcely contain himself and grew more and more hilarious. He kept walking up and down the room, exclaiming, "We, too, are on the march. . . . We, too, are on the march."

"Where?" asked the British Chargé drily. "Are you marching into the Sudan or into the ocean?"

"You will see," replied the Italian, and then, turning to me, he broke out, "We will be masters of the Mediterranean. First we will take Gibraltar. Then we will take the Suez Canal." That blurted candor was in 1938.

He was a bachelor, and often good-natured about filling a gap at my table. I remember a luncheon I was arranging for some French guests, unexpectedly arrived in Oslo. I telephoned my Italian friend, explained why his invitation was so late. Would he be good enough to come?

"Give me twenty minutes," he said, "and I will try and arrange it." He arrived late, and gaily announced to the other guests, "You see, I was having a party of my own, and I had to get hold of my Secretary of Legation to entertain them."

Then, with both candor and indiscretion, went on, "I just told my guests that I always did everything the American Minister asked me, as war is not far distant, and where will any of us turn for financial help if not to the United States?"

He either couldn't or wouldn't speak English, but he managed to publish plenty of news in his rattling Italian-French. I would match him against many an American columnist.

But to get back to the fiesta at Valstrand. Our host, Mr. Olsen, was a member of the shipping firm of Fred Olsen, founded by his father. When I made my first trip from England to Norway, the only ships of any size ran from Newcastle to Bergen, so that one had still to make a night or all-day trip by train before reaching the Norwegian capital. But the next year the Olsen Line added a very fine ship, the *Black Prince,* to their fleet and initiated a direct run from Newcastle to Oslo. And a year later, a sister ship, the *Black Watch,* was launched, and travel between the two countries was completely revolutionized from being a dreaded chore, to a positive delight. Both these ships have been confiscated now by the Nazis.

There is no denying that there is as much diplomacy in improving the techniques of communication as there is in the traditional political gestures. A still larger boat, the *Vega,* built by another company to run into Bergen, interested the whole country because it was the result of a barter arrangement. It was built in an Italian shipyard in Genoa,

I believe, and was paid for entirely, not in gold, but in dried fish, and for that reason seemed the more a national possession.

Mr. Fred Olsen, regarded everywhere not merely as the founder of his steamship line, but as a Founding Father of Modern Norway, was already dead when I arrived in Oslo, but his memory was still alive. Many times I wished that I might have talked with him; everything his hand touched seemed to burgeon. He had a knack of galvanizing people, his own employees most of all, and his sons carried on the manners and customs of the old man. Olsen Line employees had a local pride in all the company's undertakings which could only have come from close personal relations with the owner, and a sense of sharing in a rich initiative. To build and run boats profitably, the Line had to have places to carry people to, and the Olsen Line, therefore, figured in a number of enterprises like skiing hotels and bathing beaches, a whole network of amenities, and like all Norwegian pleasure places and health resorts, they were designed to please every sort of citizen, young and old, rich and poor.

I cannot say enough, nor the Norwegians either, about the air of Norway. We were always taking more of it. My own favorite places were Winge, up north, and Finse, way up on top of the world, to which one traveled on the Bergen railway. I spent unforgettable vacations at both places and meant to go back to Finse in May. In May the skilled skiers can swoop down miles from the frozen summit to where the apple blossoms are in bloom on the Hardanger Fjord. Not that I can hope to do anything heroic like that, so long and so steep, but there are dozens of shorter runs near the summit, and the air on the mountain—the air again—makes one feel as if one is off on a perpetual picnic. It is wonderful on this earth to find places where everything tastes good, everything smells good, and everyone seems young, and everyone young seems witty and wise. Ponce de Leon may or may not have discovered springs in Florida, but I am one of thousands who discovered Finse.

Mr. Lodi Fe, the Italian successor to my more ebullient friend, was my skiing partner at Finse. He fell to me naturally as we were both in the same duffer class, except that I think he was rather braver about hills. He would shake his head at me and criticize, with no hope of remedy.

"Your right foot is more ambitious than your left. Now why is that?" One day he burst out with passion, "Oh, to have been born a Norwegian! To have been *born* here!"

"But why?" I asked the Italian patriot.

"Because then," he said, grinning, "I could have learned in my childhood to be a really good skier."

I understood perfectly how the sport had absorbed him; as I remembered little Prince Harald, only three years old, but flying along on his little skis, his hand held tight by his nurse, an experienced skier and swimmer, as all good nurses should be. I told the ambitious Lodi Fe it was better to have skied and lost than never to have skied at all, and went on enjoying myself, and taking skiing lessons in the Legation garden, quite as if I might some day do as well as little Harald.

I never stopped wishing, though, that the Legation Garden were not quite such a city close. One of my dreams had been to rent a salmon river, and in the summer of '39 I was so fortunate as to secure the River Stryn near Nordfjord. Not having done any fly-fishing for years and years, it was necessary not only to lay out for rod and reel and flies and spoons (not nearly enough, for native anglers think nothing of spending hundreds of dollars on just the right this or that tackle or rod) but to learn all over again the art of casting. A long-suffering man from one of the big outfitting establishments would come around to the garden in the late afternoon while Mr. and Mrs. Cox, who shared the expense of the river with me, and I entangled our lines in the bushes and nearly broke our backs trying to imitate the supple play of muscle that ended in our teacher's fling of the wrist. Finally, the morning after the Fourth of July—we had had to stay in town for the usual Garden Party—we all set off in motors towards the West Coast, accompanied by Minister and Mrs. Sterling who had come over from Stockholm to be our first guests. We broke the journey at a mountain hotel near Otta, the place which nine months later became a center of French and British military activity.

The next day we arrived at Grotli, and we all agreed that the drive down from that place into the valley was the most dramatic scenery we had found anywhere in the world. We reached "our river" to discover that the only way to get from the main road to the cottage was to sit in a chair hung from a cable and to be pulled across, above the scampering waters. Our first swing was terrifying, but it came to be a lark, even when the head gaffer, thinking to reassure me, told me that it was full twenty years since the cable had broken and anyone had been drowned in the river. Since returning to New York, I have wished for that chair and that cable often, as a way of getting across Fifth Avenue.

Twilight and evening are best for finding the fish running. Our first evening, although a good steady rain had set in, we put on our oilskins, and after supper went forth to try our luck. I can't remember that any of us had a bite that first night, but in the morning, it was I who caught the first salmon. My friend, Mr. Thoresen, had sent me a post-card of himself near Romsdal, holding a forty-pound, a forty-five-pound, a fifty-pound fish. I was disappointed that mine weighed only twenty. It was a poor year on the Stryn and no bigger fish was caught by any of us the whole of our stay. But if my salmon *had* been larger I don't know what would have happened, for my twenty-pounder was so game that I found myself dancing down the river bank and was only saved from toppling in the rapids by the quick wits of the gaffer. Just as I slipped, he put his arms around me and clasped the rod on either side, and so we waltzed together as we reeled in the prize.

How our backs ached and how sunburned we got those first days. Notwithstanding, it was an idyllic life, with the peaceful green mountain sides, where the cut hay was fragrant and the cattle grazed across the river. We felt as far away from the turmoil of the world as if we were in midocean on a sailing ship without a radio.

Then suddenly, one day, the telephone rang. It was a message from the doyen of the diplomatic corps, Mr. Neumann, Minister from Poland, reminding me that I must be back in Oslo to welcome home the Crown Prince and Princess, back from their tour of America and visit to the World's Fair. Alas, I stayed until the last moment, waiting to catch one more fish. All would have gone as planned if the road on the way to the first ferry had not been under repair. We lost the last boat by a breath. There was nothing to do but abandon the motor and hire a fishing smack. So, for four hours, in a canvas chair put aboard for my comfort, I sailed grandly up the Sognefjord. Arrived at Laerdal, favorite salmon river of the British, at ten o'clock, I took a late dinner at the inn, and listened to the story-swapping of the last returning fishermen.

Then the inn-keeper found me a motor and I started off on another four-hour lap of my journey to catch the Oslo train at Gol. We arrived in broad daylight, though it was three a.m., after a most John Gilpinish ride. It is against the law in Norway for the man at the wheel to smoke, and so when I saw a cigarette in my chauffeur's mouth, I spoke to him, for with all the winding roads and steep precipices, I thought the law a good one. "I shall go to sleep if I don't," he said, so I said no more. There is very little complaint against this rigid rule in Norway. Both pedestrians and riders agree that it has saved many lives; as has the strict ruling about driving when under the influence of alcohol, a rule that has brought more than one prominent Norwegian into jail for three days. It is because of the firm administration of that law, and the very conservative tests applied to the breaths of slightly deviating drivers, that has made it the general rule for party-goers in Oslo to take taxis. And more than once, when I had accepted escort home from an evening party, a cautious couple have said, "You drive, Mrs. Harriman, the police are such hounds for finding trace of a good punch."

After my adventurous night of traveling, I was back in Oslo, quite in time to welcome their Royal Highnesses at the dock. There was a dinner at the Palace the next night for leading Norwegians. I was the only diplomat invited,

MY FIRST SALMON AT STRYN

CROSSING THE RIVER STRYN

". . . the only way to get from the main road to the cottage was to sit in a chair hung from a cable and to be pulled across, above the scampering waters." (Page 160)

because it was my country they had been visiting and I was the American Minister. When I made my curtsy to the King, he told me to remain behind when the others went to the dining room, for I was to go in to dinner with the Crown Prince. Then, when the other guests were seated, the King gave his arm to the Crown Princess, and Prince Olav and I followed.

Before his visit to America, all of us had noticed that the Crown Prince suffered from the shyness characteristic of his mother's relatives, the British royal family. It was with delight, I observed almost at once, that his American journey appeared to have been a liberation for him. He seemed to have developed a new ease and a ready flow of spontaneous conversation. The acclaim he had met in the United States and the gruelling round of speeches he had had to make had brought out poise and confidence. I think, too, in his stops through the Northwest where thousands of Norwegian-born American citizens greeted him, he was warmed by the realization of the bonds between the two nations.

If I had any complaint against Norway, it was that I missed Washington's Rock Creek Park and the horseback riding there. The Queen rode, of course, and a few others who had been brought up in England, but talk about horses, a calendar designed around race meetings, and the certainty of always meeting friends in the Row, there was not. There was the horse-racing at Övrevoll, a small track in the suburbs of Oslo, engagingly laid out and, with its background of hills, reminding me constantly of a miniature Santa Anita in California. It was being developed by a small group of enthusiasts, Sir Thomas Fearnley and his brother among them; and while the Queen lived, she was a regular attendant on Sunday afternoons through the spring and autumn. She often stopped in the paddock to visit her favorite horses among the many fine specimens imported from England and Ireland, especially the steeplechasers.

Boats, not horses, come first in the hearts of those who live along the Oslo Fjord. Boats and their own feet. There never were such people for walking, week-ends especially. It was nothing to learn they had risen in the morning and walked some fifteen or twenty miles one day, and back again the next. Husbands and wives, boys and girls, would set off on holidays, by train, by bus, then down some fjord in a fishing smack, then a day or two or three with big or little packs on their backs. There would be a day, or a week, up and down hills in the old-fashioned carts, drawn by farm horses often enough, then on foot again.

Nor was this active life ever just sport for sport's sake, or ridden with commercial competition. It was always a rendezvous with Nature, and the joy that comes with health.

CHAPTER XII

We Fish for Cod

Among my clippings, none ever pleased me so much as one in the Svolvaer newspaper, the morning of our arrival within the Arctic Circle. It was on the front page, in English: "Welcome to Lofoten. Today, Svolvaer and the Lofoten Islands have the great pleasure to see Her Excellency, Mrs. F. J. Harriman, the Minister of America, here. On behalf of the citizens of Svolvaer, the inhabitants of Lofoten, and about twenty-five thousand fishermen from all parts of northern Norway, Tröndelag and Möre, which today are taking part in the great Lofoten cod-fishing, we wish Her Excellency a hearty welcome to Svolvaer and the Lofoten Islands. We very much appreciate that Her Excellency has taken this strenuous trip to the north of the Polar Circle this time of the year.

"We dare hope that Her Excellency may enjoy her visit here, as we sincerely wish she must do it."

Of all the things I did in Norway, this was, I think, the happiest, the unique journey; and unexpectedly, the one that made me the most friends. For months afterward, everywhere I went, people would ask me about it; and

Norwegians would say, "Ah, so you are the one who went to Lofoten," in the tone of voice as if to say, "So now you are one of us. You have been initiated."

Traveling back from the North Cape, in the summer of '37, I had been talking to a newspaper man about how beautiful the Lofoten Islands were and how I wished I knew more of the fishermen's lives. "But if your interest is already piqued at this time of year, what would you think of it in the winter, at the height of the cod season? *Then* is the time."

"All right, I'll come back then," I said.

Early March, he said, was the great time. I forgot all about it, and yet whenever cod-fishing was mentioned, I remembered the islands in the summer and had the wish to see them in the snow. Finally, one day in March, I asked my secretary to call the travel bureau and find out what was the best way to reach the islands this time of year. Perhaps it was telepathy. The very next day, a letter from my journalist acquaintance in Trondheim recalled our conversation. He asked if I remembered my wish to see the fishing. The head of one of the coastal lines was about to invite me to travel north on one of his vessels, as his guest.

That night, sitting next to the Danish Minister, Mr. Kauffmann, now envoy to the United States, I told him about the invitation and that I and my granddaughter, Phyllis Russell, were going. He said that he and Consul General and Mrs. Askvig had been wanting, for a long time, to make a winter trip to the north—and so, like a snowball, the party began to grow. When we scrambled on the train in the sharp, clear cold of March 12th, Ship-Owner Thor Thoresen and Captain Holter of the Navy, as well as our Danish friends, were with us. And so to Trondheim, where we boarded a small, but staunch, vessel for the voyage of one night and two days. It was quite smooth, and no other word will do but lovely, as we threaded our way amongst the little islands until late afternoon. Then we were flung into the West Fjord, which is unsheltered from the full swell of the Atlantic and Arctic Oceans, for a fine tossing about. The unseahappy ones quietly vanished to their bunks, while Phyllis and I, very pleased with ourselves, stayed in the saloon playing Russian Bank. Pride goeth . . . they say; for presently the cards flew here, there and everywhere. We hung for dear life to our chairs, and then with dignity, but no more pride, we clung to the stair rail, and finally made it on our hands and knees. "We will," we said to each other, "finish the game when the boat is on more even keel."

But at sunset we were up to gaze at the Lofoten Wall, the name for the high mountains rising directly and perpendicularly out of the sea. The effect, in the snow, was of solid cut diamonds, save where the sunset left a ruby glow. The ship slowed in and made a stop at a fishing town, home of the man known as the "czar" of Lofoten. "Czar" was no title of great honor in that country where men gladly pay eighty per cent of their incomes in taxes, to make possible better conditions and social reforms for the whole working population, the firm foundation of the country. Within his area of control, the "czar" makes bitter feudal bargains. The fishermen must give him the whole of the catch; he pays them back in scrip; the scrip is good only in stores owned, managed and watched over by the "czar." Strange anachronism in the Norway of today! The "czar" owns the fishermen, body and soul. The huts where the men sleep, when they are home from the sea, are primitive bunkhouses. Six or eight men will occupy one room, cook there, and mend their nets. Some more modern quarters of two stories, I saw later; and in these the sleeping quarters and kitchens were often separated. Much this same kind of industrialist flourished in our own America in the nineteenth century. The type is dying out.

An hour farther on was Svolvaer, where we were to be lodged. It embarrassed me a little that the host of the simple and comfortable hotel had vacated his own rooms so that Phyllis and I might be as luxurious as possible. Way up north of the Arctic Circle, we had a sitting room and private dining room, a double bedroom and bath. On the walls were pictures by artists from many nations, who had spent holidays in those northern islands; and many bits of antique Norwegian furniture. From the moment we landed, we felt we were part of a play, for we were met, though we came ashore late in the evening, by a crowd of cheering fishermen, so many of them that the police had to make a lane for us to pass through. The inn was warm and cozy. Outside the snow was blowing and, in the morning, it was still storming. It was even suggested that we should stay snug and postpone the trip to the fishing grounds, but Phyllis agreed that northern weather is the very core of modern adventure. We would set off in the lifeboat provided and do as the fishermen did, hope a little, pray a little, and take whatever wind and waves there were. The decks were coated with ice, and it looked like peril to move about, so I clung to the rigging and took no chances.

We set sail in a dense snowstorm; thicker and faster came the flakes. Then, with quite a little ceremony, the Commandant of the Fleet bowed to me. "I have the honor," he said, "to appoint you Chief Boatswain for the duration of this journey on the Lifesaving Cutter *Idun,* the best cutter ever launched. However, your Excellency, to fulfill this post, you must have the robes for this office, the oilskins and the Pilot's cap—we call them in Lofoten, a 'Dory cap.' You already have your oilskins"—(I was warm inside those stiff, yellow walls)—"and I now take pleasure in placing upon your head, as a symbol of your office on this run of the *Idun,* this cap. May your Excellency keep it always as a memento of Lofoten."

I said my thank you, the crew cheered three times three, and I pulled the leather and sealskin cap down over my ears. Just about then, we discovered the stowaway. He was, it turned out, a reporter on one of the Trondheim papers. He had remained concealed until we were too far out to turn back to dump him. He was blue with cold and had to be given hot drinks; the crew gladly lending him sweaters and coats. The newspapers reported the incident as showing he was a reporter with "true American initiative."

"But without American foresight," said Phyllis. "Imagine, he might have frozen to death!"

We moved on toward our goal. I had dreamed a little of what we were to see. But when the forest of masts, extending for a mile ahead of us, came in sight, I held my breath. Four thousand boats were on the water. Never are there more than five thousand. As we came up, the sun was under a cloud. It was a dark forest on a darker sea. Then, suddenly, the sun came out and the beauty of the scene was unbelievable. The frosted masts sparkled, and the snowy mountains of the islands behind them wore tinsel wreaths.

The russet of the sails, the blue and black of the rails of some of the boats, the glittering water, all moving in the wind, were marvelous. The echo-sound apparatus was being adjusted, and the news came that a school of fish ten metres in depth was registered fifty or sixty metres beneath the surface of the water. The cutter was at once brought up in the wind and fishing lines put out. Until then, I had hardly noticed the icy weather, but I discovered that, in spite of my warm stockings and rubber boots, my feet were so numb I could not move them at all. One of the Norwegian sailors came to my rescue. He took me below, told me firmly to draw on two pairs of his own heavy, rough socks, lent me his white rubber boots and in such fashion was my circulation restored for the rest of a busy day. Up on deck, I found the Danish Minister pulling in the first cod. I threw my line and had luck as good; I got my cod, but found it no easy job to land him. Thick and fast, laughing and shouting, we drew in cod after cod. Arctic weather whets a special appetite; we talked of cooks instead of catches. Our boat was got under way and headed to a sheltered cove.

While we had been lying to, round and round us, one at a time, other boats of the fishing fleet would circle, shouting, "Show her to us. Show us the American Minister." And when I was pointed out, they should shout again, "No, no. We mean the American." Bless them, I don't blame them for not recognizing the rough-looking fellow in oilskins and cap. I certainly did not look like a woman.

It was three o'clock before we sat down to lunch. We were ravenous; and yet it was not merely appetite; what we had was one of the most delicious meals in the world. The fresh, boiled cod was served with its roe and liver and boiled

Norwegian Travel Information Office

FISHING BOATS AT LOFOTEN

"The frosted masts sparkled, and the snowy mountains of the islands behind them wore tinsel wreaths." (Page 169)

potatoes. There was beer to wash it down. How we ate, and how we laughed! There were speeches, and greetings brought from the 25,000 fishermen by the Commandant.

I think of those fishermen often, this second winter of the war. They depend for their livelihood on the cod season; these days they have no gasoline for their engines. They must fish now in little boats, without the echo machine, the Germans having confiscated the fleet. Their catch will be small—enough, perhaps, to feed their families cod, and cod is excellent food—but they cannot possibly make enough to buy anything else. In the best of times, Northern Norway depends on the south for fifty per cent of its living; now, the south has little enough to supply itself, and must also stand in fear of levies for the Nazis. I think of those fishermen, and listen to the arguments that go on. What will bring the shortening of this war, and victory least delayed—what do those fishermen think themselves?

In the late afternoon, we left the fleet and headed back toward Svolvaer. The sun sank into the sea, and fresh snowfall melted into the gray ocean. It was like a curtain descending on some fantastic opera scene. But the curtain had been lifted just long enough for us to store away a memory to last a lifetime.

As we walked from the quay to the little hotel, through clustered groups of fishermen, someone heard one of them saying, "Yes, indeed, the President of the United States is one of the greatest fishermen on earth. He wanted to come to this place himself, but he couldn't, so he sent his Minister to us." I wish the President *had* seen that fleet.

That evening we all dined with a citizen of the town, in a fine house on the hill, looking down over the harbor and the lanterns of the fisherboats at anchor. There were so many boats that there seemed to be another city nestling on the water.

And there, for the first time, I ate cod tongues. Only within an hour or two after the cod comes from the sea, can the tongues be eaten. The gourmets of the north say the cod tongue of Lofoten is better than foie gras or caviar. It *is* good. *Almost* as good as that. And anyway, I like to help the legend along, that is certain to tease the palates of those connoisseurs of food who will never see the fairy masts of Lofoten in the winter.

The principal part of the catch is made either into salted and dried cod, or stock fish. The latter is done by hanging the fish up to dry in the open air after it has been split and cleaned and the head has been removed. The large dumps of heads with their eyes looking still quite natural give a macabre effect. The most important markets today for stock fish are Italy and, for the cheaper qualities, West Africa. The production of salted and dried cod is not so simple as that of stock fish. After the head is removed, the fish is cleaned, then split, salted and pressed, again washed and finally dried. This product is especially in demand in Portugal, Spain and South American countries.

Cod is used in other forms, but by far the most important by-product of the cod fisheries is the liver, used for that famous, world-renowned tonic, Norwegian Medicinal Cod Liver Oil.

At midnight of the third day our party broke up. Consul General and Mrs. Askvig and Mr. Kauffmann and Phyllis were going further north to see the Lapp country, Finnmarken. Legation business called me back, but I left reluctantly. How comfortable we had been. I would not advise Arctic life, however, for those who are not strong, and good sailors to boot.

From that moment, I began to take more interest in the Arctic Fair which was being planned for the summer of 1940, and being planned not merely as retrospect of man's achievement in reaching both poles, but to present life in the Arctic as one of the promises of the future—not the least exciting feature of international politics.

It had been my plan to spend ten days in Bergen in the summer of 1940. I would arrive for the opening of the International Exhibition of Polar Exploration and improve the chance, then, to explore the old Hanseatic city. I could, too, take part in what would certainly have been not only a unique exhibition of mankind's heroic past, but a chance to meet explorers and scientists from all countries. Vilhjalmur Stefansson was expected to attend, and Dr. Alexander Wetmore of the Smithsonian Institution. For Harald U. Sverdrup, now head of the Scripps Institute of Oceanography at La Jolla, California, the journey would be a sort of homecoming as well, as he was formerly on the staff of the famous Bergen Museum. He was the man of science on the famous *Maud* expedition organized by Roald Amundsen.

Not the least anguishing part of this war is that it tore to tatters and postponed for years, though certainly not forever, so many enterprises that were international and humane—so much fun, so much sharing of science, so much practical hope for linked progress of all nations. The Bergen Exhibit was of special importance to aviation, for, more and more, weather forecasting depends on Arctic scientific observation. There was a sort of excitement in the fact that so many Russians from the Siberian Arctic were arriving and, toward those leaders in Arctic exploration, there was a generous and friendly feeling. Until about ten years ago, with the exception of the British Empire, Norway had been the foremost nation in modern polar exploration. But, in the last years, the Soviet Union had done more than all other nations put together, and now there was a chance for all to pool what had been learned.

The Exhibit had, for me, another touching aspect. Over it all, surely, there would have dwelt the spirit of Fridtjof Nansen, the greatest of the modern *scientific* explorers—a man who, in European politics, will be more and more discovered and remembered. How many lives he saved; how many bridges he built between warring nations and intolerant ideologies; how proud he made all who knew him, of his nation and his generation. All his life he had had official and unofficial connections with the Bergen Museum. We expected people from Alaska and Canada, from Australia and New Zealand. There was to have been, I believe, the first great exhibition of primitive art, from the Lapp people of Finland, Sweden and Norway, from the Indians and Eskimos, and from the many tribes who live on the Siberian tundra, and in the forests of the north. There would be films of the north, made for the scientific record; and that ever living, ever marvelous "Nanook of the North," made by Robert Flaherty, would be shown again. I would like to pray that we all be given war-checks, as they give rain-checks at baseball games. What was good must only be interrupted. The meeting of minds and hearts that was planned for Bergen must still take place.

CHAPTER XIII

THE NORWEGIAN WAY OF LIFE

SOMETHING IS PLAINLY wrong in many parts of the world, in the daily way of life. We use neither our hands nor our minds in a way to make us happy. "Nothing we have in Nature that is ours." One cannot generalize about a country as large as the United States. There is a way of doing things in New Mexico that is as strange and foreign to the native of Brooklyn as Provence is to Chicago, but I can honestly say that there is a Norwegian way of life that breeds strength and happiness in the faces of its people. I do not find sad that look, often faraway, stern and thoughtful, of the people of the northern valleys. They feel and think, and have good consciences. Their daily life is full of art.

Hardly a shop in Oslo but what had exhibits of the handicrafts, and these I felt, from the beginning, were an evidence of a rich and simple life throughout the whole country. For that reason, over and over again, when there was an opportunity to make an excursion by motor, I would try to direct our route to some special province or village famous for one or another of the beautiful carvings, embroidery, or iron work which came to the capital. And being a knitter of experience, and an amateur weaver myself, I knew I would learn some new stitches, and see some old looms.

On one such journey, as we rounded a curve and came on a delightful stretch of country, I stopped the motor. The sun, which had been shy all day, suddenly began to shine. A girl in a field, below a blossoming apple tree, rose from the ground where she had been sitting. At her back were the snow-capped mountains. She made an enchanting picture. Then I saw that, in her hand, she had a piece of beautiful Hardanger embroidery. Mustering my best Norwegian, I asked, "May we see your farm?" The girl dropped a curtsey and smiled. "If you will, my sisters will be pleased."

We walked along to the house, through a garden where the currants hung heavily from the bushes and withering lilacs still gave a little fragrance in the wind. Zinnias and sweet william grew thick along the path. The house of unpainted timber, without shingles, was a weathered gray. Its sombreness was relieved by lacquer-red blinds and window trim. There was the usual *stabbur* next to the house. The farmers build these stabburs, or small houses, on four legs, raised about five feet above the ground, so that rats and mice can't get in. They are, so to speak, the farmers' private banks, where they store butter, salt fish, meats and other commodities. A wealthy farmer will have a reserve put away there for two years. In the summer they hang their furs and winter clothes from the rafters. These bank buildings are their great pride and, often, they have more beautiful carving on them than on their residences.

A very old woman, in a cap, sat in the side door. "My mother," murmured the girl, with a smile and a movement of her head. As she went right on, I supposed she did not wish to trouble the old lady to meet strangers.

At the front door, the older sisters came forward, and, after a whispered explanation from our guide, begged us to come in and sit down. When I told them how interested I was in all kinds of handwork, their faces brightened and they were all eagerness to show me their treasures.

Ragnhild, as the others called her, at once went to an antique chest and brought out lovely drawn work and embroidery, yellow with age. "This was made by our grandmother for her wedding apron, and this," she said, lifting tenderly another piece that was almost too fragile to handle, "this was our great-grandmother's work." I was looking at something held dear, not merely for sentiment's sake, but as a fine old document.

Thousands of Norwegian peasant chests must hold embroidery fit for great museums. The modern copies hold to the pattern, but the work is seldom quite so fine. The old ones are real works of art and, as one touches them, as it so often is when one is handling old manuscripts and letters, the aroma of the past crowds on the senses and evokes a scene. The embroidery in my hand made me think of Italy as well, and I wondered whether some bride in this very house had been an Italian girl brought home to Norway by some seafaring son. I often wondered about that, now struck by some aspect of design in an old towel, or tablecloth, or surprised by lustrous, brown eyes in a head crowned with flaxen braids. In an antique shop on the West Coast I came on a carved and gilded Norwegian mirror that showed both Chippendale and French influence, as well as native, tastefully combined by the carver into something new and integral.

Ragnhild told me that the chest, indeed all the furniture in the farmhouse, had been made by her forebears. Their father had been drowned and their only brother, married now, was a sailor. The farm had belonged to their mother's family for generations. When her whaler husband had been lost, she had gone inland again to raise her children.

Then we talked about the embroidery. "We girls farm all the land we can, but we could not live here except that we sell our embroidery. Our mother taught us as soon as we could ply a needle. We do not remember when we were not busy so." With my first bright picture of the embroiderer, standing in a lush meadow beneath the apple tree, I found it hard to picture what she would be like in the long, dark, winter days and nights, in this northern valley. The house was small; but the usual, enormous fireplace, built of stone, stood out a foot or more in the corner of the room. This is to prevent fire hazards in the wooden buildings, and the fireplaces are so constructed that heat is thrown in three directions. Through nine months of Arctic weather, these cheerful hearths are the center of all family life. On the day I paid my visit, there would be light until eleven o'clock. The girls could embroider through the night, under the trees. But I did not stay to watch them. I was far from the inn we meant to stay in for the night, and we had a long, mountainous road to travel over. I rose to go, telling the sisters that I had made a long itinerary to see other kinds of handiwork, that I was going to the sea coast, and farther north still. They looked at each other. Would I like to see their brother's wife and children? Then they wrote her name on a piece of paper, and the name of a fishing village near Molde, and I came away.

This holding on to the ancient ways and farm economy is, I believe, common all through Scandinavia, and is organized with the utmost care, as an aid especially to small freeholders. The longer I stayed in Norway, the more interested I became. I believe that much of what I found so satisfying about the culture of the country was this conscious devotion to handwork, its recognition as necessary to the economy of the country and its part in developing the taste for durable and beautiful standards of living. In the olden days, of course, all farm households had to weave their own clothes, make their own household furniture, utensils and tools. In those days, therefore, only the handicraftsman, the artist, the competent man commanded respect. You could not buy. You could only make things. The fine handicraftsman was the "good catch" for a girl to marry; the woman who could make things was known far and wide as "desirable." With the introduction of machinery in 1830, handwork began to decline. But by the middle of the century, when already a rust was visible on the life of the countryside, a movement was set on foot to maintain the old life along with whatever advantages could be got from the machine. The question was one of national importance. By the late eighties, the country was a network of home industrial societies, schools and courses. Everything possible was done to encourage country people to use the long winter evenings for the production of beautiful handwork, a "cash crop," to be sold to the foreign and domestic market. Not only were the peasants encouraged to make things for themselves, instead of buying the cheaper machine stuff, but to augment their incomes, by developing their skills in weaving, woodworking and iron work. The winter is really the best time for anyone with a quest like mine to pay a round of visits to handicraftsmen working at "full steam." Many districts, however, in the mountains are impassable after the early snows, but the story of the winter can be read in spring and summer, in the displays of finished work to be found everywhere, each province having its great specialty. In Hardanger, it was embroidery, distinguished by an Italian influence.

Near Molde, we found Ragnhild's sister-in-law and her looms, and a very fine weaver she was. No ravelling Penelope while her husband was at sea, but a maker of fine household linens, with now and then an adventure into tapestry. I was not tempted by her choice of subjects in her tapestry. I like it better when the old patterns are reproduced from antique models. But towels we bought, and I suppose I got considerable pleasure from thinking that my own petit-point, which I was making for some of the Legation chairs, was rather better than what I found in Molde.

Such trips as mine were always voyages of discovery. On that same journey, I believe, on a mountain side, near Romsdal, we found a wood carver who was as truly an artist as any of the great ones. He would have written himself down for the census as a farmer, never as an artist. He had not studied with anyone, but through many long, cold winters, with his knife and with his wood, he had worked "to please himself." One of his cabinets was as delicate and exquisite as lace work. I had never seen anything like it before and offered to buy it. He said that he had carved it for his wife and so, of course, could not take any money for it. But he

A CHARACTERISTIC NORWEGIAN TOWN

INTERIOR OF A NORWEGIAN FARMHOUSE

"The house was small; but the usual enormous fireplace, built of stone, stood . . . in the corner of the room." (Page 178)

would give it to us! It was a curious experience. His face shone. Money he could not take for anything he had loved to make for a beloved one. His expression, as he tried to explain to us, and the strange tapestry of the knitting women of Selbu, I shall long remember.

In the old days, it was a custom in the valleys near Selbu, for the bride, on her wedding day, to present each one of her guests with a pair of mittens. That is why the little girls learned to knit even before they learned to read, and what is the fun of knitting all your girlhood, mittens that are all alike? The nicest little differences, the most charming variations, became a specialty of the mittens of Selbu. And now the farm land being poor, not the best, at any rate, you can see, in and out of the houses of Selbu, three thousand women knitting. Like the women in "The Tale of Two Cities," they knit from morning until night, making mittens—mostly black and white, with the reindeer design upon them. Everyone who skis or bobsleds must have seen at least a pair, for between a hundred and a hundred and fifty thousand a year for America is an average export. The only money figure I have goes back to 1937, when the women cleared 137,000 kronen, which is over $32,000. I might not have thought of those dour French women, knitting in the Dickens story, if one of the local clergymen had not taken me aside to tell me in all seriousness, "They cannot stop. They cannot stop. They are becoming a community of neurotics. They will knit themselves crazy. They knit and they knit and will concentrate on nothing else. I have tried to get them to do other things. Other things they will not do."

All over the world there are men who fear the worst when their women take to knitting, and perhaps he was only one of them. We acquired many pairs of mittens with delight and continued to study the part handicraft played in the total economy of the country and decided to report on mittens and tablecloths, for the Department of State to pass on to the Department of Agriculture. If 450,000 households in Norway can earn $11,750,000 annually, so beautifully and creatively, no time was wasted that I spent on a report which might stimulate some such activity in our own country. I enjoyed all the traveling, the people I met. I bought some beautiful objects and some were given to me with touching speeches about our two countries. I felt that I saw new vistas of solving many problems.

Someone told me the story of a young woman who began her weaving for the Home Industries Organization at Hedmarken at the end of the last century. Her work was so beautiful and flawless that inquiries were made about her. Only then was it discovered in Oslo that she was a cripple without hands. She had been taught to weave in a public institution and had learned to use her toes. The Husflid (The Home Industries) found a market for her which she could never have found herself. She was able to build a little house for herself, and to have a life, admired for her art, instead of becoming a public charge. Many of the old women, too, keep their independence which they prize most highly, well on beyond the seventies, if they are skilful basketmakers or knitters.

What Henry Wallace, what AE, what M. L. Wilson would understand, are all the implications of this encouragement of handicraft in the Norwegian countryside. There is a life of art as there is of religion. There is a kind of community democracy that is hurt by the importation of outside goods sold a penny cheaper, but without romance in their making. There is a kind of brotherhood of man, and understanding of neighborly needs, in the sort of encouragement given in the village stores of Norway to the chairmaker, the weaver, the candlestick-maker, the andiron-maker, etc. These artists put into their designs all that is common in the life around them—the color of the autumn leaves, the prow of some old ship . . . The good name, the respect gained by a local artist, means a sense of richness in the village, a sense of having the very source of creativeness at hand. We, who buy cheap goods, however wonderful, from half way across the world, are letting the lives of our own people go barren of some of life's deepest satisfactions. There are three thousand counties in the United States and I could wish for every one the same pride in their quilt makers, their rag rug hookers, their mince pie makers, their nut bowl makers, as the provinces of Norway have for their local chest designers, the makers of mufflers and mittens, of waistcoats and towels and tapestries.

The wise direction, the careful accounting of small committees, all over Norway, prevent exploitation of the handiworkers and create fresh markets for their work in the cities and abroad. The quality of yarn and dye is overseen. In some places, common workshops have been built, especially for weavers. Teachers, who believe in the maintenance of the old traditions, are sent into the mountains. Clothes for workers and clothes for sport assume a new gaiety because of the making of them in the old way. A woman will belong to a weaving society, as we might belong to a bridge club. And sometimes whole families, men and women together, will weave, as a way of passing a family evening. What we do by way of training for the blind, in a way, the Norwegians try to do for everybody. "Those who can use their hands have more than one pair of eyes" is an old saying.

CHAPTER XIV

Up the Gulf to Leningrad

"Grow old along with me, the best is yet to be, the last of life for which the first was made." On my birthday in July, 1939, I stood in Frogner Park in Oslo and repeated those lines to myself and Kim with complete sincerity. I felt that every year our values become more clear and that the small irritations of life count less, and so we are increasingly contented. Kim, my eleven-year-old police dog, had been my constant companion since he was six months old. That day, when he looked up at me with his gentle eyes, it didn't, fortunately, enter my mind that, in just a year's time, I would be forced to give orders to have him chloroformed. As dogs go, he had lived to a fine old age, but the terribly severe northern winters had given him rheumatism. He had a perfect nature, which was never ruffled except by motorcycles. He had once been run over by one and, from that day, he had a vengeful habit of giving chase and barking angrily, whenever a motorcyclist went by. I could not cure him, and even felt sorry when my other dog, Viking, a Norwegian elkhound, cheated Kim out of a double revenge.

It happened on the morning of the German invasion. A Nazi officer, on a motorcycle, came down the street past the Legation. Viking must have instinctively hated Nazis—cycles had never bothered *him* before—for he rushed the officer, toppled him and his machine, badly messing the invader's regalia in the slush and snow. Though his own shoulder was painfully torn in the process, so that it was necessary to send him to the veterinary, he wore a definite air of satisfaction.

Kim would so have liked to do that, to that particular target! It really didn't seem fair! I used to call Kim my sixth column. He had a way of sensing strangers long before they were heard or seen by anybody else. He would follow me upstairs and down, a constant guard; and when I went away from home, he would wander about the house disconsolate. I acquired my Washington house and Kim at the same time. It hurts to think of living at Uplands without him. Good Kim, I ought not to complain. Wherever there is a dog's heaven, there he surely is.

In Frogner Park is the famous bridge of Gustav Wigeland, and nearby the studio, given him by the city of Oslo. Wigeland's gigantic and ambitious plans are for a kind of *comédie humaine* in stone and bronze, to celebrate life itself, man's span from youth to age, our common experience of being born and living and coming to the end. A visitor once, in speaking of him, put it this way—"I think, in the future, Oslo will be a place of pilgrimage. Whatever the rest of the world has to offer in tremendous political adventure, here, as to a church, one may come to think and pray. Wigeland's sculpture portrays the individual biological story of each one of us."

On the bridge there are thirty-six statues, mounted on the balustrades. In the far end of the park is a monolith from which radiate long allées. No such ambitious scheme has ever been commissioned since Michael Angelo's time. Wigeland is growing old; he has been at work for over twenty years; and under the strangest and most tolerant patronage, unimaginable in America. Few who have paid for his work have ever been allowed in his studio, including the officials of Oslo, who promoted the subsidy from the city. Visitors come from the corners of the earth wanting to see him or his work; the door will be bolted against them. His wife will explain, often sadly, that time is short, the artist must work. Yet several times a year, almost without warning, the studio will be thrown open and hundreds of the simple folk of Oslo and a few friends will go in and see everything. Last year more visitors were allowed, and several times I had the chance to study the stone figures on which the cutters were still working, and the hundreds, even thousands, of small models and drawings which are the artist's sketchbook.

Wigeland and his project have their critics; the strange artist has his feuds; but both in the great magnum opus, and in the early work in the National Museum and in the garden of the Theile Museum in Stockholm, it is plain that, in Norway, works one of the great artists of our time. He speaks for individual man, when the world is dealing in masses, and Europe is wet with blood.

The Norwegians, many of them, are even prouder of their other great hermit, the painter, Edvard Munch, whom they place above Picasso or any other modern master of color. When the New York Museum of Modern Art wrote the Legation asking our help in getting a painting of Munch's for their 1939 exhibition, we thought it would be a simple and routine matter. But we discovered the painter to be so much a recluse, that no stranger could hope to conclude any personal dealings with him. Through the kindness of Mr. Mustad, a great collector of his works, the Museum was eventually lent a picture from the Mustad Collection. It was an early work—"The Tempest." "The Sick Girl," the most widely known of the Munch pictures, he has painted five times, but never copying from a previous version. One of these copies was presented to the Tate Gallery in London by Mr. Thomas Olsen, the ship-owner.

Edvard Munch was, until the Nazis began to promote simple, calendar art for Nazi warriors and breeders, one of the most highly prized painters in German art galleries. Norwegian museums forgave the insults heaped on Munch, amongst other moderns, when the purge of Matisse, Picasso and the rest was on, and cheerfully bought for their own walls Munches they had long envied Munich and Berlin. And, only this last year, Mr. Rolf Stenersen, banker and writer, presented a museum to the city of Oslo, a beautiful building, set in the working-class quarter of the town, to which his collection of Munch pictures is to be given intact. It is noteworthy that, as a nation, the Norwegians take pride in their artists. They feel it an honor to support them, to buy canvasses for their own homes, and make a place for art purchases in municipal budgets. Their wood carvers, their etchers, their sculptors, are as known by name to the population at large as their skiers, or, with us, our columnists and baseball players.

"I wish I could see all the museums in Europe," I said, half aloud to Kim, as I was walking past the Wigeland

Studio that July evening. And, almost like the three wishes in the fairy tale, the unexpected came to pass.

The next day two American ladies arrived to call at about half-past twelve. They were in Oslo, spending a shore day on the Baltic Cruise of the S.S. *Franconia.* I had never met either of them before, but I knew friends of both Mrs. Mortimer and Mme. Ardenghi. They were obviously enjoying their cruise tremendously.

"Going to Russia?" I exclaimed. "I've been longing for years to go."

"Do come with us," they said at once.

"I think I will," I said, with a premonition, somehow, that I would go. The obstacles were many! It generally takes two weeks or longer to obtain a visa for the U.S.S.R. It was midsummer and Saturday, and most Consulates closed at midday. Perhaps the ship was full. I telephoned to the Captain, who put me in touch with the Raymond Whitcomb man on board. There was still a vacant room. "Hold it," I said, "until I can talk with the Russian Consul."

The Consulate "didn't answer." I tried the Legation. The Minister was an hour out of town and no one else could help me. It was already half-past two and the steamer was to sail at five. But the hunch that I was going still persisted. I called the maid and told her to pack my bags for a fortnight's cruise. In another hour we were rung up and told that the Minister was so pleased that I wanted to visit his country that he had motored in to town, and would I send my passport around at once? He had been two years in Oslo but, as he spoke no word of any language but Russian, his usefulness was almost nil and, indeed, a short time after my return, he was recalled. He has my personal gratitude forever for graciously making this trip possible. My secretary rushed off for a Finnish visa. At a quarter to five I stepped triumphantly aboard the ship. The staff at the Legation, I think, considered me quite mad but, as I have never been more rewarded for following an impulse than on that Baltic Cruise, I think it wise to say a word for madness.

Our first stop was at the Island of Gotland. The lovely walled town of Visby, with its narrow streets and pretty houses, had that effect of stage design you sometimes find in old English villages. From the sea, ruins of churches and cathedrals punctuated the landscape. Their walls tower above the modern buildings. How our Garden Club members would gasp if they could see the flowers. There are giant standard fuchsias and roses five and six feet tall. The rose plants are like small trees. Ivy clambers like jungle over the house walls. It was all a beautiful dream—all but the round cobblestones in every street. We longed for soldiers' boots, as the stones crippled our modern feet.

The church ruins interested everybody, and two, in particular, tickled my fancy. The twin churches, Drotten and St. Lars, were built in the twelfth century by a father for his two daughters who, having quarreled, refused to worship under the same roof.

The day was charming and the evening even better. We sat in the roofless cathedral of St. Nicholas, at first under the rosy light of the dying sun. Then the stars came out one by one in the deep, blue sky. We witnessed a musical miracle play whose plot was built around the most famous Gotlander of the Middle Ages, Petrus de Dacia. He lived in the thirteenth century and was a Prior of the Dominican Monastery of St. Nicholas, of which these were the ruins. His grave, legend has it, is in the chancel. The drama was about the conflict he experienced between celestial and terrestrial love, for he adored the pious woman, Christina. The beautiful music of the organ, the fine voices, the setting of the ancient ruins, wrought on us. It was an impressive and stirring performance. As we came away, I overheard people saying that they found greater qualities in it than in the Passion Play at Oberammergau. I could not judge, as I have seen only the play at Visby.

I had meant to keep a diary on the cruise, but by the time we reached Stockholm I was down to dots and dashes and promises to myself to write at length tomorrow. I do remember that date because I met, for the first time, Mme. Alexandra Kollontay, the Soviet Minister to Sweden. She had been the first woman diplomatic officer in the world, and had served the Soviets first in Mexico, and then in Oslo, whence she was transferred to Stockholm. She has become in the last few months, owing to the death of the Norwegian Minister, doyenne of the diplomatic corps in Sweden. I liked her from the first and wish the fanciful writers of the popular press knew how much better copy she really is than their silly stories have tried to make her out. Her dignity, her directness, her cleverness, make an instant impression. And how she admires and appreciates the Scandinavian countries. Half Finnish herself, born there, daughter of an officer in the Czar's army, she is an authority on the care of women and children. Her book of twenty years ago is still an international authority on the subject. She is a dancer who can manage a court train, and one of the world's most facile linguists. What luck her country has in her services! I have seen her many times since, and always to my intense interest. I would rather read her memoirs of what has happened in our time, than that of any other woman. She ought to do them, but perhaps the Soviet theory of one light and one only on every story, holds her back.

The cruise went to Tallinn. No notes at all, except a hasty, "Tallinn begins to look more like Russia, they say, and less like Scandinavia. Saw the small house where Peter the Great lived; and the palace he built for his wife, Catherine."

Tallinn is one of the most beautiful of the Hanseatic cities, and as we pottered around the market place buying the leather things for which Esthonia is famous, I mixed thought of the ancient Baltic past with questions to the little merchants and peasants about the future. No one who travels in the Baltic can fail to have a glowing awareness of the Hanseatic past. It struck me sharply in Bergen at the Hanseatic Museum, now lodged in one of the ancient counting houses of the German Merchants Company which had a stranglehold on the commerce of Bergen for centuries. The whole medieval world comes back with a rush as you stand in that museum with its tiny rooms, its beds in cupboards, whips for lazy apprentices' shoulders, false weights for the fish, and light screens in the windows so the merchants could watch operations on the quay below without being visible to the seamen. It was all so vivid; so hateful, too; and yet, I understand some of the terrific romantic pull for the Germans who had been masters of that trade and sea. All round the Baltic, the buildings, the statues and monuments tie that league of cities together still; behind them, new life and new ideals sprang up. In the Esthonian market place, we heard expressions of dread lest little Esthonia might lose its independence again. At the same time, they spoke of what seemed like healthy trade. Wheat and dairy products were being sent to the Soviet Union in return for machinery.

In Leningrad my pen found ink once more. I have pages of jottings, set down as impression after impression was made upon me. The people were so badly dressed and their faces seemed to me so sad. I had heard of the melancholy Slavic visage. I did not expect the gaily clothed, free-swinging athletes of the north. But neither had I been prepared for the air of indifference and lassitude I observed in the crowd of slow-moving passers-by; nor had I been prepared for the background. The Neva flows through more grandiose architecture than Paris. The city needed paint; but it had been planned by great architects. It was an imperial city, and in the northern summer, Leningrad was old St. Petersburg still.

Nobody wore any hats. The women were dressed in sweaters and linen skirts, or rather inferior cotton frocks. Some had handkerchiefs on their heads. Nearly everyone had canvas shoes, sneakers or sandals, and many were stockingless. They all took notice of our footgear. The men were most of them in shirtsleeves or cotton Russian blouses.

Our guide went on in a pleasant, relentless, explanatory voice all about the energy of the people being concentrated on building up the basic or heavy industries which had been destroyed by the revolution, or had been non-existent. "The other countries," she said, "had no confidence in our experiment, so we couldn't borrow." Now, they had money . . . now, they would initiate . . . now, there would be light industries and shoe plants . . . I hardly listened, I was so interested in things to see, even in the pouring rain, which seemed to increase the gloominess by the minute. It was certainly no weather for either canvas sneakers or expensive American pumps.

We drove first to the Winter Palace, which isn't at all to be judged by photographs. We saw the arcade built to commemorate the defeat of Napoleon. The Russians remember their part in those wars, and in the west we remember Waterloo! I stood a long time before the column of Alexander III, the Czar who "freed the serfs." In Russia his monuments still stand; in the west we remember Lincoln.

On the Square of Mars, we stopped to look at the old British Embassy, nearly a block square, an impressive building still, though the blue paint was peeling from its walls, and the gala entertainments that once went on within are only memories. Opposite is the Palace presented by the Empress Catherine to Orloff, one of her lovers. He was brother to the Orloff who killed her husband, Peter II. In those days, an immense parade ground lay in front of these buildings; now there are extensive gardens with many flowerbeds, dedicated to those fallen in the revolution, and buried there in a common grave.

My memory of Leningrad is strictly tourist. I moved rapidly, not to lose track of the others, and always aware that the whistle would blow, as it were, to leave. My memories are like a packet of postcards—the Blue Mosque, built in the time of Nicholas II, was of a ravishing color. Its blue and white mosaic tiles were a reminder that the empire of the Czars, and the Union of the Soviets alike, stretch far to the south and east, to Persia and to Samarkand, to the lands of ancient tiles and priceless vases.

The Hermitage, of course, was the best of it all. I remembered Ambassador Isvolski in Paris, in 1919, describing how he and others had made trips to Petrograd to preserve and assemble its art treasures. But he had conveyed no real idea to me of the unbelievable riches of the place, the enormous malachite and lapis lazuli vases and epergnes, seven feet high and beautiful beyond compare even with tales of the Arabian Nights. They say that many of the Rembrandts have been sold abroad, but there are beautiful ones left, among them the famous "Goddess of Spring," said to be a painting of his wife. We saw some fine El Grecos. We stood under countless rows of crystal chandeliers, collected from the Czar's Winter Palace. We were let into the famous Gold Room. The door was locked after us, while we gazed at the ancient golden ornaments of the Scythians, and the famous collection of snuff boxes and priceless jewelled toys, sent to the Czars from emperors and princes—watches, rings, plates.

We admired the many bridges, wide and handsomely embellished, and the gilded domes and spires of the Admiralty and the churches. Leningrad, Peter's City.

At luncheon in the Hotel Metropole, I kept questioning myself: What did it all add up to? The waiters were in soiled jackets and Emma, our guide, rather spoiled my appetite by the way she slashed her food with her knife and poked her elbow into me, and yet she spoke good English, and I spoke no Russian. She was obviously intelligent, though she had a fanatical gleam when she talked about "our system."

After lunch we drove out to Peterhof, where we saw the one-story lodge built by Peter on the shore of the Baltic, a building intimate and charming. There it is, intact, just as it was when the last of the Great Peter's heirs lived in it, and hung beside the bed is Great Peter's uniform.

From there, we went to the large palace, called the Russian Versailles, with its waterfalls and canal running a quarter of a mile to the sea. It seemed rather shabby to me. It was a summer home at times for the late Czar and his family. I made a note of the enchanting effect in the ballroom of having candles in hurricane shades on one side, with full-length mirrors reflecting them upon the other. We ate our dinner on the ship, and took the night train for Moscow.

Our porter was very attentive, almost jovial, in fact. I had no idea he was part of a change for a gayer city. I rather dreaded our arrival in the morning. But the train, wider than ours, and the old wooden car we were in, built in Belgium in 1913, were comfortable, and we slept well.

Moscow is not at all "more Leningrad." The tempo, the expressions on the faces of the people, are brisk and vital. We saw many women dressed not unlike ourselves—not such good shoes or stockings, but the same general styles. There was no stinting on cosmetics; the stories about the shutting down of beauty parlors cannot have been wholly true. We were taken to the Hotel Metropole on the Theater Square, opposite the Bolshoi Opera House and, after a hasty breakfast of tea and coffee and eggs and bread and cheese and sweet rolls, and hardly any time for tidying up, off we went again. A block or two away, facing the Kremlin, we passed the American Embassy with its imposing façade of pilasters, in the French style. A shallow building though, and, I was told later, not at all well built.

Then we saw the Red Square. It was always called the Red Square, even before the Revolution, for red is the color of Life. It is the central artery of the city, and very impressive. The Kremlin wall is of greenish granite, in front of which the Government has now planted, at intervals of fifteen feet, blue or Norway spruce, the tips of whose branches shine like silver. In the foreground is Lenin's Tomb, red and black granite, modern in design, yet taking its inspiration from the simple, wooden structure which preceded it as Lenin's first resting-place after his death in 1923. Outside it, a queue of two or three thousand people were waiting their turn to go inside and see him where he lies, strangely preserved. At the end of the square is St. Basil's chapel, whose Italian builder was blinded by Ivan the Terrible at its completion, lest he should build another church more curious and wonderful for someone else.

We were tourists. We did not stop to think many thoughts. Tretiakov Gallery was only one thing on our list. I think we did that museum at a jog trot—hundreds, no, thousands of pictures—the guide, in a low, guttural voice supplying the names of the painters and seeming to urge us both to hurry and to stop and really look. What struck me was that so many of the pictures were of hideous sights—executions and banishments, chained prisoners in Siberia, Ivan the Terrible in his madness. This was the Russian past.

Lunch at the hotel was hearty and delicious—caviar, broiled chicken, and ice cream. We were delighted with our guide, who was, beside being all that a guide should be—patient, knowledgable and gay—a very great beauty. Valja Molodnina had a profile like those on some Roman coins. She had a short upper lip, an oval face, a filmy, white skin, and fluffy, red-gold hair. She was twenty-six and determined not to marry. You can see what kind of impertinent tourists we were! We inquired about everything which interested us, and many personal things did. Valja wouldn't marry because she couldn't find a man good enough! Her father was an electrical engineer, and her mother a believer who still goes to church.

If a group in a community can support a church, apparently, they can have one. It must be very hard on the old people who still have religious faith, but no money. Though now I come to remember, no old people are seen anywhere in the cities. But many pregnant women were there. I was accosted by a beggar only once while in Russia—it is against the law, as is the taking of tips—and she, carrying a baby which didn't look a year old, was far gone towards producing another. In Leningrad, before the Revolution, I am told there were 50,000 beggars!

What I wanted to do was prowl about by myself, as I love to do in other cities. I wanted to go more slowly, and with no information in my ear, however educative. "They will follow you if you go off alone," someone said. Nobody seemed to be watching me but the elevator girl, who was staring at my feet. I held one up, and she leaned over to run her finger down my silk stocking. I wanted to give her a pair, but was not quite sure what the effect would be on her fellow workers. I cannot forget her "ooo-oo" of satisfaction at their silky surface. The Metropole was a good hotel, clean, the housemaids attractive in their neat, brown uniforms, their starched caps and aprons, and cheerful countenances. Starched caps make a revolutionary country more attractive, and maybe, after all, are no sign of waning power.

I never did get straight a great many things. We had been handed over on the dock in Leningrad, by the Raymond Whitcomb Tourist Agency, to Intourist, the official Russian organization. I was told not to take much American money into the country and, therefore, changed only twenty-five dollars, receiving five roubles for a dollar. The stewardesses on the boat, however, received twelve roubles for a dollar, because, or so it was explained to me, "stewardesses are not capitalists." Afterwards, someone told us that the Russians get twenty roubles to the dollar.

Intourist routed us, then, to the Nove Deriche convent. For what we found, exquisite is an inadequate word. There were several buildings, but we were shown only one, the chapel. It was small and high, more like a tower than a church. If its richness had not been so beautiful, the little jewel box would have been oppressive. Every available surface of pillar or wall was frescoed. The reredos ran from floor to ceiling and to each wall. It is a succession of ikons (which word in Russia seems to cover every painting or gadget of a religious nature) paintings about thirty feet high, inlaid with precious stones. There were precious stones, too, mostly pearls, in the priests' robes, preserved in glass cases, and an incredible amount of gold embroidery. It came to me forcibly what great power the church had enjoyed through its riches. What sweating work the nuns must have done through the centuries to produce this luxury. I was dazzled; and thoughtful.

As we left the convent, the rain began to fall in torrents and steadily increased as we proceeded to the next item on our program—Lenin's tomb. The queue was even longer than it had been when I passed it early in the day. People hardly shifted on their feet, but stood patiently in line through the drenching, and no one at all showed resentment when the tourist crowd was routed in at the head of the line. We entered the tomb. The passageway is of solid marble, and though not so long, recalled to mind the way into the tomb of the Sacred Bull Apis, in Egypt. Rounding a corner, we found ourselves in a little crypt and looked down at Lenin in his coffin. The face is thinner and more delicate than in the photographs of him addressing the Congress of Soviets. His long illness accounts for that, and for the way the bone structure of the face almost makes one think it is a marble mask. The hands are sensitive and beautiful. We moved through the little room silently and too quickly. Now, long after, I remember best from Moscow the Kremlin wall, and that face in the glass coffin. There are those who say that the process of deification of Lenin is well along; others who argue that, as time passes and life in the Soviet Union takes fresh political forms, though perhaps no new direction, Lenin will be both historic figure and legend, to leaven the life of the people.

Mr. Grummen, Chargé d'affaires, had sent to meet me on my arrival. He, himself, was in the midst of negotiating the commercial agreement, renewed and signed now annually with the U.S.S.R. Late in the afternoon, he came and took me to the Bohlens' flat. The Bohlens were away in Sweden on leave. Mr. Chipman, the second secretary, acted as host and we drank beer and ate nuts. Then I went back to the hotel, ate my dinner alone, fell into bed at nine, and wondered what stuff our other tourists were made of. They had departed for a concert and, no doubt, supper afterwards.

Sunday morning, I see by my diary, was started with the subway. The station we entered had a very long escalator. I was ashamed to say that I am always afraid of escalators, never being sure I will jump off at the right moment—but I braved it. When we had ridden through several stations and seen the dignity and beauty, the shining marble walls, the cleanliness, and, above all, these people's pride in their public conveyance, I began to get some idea of the upside down in the Soviet Union. What they wanted to have perfect was the common denominator of the lives of the masses. They were all like men showing off their private yachts.

Back from the subways, there were the motors, standing in front of the hotel. Mrs. Mortimer laughed. "I see why so many people die or commit suicide on round-the-world cruises," she said. I forbore to add, "or get a new lease on this interesting life." And so to see the Volga-Moscow canal out at Krinski river port, with zestful explanations about the future from our guide. The canal starts about five miles from Moscow and goes to the city of Lainin on the Volga and then to the Caspian Sea. A great engineering feat, certainly, and when large ships eventually are carriers direct from Leningrad to the Caspian, new trade routes and new manufacturing centers will be established.

After lunch Mr. Grummen came again, this time with Dean Root of Princeton, and drove us three-quarters of an hour into the country where the Chipmans, the Bohlens and the Military Attaché shared a Datcha, or little summer house. The French and German secretaries were there and Mr. Vereker, Counsellor of the British Embassy, turned up. In all, quite a little patch of Western Europe. Mr. Vereker, an ex-Grenadier Guardsman, and I soon were gossiping about old friends. With him was Mr. Strang, then in Moscow negotiating the British-French-Russian Pact—the Pact that we now remember as the Pact before the German-Russian Pact. I looked across at Mr. Strang and thought, at the time, that I had never seen a more clever face. The others chaffed him and called him The Sphinx, for he told us nothing at all of what was going on, nor of his hopes or fears. I think he must be above having either. I remember wondering if this type of man would really bring it off, for it is plain that the Russians have some sort of half-hidden inferiority complex—the number of times they insist on their size and importance makes you feel it—and perhaps someone better known, a Duke or Lloyd George, would have pleased them more.

After tea, we went along to see the residence of our Ambassador, a large house with a fine garden; but the British have a view of the Kremlin, and I should like that better. I stopped to look again at the Kremlin wall and the planting which so heightens the effect of the ancient bricks and granite; and paused again before the Holy Gate, erected by the architect Solarum in 1491. Through that gate, so much of Russian history has gone its way in glory and in sorrow. Through it went the Czars to their coronations; before it took place the executions of friend and foe in the days of Ivan the Terrible. Through that gate passed Napoleon, the temporary conqueror and uniter of all Europe.

During my stay in Moscow, I purposely avoided discussing the Soviet system. I wanted to use my eyes and ears—such an opportunity might not occur again. Only now could I have the chance to see for myself, and to enjoy—for I did enjoy—whole hours of Soviet propaganda and sightseeing. I have no patience with people who cannot take propaganda with salt and let it go at that.

The Russians have done many new things, sometimes expanded old middle-class institutions into services for the masses. Sometimes, they do one exciting experiment and claim it is nation-wide. This is a way all nations have. I had heard so much about children's clinics and maternity centers that I wanted to be sure to see one in operation. I wanted to see some factories, too, but those were closed to us—why, I cannot tell. The children's center we went to, they said, was one of twenty-three, one for every district of Moscow. Once you look at the world wholly from the point of view of a woman factory worker, I do not see how you can be anything but pleased and excited about these maternity and child services. You do not leave your children at home, but take them along to the factory and check them at day nurseries where it is possible to have one doctor look after all. Women who take for granted calling a specialist for every degree of fever their own children have, ought to be the first to delight in clinics. The state undertakes to run summer homes for the factories, and the business of "fresh air funds," which we all admire in America, is made universal, in the name of the workers themselves. I was especially interested in the pleasant nurse and uniformed attendant who showed us the two floors of educational propaganda. It was all so colorful, fresh and full of information. Great use had been made of enlarged photographs and models. As abortion is illegal now in the Soviet Union, there was considerable information about birth control. Naturally the Government prefers that women, for their own sakes, have children and bring them into the world in health. All sorts of exhibits teach posture for pregnant women; dummy trays of papier-mâché show what diets are healthy. Model layettes and clothes for mothers are exhibited on racks, and women are shown how to cut them out and make them. The simple, scientific frankness with which the nurse discusses the physical processes of birth with the women, made me wish that I could have set down, word for word, the way in which the "lesson" was given. What was thrilling was the excitement in the staff about correct feeding. They wanted all children to be taught to sleep and have the right naps. There was a great case of modern toys—how many of them really just old peasant toys, which had trained baby fingers for centuries!

I took two long walks alone on the Moscow streets. I saw very few displays that were attractive in the shops, and had no way of discovering whether that was because there were no goods, or no window dressers.

I was truly sorry to say goodbye to Moscow, to the Kremlin where I had seen the moon at night behind the two artificial red stars, and to the cupolas of churches, crosses gone and stars instead, but cupolas intact.

Then Leningrad again. I gathered a much better impression than I had on the first visit. Perhaps because the sun shone! I dwell on details of what I saw, because I find so many people who think that all, or many, of the beautiful treasures were destroyed in the revolution while, as far as I could see, all were scrupulously preserved for the public.

We drove out International Perspective Avenue to Pushkin and, on the way, saw the new City Hall and much other building going on, principally flats. The City Hall is very finely proportioned, with a circular building, like the Temple of the Winds, at the back. Here, in niches, will be busts of all important men from the Soviet point of view. New times, new names in Halls of Fame. An American expert on brick work who has seen the City Hall, I am bound to record, insists none of the brick work is adequately done, and will not last.

At Pushkin is the Palace of Alexander where the Czar and his family were arrested in 1917. On entering one sees, first, three lay figures wearing the court dresses of the Czarina. No gowns I ever saw were quite as rich. One was pale blue velvet, the train three yards long, with a bodice heavily embroidered in silver. Another was white, encrusted with gold embroidery. There was a long procession of salons, *all* of the walls made of white marble. Figures of footmen in the red and gold livery of the Court stood attentively in each room. All the bibelots were in place. At the far end were the private apartments of the Czar and the family. They were heartbreaking. The toilet things were on the Czarina's dressing table, just as she had left them, even her scent bottles. In the glass cupboards were quantities of frocks of all descriptions, and the enormous hats of that period. The walls of her bedroom were covered with ikons and crucifixes—as close together as possible. The curtains were of English chintz. In her boudoir there were photographs, unframed on the walls, of all her relatives, including the English Royal Family. The rooms were intolerably cluttered with knickknacks, but there was a very nice English atmosphere. The guide, rather bitterly, said that the rooms were a key to the kind of woman the Czarina was—"just a small German Princess with no training for her position." I suggested to her that the Czarina's mother, Princess Alice, had been the daughter of Queen Victoria, so must have had some knowledge of what was expected of her. The guide, surprised, said that she had never known that before! In each room of the Czar's there was a painting or large photograph of his wife and in one, a marble bust. She was an extraordinary beauty. The desk where the Czar was sitting when arrested, and the pen he was writing with, are just as he left them. On the work table where the Czarina was sewing, nothing has been touched. It is as if they had walked out yesterday. It is admirable the way everything has been left intact everywhere, in Russia, so different from the havoc after the French Revolution.

In Catherine's Palace, to which we went next, all the rare Chinese porcelains are preserved. This Palace must be at least a quarter of a mile long, and room follows room, each more exquisite than the last. Walls of lapis lazuli, malachite, amber, mother-of-pearl; and silks, with a Chinese influence, made in France. There is a magnificent collection of Chinese porcelains in three rooms, used not as an exhibit, but as ornaments.

Gazing at all this ultra luxury which flourished while the lot of the majority of the Russians under the Czars was what it was, the revolutionary outburst is easily understood. Whether they find the answer under the present regime is still to be seen. They had to begin from scratch, to rebuild what had been destroyed by the revolution in the way of a system of living. What they have done in twenty years, in a material way, is amazing. They ask to be left alone to work out their own problems. That is what I was told by people both high and low. I have also asked Russian diplomats about the mass political executions, and their stock reply is that they are still in the revolution and must stamp out disloyalty.

I do not attempt to pass judgment on political Russia, on the basis of a five days' visit. The question is whether the material gains are worth the human sacrifice.

For us, from the Western world, it is difficult to accustom

ourselves to one class, one level of life—it is monotonous and drab to look at. It offends us to see men eating dinner at the best hotels in their shirt sleeves and unshaven, but as many of the women in Moscow are now rouged and powdered, perhaps the men will eventually put their collars on. But the tales of the continual disappearance of people is horrifying. The world should know more of the exact truth of what does go on.

We sailed away from Leningrad in the first week of August, cheerful, but puzzled. I could not be sure whether I knew much about Russia at all, whether I had eaten a main course, or had only tasted zakuzka. The impact of Moscow upon me, the sense of its being, not only the Mother Moscow of the Kremlin Walls and little churches, but a tremendous world city with wide streets, and a center of thousands of engineering and educational schemes, was balanced by a curious sense of having discovered, mostly, new distances. Always you felt in Russia that thousands of miles to the east, the earth went on to Asia and to the Pacific. And beyond the Pacific was America.

The last stop of our cruise ship was Danzig. And the Danzig of August, 1939, made me think a hundred times of Frank Simonds. "The Polish Corridor will be the excuse for another war." There was a whole division of German soldiers in Danzig—you collided with one of them at almost every step. The ancient buildings helped me complete my picture of the Hanseatic Baltic; this we forgot again, in our sense of its modern improvements and its glowing life, for we drove to the beach and seaport at Zoppet and admired the new hotels and villas. With our Consul, Mr. Kuykendahl, I made a further trip to the Polish port of Gdynia, pride of the Polish Republic, but the fortifications and barricades we saw there struck the heart.

Behind, in Moscow, the British were negotiating! After all, soldiers and songs and general rampaging propaganda had been going on for a long time in Danzig. Fevers sometimes recede; they do not always drive the patient mad.

But when we left Danzig, I had a whole picture, something I never ceased to be grateful for, in my official life in Scandinavia during the bitter year that followed. I had had a lesson in geography. Places, people, frontiers, all were real to me. I had glimpsed how, for centuries, Swedes and Germans and Russians and British had fought and contrived to hold sway over the Baltic. But a German-Russian Pact was the last thing I expected. I had not looked as deep as that.

CHAPTER XV

No Reprieve

BACK FROM THE Baltic, the autumn calendar began to turn like a merry-go-round. It would begin with the mid-August meeting of the Interparliamentary Union. I looked forward to a visit from Senator Barkley of Kentucky, and had taken it for granted that it would be he who would arrive as head of the American delegation, since the custom heretofore had been to elect the leader of the majority party in the Senate as chairman. But no—the Oslo papers announced the imminent arrival of Hamilton Fish. And thereby hangs a tale of political maneuvering which I did not catch on to until later.

True, in former years, the representation at the Union meetings had been more of a duty and chore than anything else. But someone saw a platform in it, and I was entertained but not a little surprised when it came out that, in true go-getter fashion, Mr. Fish's friends had packed the committee meeting which elected the chairman and bore off the chairmanship as they might have a scalp. Anyway, my old friend Senator Barkley did not come and my old friend Hamilton Fish did. A good many of the American delegates had brought their wives and we kept more or less open house at the Legation and nearly everyone came for either lunch or dinner. The weather was still mild, so we held our own big reception in the garden, stringing lanterns from the trees and making the event as much an amiable fiesta of peaceful times as possible. The Parliamentarians, elegant, brightened with medals and orders on their shining shirt fronts, looked very much like a Court occasion. Senator Green of Rhode Island was a house guest, and my sister Elise Mairs had to my joy arrived from England to visit me, and we set out in high spirits for the opening meeting of the Interparliamentary Union, which was to take place in the handsome Assembly Hall of the University, famous for its Munch frescoes.

The American chairman did not appear, and we made a game of comparing one delegation with another, and gathering this and that about the political parties in the many countries with representative assemblies. Our American was not present because he was busy with the Press and despatches about his spectacular arrival from Berlin that day in Herr von Ribbentrop's private plane. That and everything he did later made headlines in the Oslo papers and, to be frank, made the American Legation just a little jittery. At a business meeting, one of the following days, he announced that he had the promise of a billion dollars from the United States for aid to refugees, if he could secure the coöperation of the Union. People gasped—a million was understandable, but we in the north were not used to counting in billions or even to orating about such sums. There was also a statement about preventing war, which the Press gobbled up. He gave out the interviews, but it was the Legation which drew the questions and the bombardment of excited requests for details. We had none! And as far as I know the billion dollars has never been heard of since.

The Interparliamentary Union was founded to meet annually for the purpose of exchanging ideas and for discussion of politics, between countries in various parts of the world. Perhaps the question of a united policy on refugees ought to have been discussed in Oslo in August, 1939. Certainly behind the scenes no one could forget the problem, but the Union had no powers of action, and the subject was not on the agenda; and I am afraid that the most important decision taken at the handsome banquet held at the Grand Hotel on the last evening was to foregather in 1940 in London. My dinner partner at that banquet was the distinguished Prime Minister of Denmark. He spoke neither English nor French. My German is scantier than my Norwegian, but Norwegian is much nearer Danish than is Swedish, and we got along rather well in a simple, conventional interchange which might have done very well in a schoolroom. For the thousandth time I said to myself that the day would surely come when there would be one international language, and that a study of that language would be compulsory even for Hottentots. How I envied most Europeans their fluency; and how many times I had wished I could serve my country, saying exactly what I wanted to say in Norwegian, instead of saying mildly what I *could* say.

On the heels of the Union meeting came wires that Secretary Morgenthau, his wife and two sons and his daughter were in Finland, and would be coming through Oslo. The Legation was delighted. Anne Morgan and her friend, Mrs. Lovett, arrived on their way back from a vacation on the

River Stryn where we ourselves had fished earlier in the season. The morning they were to take the plane for Sweden, the news that made the whole world reel came through, that Germany and Russia had agreed on a pact which only awaited the signatures of Von Ribbentrop and Molotoff, to become effective.

Our own Chancery was as dumfounded as all the others. We looked at each other and said, "What next?" It was like the uneasy moment when a great ship is launched or, as someone said, more like watching the fuse of a bomb slowly burning before fascinated eyes. Yet the intent of the pact, the signers said, was "peace." The general feeling in Norwegian Government circles was that Russia had now been given a free hand in all the countries that had once belonged to her, such as the Baltic States—all of which has come true.

When one guest came downstairs later and we broke the news to her, she said quite calmly that, oh, yes, she had heard the news at seven o'clock on the radio. She was the only calm one present for, not having followed the tenseness of European politics as closely as we had, one treaty or pact was rather like another to her, and she had not dreamed of waking anybody up. I called Anne Morgan. To her the news had a tragic portent. She cancelled her trip to Sweden within the hour and arranged to fly at once to Paris.

By August 26th, when the Morgenthau family arrived, there was a furor throughout Europe, as tourists and refugees tried to move fast lest the storm imprison them on a doomed continent. We at the Legation were all busy about passage home for our cabinet Minister. I arranged a luncheon one day for the Secretary and for Mr. Thorp, the new

Minister of Finance, and Mr. Rygg, president of the Bank of Norway, who spoke English, as the Minister did not, and served as interpreter at what I hope was an encouraging conversation on what to the two Norwegians must have been a dark day. They were Europeans, and they had seen four years of war in their youth.

Mrs. Morgenthau, as always, was delightful and one of the most intelligent sightseers we ever had in Oslo. She had read so much, she has such a fine eye for little things. The Secretary of the Treasury had little chance to be a tourist. In vain he explained to the Press that he was on a holiday. He could hardly stir a step for the interviewers.

"How about President Roosevelt's peace appeal last night?"

There were newspaper men from all over Europe, correspondents for Balkan papers, for British papers.

"What about American neutrality in the event of a European war?"

He had one answer. "I hope there will be no war." He spoke as an American, as Secretary of the Treasury, and I used to think, too, he spoke as the great conservator, the man who loved forests and hated fires.

The tension grew more ominous, but there was no panic. Passage was still difficult to get and the Morgenthau party went off to see something of the West Coast, in the hands of capable Mr. Bache of Bennett's Tourist Bureau. Bennett's Bureau—I used to feel as if that organization were the kindly Third Secretary of the American Legation, for in how many troubles did we not say "Ring Mr. Bache." Mr. Bache was our right hand when friends or strangers came, wanting to see the sights of Norway; he was the ever patient and imaginative counsellor when the refugees came through; he was long suffering but in such a courteous way that we hardly knew ourselves when we put a burden on him, whether we had asked a favor or granted one.

Our Secretary's traveling difficulties were taken care of when a U. S. destroyer was sent to Bergen to take him to Halifax; and an officer of the S.S. *Bergensfjord* arranged passage on that ship for the family.

On September 1st, the expected news came. The Nazis invaded Poland, and the most bloody and butcherous episode in modern war occurred.

September 3rd, the pact between Great Britain and Poland was fulfilled.

War was declared. Worse than 1914 had come again.

Our business in Oslo was to report each turn of events, each discussion of possibilities with the Norwegian Government, caught again with the terrible task of maintaining neutrality in a bloody struggle; and this time with a far-flung fleet, tempting to both belligerents as a prize, dangerous as a potential enemy.

For myself, there was less "high politics" in the days that followed—although new problems loomed on every hand for the neutrals, and there was double the work of reporting on the international situation—than just "getting people's papers in order." How long the war would last—what part America would have to play—nothing was clear. There were upwards of a hundred thousand American citizens living in Europe, not counting the tourists, calm and frightened, who had come for a last venture on the continent. Some of these citizens were native born, some were born in the countries to which they had now returned with the protection of American passports. There were more than two thousand American citizens living in Norway, I knew from the fairly accurate world census of Americans living abroad which the State Department had released to the Press in the spring of 1938. There were more than twenty-five thousand Americans living in Italy, more than twelve thousand living in France, nearly six thousand in Germany.

Ever since the last war, the emphasis on nationality had been growing. The old world of the turn of the century, when the need for passports to visit Turkey and Russia was looked on as a relic of times past, was gone. The horror of locust tourists who settled on countries whose money was rocketing in inflation, the slowly growing police surveillance in all countries, the fleeing refugees seeking political freedom or bread, had gradually made passports more precious than jewels. People could make fortunes falsifying them; everywhere they were necessary. From time to time, and in a mixed hope of encouraging tourist trade and restoring amiable international relations in certain countries, visas became unnecessary, and the price of them no longer a deterrent to travel.

The State Department laid down the policy of strict passport control. No new ones were to be issued except under careful checking. For United States Nationals, according to a statement issued on the 4th of September, 1939, no passports would be valid unless State Department authorities deemed the traveler's reasons for moving about in the danger zone imperative. It was the best way to effect the removal from the path of military operations on land and sea all our Nationals who might, as had been the case with the passengers on the *Lusitania,* become a casus belli. There would be, if the Department could help it, no *Lusitania* incident because there would be no passengers!

The Consul General in Oslo and I decided it would be wise to ask every American citizen in Norway to register at the nearest consulate. I was especially anxious to have this done because I had overheard some women talking, one of whom said she always voted in Norway where she had come to live after her marriage, but that she had kept her American passport. We foresaw an endless amount of work in sorting our Nationals in case the storm came north, and wanted to get it out of the way. We *were* in the danger zone already —at least the waters around us were.

We issued a call through the Press and the news was on the radio, and in no time the consulates were swamped, and with cases "corny" and some ridiculous. There was Mr. B. He regarded his passport as somehow a ticket to heaven, a meal ticket, his most precious possession certainly. He had gotten into a scrape in Norway and had lost his job. As he was an American citizen, he put it to me that I was responsible for seeing that he made a living. I did all I could to tide him over and to help him hunt for work. But when his letters of appeal continued and he wrote that I stood in the place of Mother to all the Americans in Norway and must be responsible for the rent of his apartment, I had to call a halt.

"He had a nice idea while it lasted," said one of the clerks, laughing.

Most of our citizens behaved rather well, considering how far they were from home, and how unknowable the situation. But I will not soon forget one man who used to eye me menacingly:

"I am a friend of Congressman X, an intimate friend of Senator Y, and I intend letting these men know how I have been treated by you."

He had no taste for taking his turn. He and his party finally went off on a small freight ship, very comfortably, I thought; and his cronies, Congressman X and Senator Y have not, to date, carried out his threat.

Some tourists I had less sympathy for. These were the ones whom we advised to stay quietly in Oslo while passage was being arranged but who would dash off to take side trips, and then suddenly turn up again from Finland or Sweden in a panic and demand hysterically that they be gotten out by nightfall. Other tourists, rather sweetly and delightfully, finding it hard to believe that tickets were not favors like rabbits out of a hat, used to fill the Legation with flowers and hope for the best.

There was one dear and methodical lady who came, week after week, and had the same interview all over again. All her children but one lived in the United States, but she had planned to spend the winter with the other in Norway. Should she stay? Should she go? Would the war come to Norway? Since she was in Norway and travel overseas was rather dangerous, I used to say, "Stay on a while. There seems to be no immediate danger." But when the Finnish War came, I used to beg her to go while the going was good. Alas, my advice was not taken. She would buy her passage and then she would not use it; and it was she who turned up, trembling and pale, the morning of the Norwegian invasion when it was too late. She finally escaped through Siberia, at enormous inconvenience to herself and others.

As the blows continued to fall in Poland, our own refugees, with diplomatic passports, began to arrive in Oslo—the wives and children of our Foreign Service officials in the belligerent countries. They came in flocks to seek shelter in our quiet corner of the world. Many of them had fled the storm without baggage, only the clothes they stood in, and with their children tagging at their skirts. Troop trains had wrecked all travel schedules, regulations about exchange made what money one had often useless. But the worst for the women who came up from Warsaw and Lvov and Cracow was that, for weeks, there was no news. Their husbands were somewhere. Dead? Or alive? They did not know. Each time any of them came to the Legation, it seemed to me they had grown paler and thinner, so great was the strain. Some had come by train, some by little boats down the Baltic, and into Norway over Sweden. I learned more geography in those first weeks, the names of towns where long and painful waits had delayed journeys, this town with no hotel, that one where the children got ill. As the days lengthened into weeks, our refugees formed the custom of coming in little groups of twos and threes to the Legation, asking for news. Even their great courage and restraint could not hide it—they were afraid. So was I, that this time no news was bad news. Then one evening I had word from Alex Kirke, our Chargé in Berlin, that one of the Warsaw secretaries had got out as far as Roumania and had telephoned that his colleagues were safe and would follow him the next day. I seized the telephone with delight, and called the waiting wives at their hotels. There is no fate so happy as to be the bearer of good tidings, yet I could feel how near the breaking point more than one of them had been. In their great relief, they could hardly speak more than the soft sigh of relief.

The waiting had been hard, and none of us knew how long it might have to go on. Boats to America, boats to England, were few and far between. Refugees crowded Oslo and Bergen and mountain spots between. The daily accounts of sinkings on the North Sea, in the Baltic, in the North Atlantic, were not pleasant reading for prospective travelers, but everything is easier if it is borne in company. So, presently, we set up the custom of being together, the wives of the Legation and Consulate staff, and the refugees and American wives of many Norwegians. We organized a Red Cross Committee to meet every Tuesday and Friday at the Legation to knit and sew and listen to the radio and have tea.

One of our special duties was to make layettes for the wives of the fishermen in the north. This was usually the service of the Oslo women, but the war crisis had given them so much emergency work that they had been obliged to curtail it. That we Americans stepped in made for wonderfully good feeling, not only among ourselves but the Norwegians; and somehow I liked the idea of our working for the children of the fishermen—it brought back Lofoten. We began these meetings in September and they were attended without fail until April when the invasion scattered us again. Margaret Cox was a great help, constant in attendance, and taking over when I had official business, and the consulate wives were one and all good troopers. Mrs. Mejlaender, the American wife of a Norwegian, took on the job of assembling the finished layettes and of distributing both baby clothes and the helmets, stockings and sweaters we were knitting, when Miss Boardman, who had helped me organize, had left. Why should it be more attractive to knit for soldiers than for courageous fishermen? We found it wasn't. We knitted for those to whom we were beholden. I especially was grateful for the chance to know better my exiled countrywomen. When I saw in some American newspaper—the clippings were always tumbling in—that the Department of State had a laugh over "teacup diplomacy in Norway," I merely smiled. Too many Norwegians had gone out of their way to tell me that no single thing had lain more gratefully on Norwegian hearts than the way a group of American women, official and unofficial, had understood their problems and lent a hand.

I used to get a special "kick" out of the meetings, from sheer pride in the taste of our Foreign Service. The wives were all well above the average in looks—a witty, agreeable set of women, with varied talents. We did not find out each other's virtues all at once. There was one particularly charming woman, a Russian, wife of one of our Embassy Attachés in Berlin, who had come north with her two small children. Only after a month did we learn that she was a singer. Marie Maximovitch was soon asked to be soloist with the Oslo Symphony Orchestra. And when we read the critiques in the newspapers the morning after the concert, a wave of pride went over all of us, and when she was given a license to teach her singing method to Norwegian teachers—a privilege seldom accorded to foreigners—we were all delighted. The invasion came just as she had started her classes, and once more, a child under each arm and a Nannie trailing with the bags, she was off. I shall always want to hear her sing again.

Early in November, a leading Norwegian said to me that

had he had a son he would have had him reared in England and become a British subject.

"Why?" I asked, startled.

I kept thinking it over and I remember late in November bringing up the subject again and taxing him with having made such an unpatriotic statement.

"But, Mrs. Harriman," he said, "with things as they are, I see no future for the small nations."

He said this, as a matter of fact, the night before the Soviet airplanes dropped bombs on Helsinki; and I felt that he had spoken out of second sight.

All through October and November in Norway, as elsewhere, people spoke about a phoney war—this in the American papers. The Norwegians were rightly irritated.

"Nothing may be being lost behind the Maginot Line," they would say, "but we, the neutrals, are losing ships every day."

I spoke to one of the great ship-owners at dinner. "You must live in daily deadly fear of losing your beautiful boats."

"A boat, oh, yes, but that does not count. It is the fine men who go down with her who matter."

We scanned the papers daily for news of mines and torpedoed boats, and as the stormy weather made navigation difficult at best along new courses, the war came closer and closer. One morning it would be a boat we knew, its captain the uncle of my secretary. His ship was struck by a magnetic mine and nearly all hands were lost within a few minutes.

The Great Countries versus the Little Neutrals, so the war seemed to many in the north, as losses among their ships grew and grew. And we at the Legation shared their anxiety, and hung upon the radio less for news from London and Paris than for shipwrecks and sinkings in the Baltic and the North Sea.

The Finnish-Russian War was a surprise to some and a foregone conclusion for others. A friend from Finland, traveling through, had predicted a long-drawn-out dispute but no war and because, in the winter of 1939, one wanted to think that somehow the war would be one of waiting and not of terrible striking, I allowed myself to be a little cheered. But the war broke; and for Norway, it came closer and closer. Few Americans study the map and few know how Northern Norway and Finland are joined. We felt in Oslo as if Norway were the goal, and the ice-free port the Russians have wanted for centuries might be grabbed.

"The ice-free port," people in Oslo would repeat. "We, too, shall be a victim."

At one party, some woman ventured to break into the talk of Russian aggression with a remark that the Nazis might want Southern Norway. But the poor woman was hooted down as ridiculous, and a war-monger!

In the north, a division of the Norwegian Army was mobilized and stood guard on the frontier. When later the Germans came in, this was the only armed force prepared to meet the attack. The Government discussed military assistance to Finland, but both Norway and Sweden felt assured that if this assistance were given, the Germans would intervene on the side of Russia. Five hundred volunteers went to fight with the Finns. A medical unit and ambulance was sent off to the Finnish front, under charge of Professor Holst, one of the famous surgeons of Scandinavia, and we heard stories of heroic endeavor and service in the terrible cold of the Finnish winter. As the Finnish War went on from week to unexpected week, the staying power of the Finns was our marvel and the world's. And because the ski troops in Finland were so wonderful, the Norwegians, in a strange way, began to think of themselves as a nation not only strong in peace but with unexpected resources in case of war. It was just a way of looking at themselves, of gathering strength for resistance in a world gone mad.

In the first days of the war, more than ever, the Legation got the impact of the strangled hopes in Europe. Somehow, people felt, some way, America might save the situation. On the day before the actual invasion of Poland, when one more account, true or false, of the killing of some Germans along the frontier was being reported, Professor Keilhau of the University of Oslo came with a cable to be forwarded to President Roosevelt begging him, in the name of an Oslo Peace Society, to intercede. Hope died slowly.

Day after day during the Finnish War I was visited by persons and delegations begging me to ask the President to make some official gesture which would show Russia how strong the feeling in America was against all aggression. One old gentleman in Bergen asked Mr. Halvorsen, the ship-owner, to call on me and beg for "a convoyed hospital ship to Petsamo to put fear into the hearts of the Soviets." Mr. Halvorsen, who had been decorated by Hitler and was commonly known for his sympathy with German aspirations, was himself wrought up over the invasion of a Scandinavian country.

Sometimes I felt like a phonograph record, and always helpless, as I explained to him and to all petitioners that America was governed by the Neutrality Act and that, no matter how sympathetic the American people and their government might be, American foreign policy was planned to keep the European war to that continent, and to do everything possible to prevent the extension of the field of operations and the number of warring nations involved. One journalist, with whom the Legation had long been on friendly terms, at the height of the Finnish-Russian agony, when things looked darkest for the Finns, came to me all but on the verge of tears. In the greatest agitation, he walked up and down repeating, "Only your President can stop this tragic business. Please get him to act." His theme was that America was so rich and powerful that she could do anything with impunity. The world would listen to her through fear.

He was like a child. In his anguish, he had forgotten all the infinite complications and implications of international politics. To millions of simple people in the world, the United States was still the Western World, the Santa Claus whose bag was bottomless. In the north that winter, it was easy for an American to feel what numbers of people felt—that Santa Claus was Shylock. And sometimes when I read in the Norwegian press accounts of the debate in Congress on the Finnish loan, my skin would prickle as the writers intended it should. It was hard for the Finns to see what difference thirty million or sixty million dollars made to us. It never had in previous loans to other nations.

Our life was lived in layers—we were part of a world at war—again, we were "safe in Norway," and then, for all of us Americans, there was a sense of special community and concern for each other.

Everybody at the Legation took a particular interest in a Montana girl who was in Oslo—Mrs. Ronhovde, a niece of

Jeannette Rankin, our first congresswoman. We liked her the minute she came to call and, through the winter, she drew my admiration and affection. Her husband, a professor, had come to Oslo on a fellowship for a six months' research study of Norwegian Territorial Claims in the Polar Regions. They had with them two enchanting children, a beautiful black-eyed boy of three and a curly-headed, blonde girl of less than a year. Where Mrs. Ronhovde got her technique I do not know but, if I am ever asked to give out ribbons for the best-brought-up children I have ever seen, two ribbons very blue shall go to Montana. The professor's work went well and the time came for him to turn over his report to the Foreign Office to okay, and to delete, for publication, anything they might deem indiscreet, for they had allowed him to examine all the Foreign Office files on the understanding that he would prepare only one copy of his report and allow them to keep private what they wanted. The war in Norway was Professor Ronhovde's misfortune. He turned in his work—the Foreign Office was so occupied with the crisis that the checking of a paper on an outside matter seemed of secondary importance. He was not one to insist or nag; but finally, anxious to leave, he exacted from the Foreign Office a promise to hand over his report by April 1st. But April 9th came, and the invasion. He found himself without his report, which was part of his life's work, and he had to leave for Sweden without the money he had deposited in an Oslo bank.

I was in Stockholm when the Ronhovdes arrived. As quietly as in Oslo, they patiently began their plans for return. For some reason, while others got visas, the German Legation never had any for them. We considered whether there was any reason; perhaps the free-spoken Montana girl had been too much the democrat in the years when she had studied in Germany. Finally they decided to take the long way home, as so many of the German emigrés had. And that took time. For Soviet visas are hard to get. Then there was the business of stocking food for so long a journey for the two babies. And then, the night they left, there came through from the German Legation permission to travel over Berlin to Genoa! It was then too late. Their patience won us all. And we worked hard to get their money out of Oslo.

"This young American couple is just too good to be true," we used to say to each other. They are now stationed in a New Jersey college; I wonder if they are producing the same feeling of gratitude at home.

Another unique American woman whom I might have missed in Washington, or even in Norway, was Louise Arner Boyd of San Francisco. She was an autumn visitor my first two years in Oslo and was there again at the outbreak of the war. She would arrive in Oslo and, for half a day, spend her time ridding herself of the ravages of rough travel, and then would appear for lunch at the Legation as soignée and smart as if she had just stepped out of a Paris dressmaker's. My other guests would always be astonished to learn that this fragile-looking woman had ever done anything more strenuous than to play bridge or an occasional game of golf. I was surprised myself when I first learned that this was the Miss Boyd who had organized, financed and led six expeditions into the Arctic on a sailing ship, and who had more distinguished medals and degrees than most women have costume jewelry.

She had gone on a North Cape cruise one summer with her family, like any other pleasure-seeking tourist, and lost her heart to the north. After the death of her parents, she threw herself into science, first as a distraction and then as a creative endeavor. She set out to make a contribution to oceanography. She was accompanied on the last three trips by distinguished scientists, she herself serving as the photographer of the expeditions, and besides her book on Polish countrysides, was known for her study of the "Fjord Region of East Greenland." Her reappearances from year to year always meant one or more "hydrographical luncheons." Her expeditions took extensive soundings between the west coast of Norway and Jan Mayan Island and northeast Greenland, and in the fjords and bays of northeast Greenland from Scoresby Sound to the northern part of Ile de France. She had been in the Greenland Sea off Spitzbergen, and north of Svalbard among the Seeven Islands. The Norwegians, few of whom knew that part of their country as well as she, were intensely interested in the extensive collections of moss and flora she had made, and King Haakon had bestowed on her the Order of St. Olaf. And presently I discovered that the dash of red on her frock was the ribbon of the Chevaliers of the Legion of Honor of France. But what seemed to have satisfied her most among her honors was that a barren stretch of the Greenland coast had been named Louise Boyd Land.

Oslo was distinctly not a great news center—good news of simple living is not worth cable tolls—but now and then one of the American newspaper men would include the northern capital on his beat. And it was an especial pleasure to talk with young men like William Stoneman from the

Chicago Daily News office in London, who came through twice, or three times, on tours of Scandinavia, watching the pre-war moves in international politics; and Marquis Childs of the *St. Louis Post-Dispatch,* who spent time in Oslo on both his expeditions to study Sweden. His keen sense of domestic politics, his lively comparisons between American and Scandinavian manners and economic life, were a delight. It was after a visit of his that someone suggested that the Foreign Office ought to keep Legations supplied with visiting newspaper men from home as part of the service.

CHAPTER XVI

I Cover the "City of Flint"

For years the city of Flint meant to me an industrial town in Michigan, in the press chiefly when General Motors workmen went on strike. Not so since last year. In the Legation, we came to speak of the "Saga of the *City of Flint.*" Others may already have forgotten the American ship, taken captive by the Germans October 9, 1939, on the pretext that she was carrying contraband to England. But I get ahead of my story.

We spent days and days running down rumors, and in the end wrote our part of it with quick action, in a few hours. Our first knowledge in Oslo of any trouble was a cable from Washington asking for news of the missing ship. We had none. Our second wind of her was a day or two later, when Mr. Sterling, American Minister in Sweden, who must also have had an inquiry from the State Department, telephoned me that a newspaper man in Stockholm had heard from a correspondent in Tromsö that the *City of Flint* had been there to get water. "This is your pigeon," Fred Sterling said, "and here is the Tromsö man's name and address."

The Foreign Office in Oslo disclaimed all knowledge of

the ship's whereabouts. Our friends in shipping offices shook their heads. But I had luck with my call to Tromsö. My man at the other end of the wire reported that the ship had indeed been in the harbor, but she had left and gone on north, presumably making for the port of Murmansk, the still ice-free harbor, in northern Russia. No one could be sure, of course; so I made a pact with him, that he should let me know immediately, should she return, or if he got the slightest clue to any of her movements. The next morning the Oslo papers carried a long statement from an Englishman who had been landed with the British crew at Tromsö. This crew, from the torpedoed British ship, *Stone Gate,* with a German prize crew, had been put on board the *City of Flint,* in the North Atlantic, by the pocket battleship *Deutschland.* We got just a whiff of the mysterious war upon the sea, and a hint of the jockeying for legal positions that was going on.

The Foreign Office still denied all knowledge of our ship's whereabouts. Our Consul at Bergen, therefore, was asked to communicate with the British, if and when they arrived, en route to England. This he did, and got from them the same story we had read in the newspapers, an account that turned out later to have been, in parts, more sensational than accurate.

Days went by. No word of the *City of Flint.* But we didn't relax our efforts or cease our inquiries. All of us in the Legation felt somewhat thwarted, and at least one of the staff was annoyed—as one might be if an unfinished detective story were snatched from one's hands. Where *was* the beastly ship?

Then, suddenly, one evening, I heard from my Tromsö acquaintance again. The *City of Flint* had hove into Tromsö harbor. But no one had been allowed aboard her except the German Consul. She had left for the south under convoy. Excitement in the Legation, and in Oslo; rumors rose and flew like a covey of birds. She had been sighted off the Lofoten Islands—she was coming up the West Fjord. We never got the same rumor twice.

Friday, November 3rd, is a Norwegian national holiday, like our own Thanksgiving. The Chancery was closed, and I promised myself a long, lazy afternoon and evening doing needlework and reading Daniele Varé's "Laughing Diplomat." At three o'clock, the office telephone, switched to my sitting room, rang: "Copenhagen calling." It was Ralph Peters, United Press correspondent in Denmark. "What news have you got of the *City of Flint?"* We had none, I told him, beyond the report from Tromsö, four days before, that she had left that port. "We have reason to believe she is off Bergen," he said. Then an Oslo paper called. I laid down my work and my book. I would call Bergen. Consul Dunlop was at home, having as quiet a holiday as I, but he agreed to go forth in the town and see what he could find and hear. An hour later, he called back. The ship had not been sighted, and he thought she had not yet had time to have come so far south.

Copenhagen rang again. What had I heard from Bergen? Nothing, I said, and, giving up all idea of trying to read, picked up my embroidery frame—a final gesture toward my rapidly vanishing restful afternoon. For three or four hours the telephone continued to ring, and between matching silks, I kept on telling all inquirers that I had no news. At seven, Copenhagen called again. Someone had informed them the *City of Flint* was at Haugesund, seventy-five miles south of Bergen; was this true, and could I check it? Their report was that she had one or more ill sailors aboard. A boat had been seen going off to her, with a doctor. He could not verify this, as the telephone operators had been instructed not to put anyone through to the Naval authorities.

I began to get some idea of the technique and expense of modern news-gathering. I felt like a cub reporter—and I had my assignment to find out about the *City of Flint* for Washington. I tried to think what my various newspaper friends would do. I had an idea. I called in the butler—secretaries were gone their various ways for the day and my Norwegian was insufficiently fluent to cope with Long Distance—and told him to call the Officer of the Port, if there was such a person, at Haugesund. "Tell the operator," I said, "that it is very important, that the American Minister wishes to speak to him." To my surprise I got through, but the officer at the other end was only second base. "I can say nothing," he replied, "but we are reporting everything to the Chief of Operations in Oslo, so you might ask him." Now I knew the trail was hot. Curiouser and curiouser.

I called the Admiral. He answered the phone himself. "Why don't you talk to the Foreign Office?" I told him I had tried, but it was closed on the holiday. The Admiral hemmed, at which point a long distance call from Bergen was cut in for him, and I thought he seemed very glad of the interruption.

I, too, called Bergen and got Consul Dunlop. "You try," I said. "You're nearer. Maybe you can get in contact with someone at Haugesund." By eleven o'clock, Peters had called me five times from Copenhagen, and the Oslo papers were making persistent periodic inquiries. "Your papers must be very rich," I said to Peters finally. He laughed.

At midnight, I went to bed and to sleep. But at half past one, the whirr of the telephone, that special long distance whirr. Dunlop was on the line and had good news. He had found the mystery ship, found her at Haugesund, the prize crew interned, and the American Captain again in command. Then he said, "Admiral Tank-Nielsen told me he was telephoning you, to relieve your anxiety, even before he tells the authorities, that the job is finished." I am told only cub reporters, with their first beat, will understand how swift I suddenly became.

I must get it coded and off to Washington. I called the Secretary of Legation. No answer. I finally reached one of the clerks, whose telephone was at his bedside. He would come to the Legation at once.

No one was stirring in the house. In spite of all the telephone bells, the servants were still asleep. I dressed hastily, went down and let the clerk in. We went over the cable I had drafted and put it into code. Another phone call, from the Admiral in Bergen, and we inserted further details in my report. We had difficulty trying to switch the telephone from my personal quarters to the office, and finally had to rouse the butler, who appeared in a wrapper, very sleepy. I was left to wonder what might happen in case of illness, or fire, with such a household of sound sleepers.

More bells. Consul General Beck was at the door; Consul Dunlop had called him, too, and he kindly took the message and drove off to the cable office at 3:45 A.M. (9:45 P.M. Washington time, it was received). We had beaten the Press at their own game; and then suddenly, I began to feel guilty and wonder what the newspaper crowd would say, since my beat came on one of their "tips." My chief was in Washington. I had to give the news there first. All the same, I thought a long time about it and was rather relieved to learn that, even if it had been advisable to call Copenhagen, there had been no chance to get through, as the telephone was so constantly in use.

At 4:00 A.M. I put out my light. At seven-thirty the bell was jangling again. Dunlop was telling me the *City of Flint* had sailed for Bergen under escort of the Norwegian ship *Olav Trygvason*. This is the ship that later badly damaged the *Emden* and sank two other German ships. Another cable was coded, and directly after breakfast I wrote a résumé of the night's work and had it put on the desk of the Secretary of the Legation in the Chancery.

Toward noon, Captain Gainard himself, master of the *City of Flint,* reported the ship's safe arrival at Bergen. "The pursuit of the phantom ship" was over. It was Saturday and there was no night train to Bergen, but I could and would leave Sunday night and see him early Monday morning. As my secretary used to say, we now had to "get to dealing" with a tangible problem.

The Foreign Minister asked me to see him Sunday afternoon, that he might tell me the latest developments in the case, from his side, before I left town. The German Chargé had visited him twice on Saturday threatening "dire consequences" if Norway did not return the *City of Flint* to Germany. I had never seen Dr. Koht so disturbed. He said that Norway had acted strictly in accordance with the Hague Convention, and would not retreat one step. He gave me all the papers in the case, and on my return to the Legation, Ray Cox and I sent off more cables. Then my private secretary and I took the train.

In the dining car at breakfast the next morning, there across the aisle from me sat the German Naval Attaché, bound on the same errand, but from another angle! As, for the time being, we were enemies of sorts, I quickly withdrew my eyes and was careful not to let them stray across No Man's Land during the rest of the meal.

Stepping from the train, I met an enthusiastic welcome from our Consul. A man with a camera seemed to jump from behind every post, and this was my first realization of the widespread and intense interest the incident had aroused.

Captain Gainard was busy in the consulate making out his long affidavited report. Through the whole story, the Captain seems to have been a strict but kind disciplinarian. If I were a man I would take off my hat to him. What patience it must take to weld into a good ship's company a heterogeneous set of men of many trades and nationalities, each with its own demands and traditions, and keep them cheerful under orders. Whatever it takes, the Captain had it. Twenty-nine years in the American Navy behind him, and some years in the Naval Reserve, he knew his job, and might have qualified as a diplomat as well. He was humorous, full of the wisdom of the seas, and within half an hour, all of us in the party felt we had known him all our lives, and were being proud of an old friend.

I listened carefully to the Captain's story. The Boarding Officer from the *Deutschland* had, after some conversation about the engines on the *City of Flint,* conveyed the message. The *City of Flint* was to take on a Prize Crew and the ship would proceed to Germany with the thirty-eight British prisoners. In the meantime the *City of Flint* radio was out of order. One feature of the events which followed was that, of the four German radio operators who came aboard with the new crew, none of them knew enough to repair the apparatus, and no communication with Berlin was, therefore, possible. The English prisoners were brought aboard, told to accept whatever accommodations were given them, and Lieutenant Hans Pushbach, a German officer who had seen service in the first World War, addressed the Americans in English. He told them they were bound for Germany. "My soldiers will be a military guard and you will get your orders from your Captain. You must obey these. If there is any refusal or interference I will kill you. I have sufficient means here to sink the ship. If there is interference, I must act with war measures. My country is at war and whether we like it or not, we must do certain things we would not ordinarily do."

So began the strange journey, the Germans with their machine gun aboard, and each going about with hand grenades in his pocket. The American Captain was still in command of navigation. To a layman, maneuvers of the two Nationals were like chess. Both German and American wished to save the ship, each was under orders; both aware that even in the middle of a war some fine observance of the international law of the sea is a duty, and a possible advantage, for belligerents and neutrals alike.

Captain Gainard, speaking quietly in Consul Dunlop's office, was undramatic and matter-of-fact, but he was reciting a saga all the same—how the boat, under armed guard, had gone far, far north of the Orkneys to avoid the Royal Navy cruising "toward Germany." Sometimes the British Captain would join his German and American colleagues. The American and British crews night after night got together and hatched plots for throwing the Germans overboard, but what the German Captain called "monkey business," which would have risked the lives of all on board, never quite came off.

I listened to all the reasons, in law, why the Germans had a right to be aboard and why, if the Americans had challenged their claim that the cargo was contraband and tried to put them off, the Americans, not the Germans, would have been guilty of piracy. With no sending apparatus, and only small receiving sets which gave the men of three nations the benefit of Lowell Thomas and Lord Haw Haw, the *City of Flint* had passed out of knowledge of the world. That was apparently when the State Department began to make inquiries, for the ship should have reported to the Maritime Commission on the 12th of October. And there had been only silence.

The Germans had painted out the ship's name and marking, and labeled her the *Alf,* and Danish. But, as Captain Gainard kept on saying, the *City of Flint* was a Hog Island ship, with shape and carriage unlike the bottoms from any other shipyard in the world. But as, from the time they left the *Deutschland,* they had encountered no other vessel, no one identified the *Alf* as the missing American ship. On the morning of October 20th they had found themselves off Tromsö.

Then followed the incident of the water supply. One has to know international law to understand the fine points of the play between the two captains and the Norwegian authorities. If short of water, the ship could put in to neutral ports. Captain Gainard put in and waited, hoping the Norwegian authorities would discover that there was no real shortage of water and so detain the boat; but no, the Norwegian authorities, whether knowingly or not, played the game otherwise and conventionally. Once tanked, the ship could not loiter, but must move on. The Norwegians, with copies of the British rules for neutral nations in hand, required only that the *Alf* become forthwith the *City of Flint* again. The painters swung down the ship's side. The British passengers were put ashore and with them the one Scotch member of the American crew, one more man escaped by the skin of his teeth. Then the Norwegian officials said, "Go, now."

The affair of the *City of Flint* was one small detail in a great war, but as the Captain talked, the war itself, so chaotic and menacing, took more definite shape. How to get to Germany, with the battleships of two nations looking for each other and for the American pawn, how not to be sunk, or avoid the rocks of an unfamiliar coast? The first objective was Hammerfest, and thence down the coast hugging the shore toward Germany. But a great fog hung over Hammerfest. They kept moving off North Cape, thence to Kola Bay, and Murmansk! But in that harbor where so many German ships, including the *Bremen* and the *St. Louis,* lay waiting, and where so many British ships were loading, they were in a fresh predicament. None of their messages written to the American Ambassador in Moscow were sent; no one, not even the Captain, was allowed ashore; the radio sending apparatus continued useless.

THE "CITY OF FLINT" AT HAUGESUND, NORWAY

A female Russian immigration officer came aboard. She pointed to the Captain's wedding ring and asked, "Gold?" When he replied in the affirmative, she made signs to him to take it off. After inspecting it closely, she handed it back to him and hissed, "Capitalist."

The German crew was taken ashore. Captain Gainard expected that he had seen the last of them, for was not Murmansk a neutral port? The Russians, as all the world knows now, had their troubles deciding what to do with the German crew and ended by sending them once more aboard the *City of Flint.*

Back toward Germany, within the three-mile limit, off Petsamo and the Finnish coast, as went all the ships trying to run the British blockade, now ran her course. The *Flint* was met by the Norwegian destroyer *Stegg,* and the Neutrality Patrol examined her, removed the Russian customs seals from the hatches, and made a cursory examination of the cargo. Another destroyer, the *Aegir,* and the mine-layer, *Olav Trygvason,* proceeded to convoy the American ship down the fjords, desperately trying to avoid any action in neutral waters. All the world knows the story.

There was the incident of the British cruiser which tried to invite the American ship into a convoy, and signaled her, "We wish we had met you without your friends." At Haugesund, the Germans sent for a doctor—under international law, this was allowable, although the pretense of illness aboard was soon exploded. Meantime, the German ship, the *Schwaben,* had conveyed orders to the German Lieutenant Pushbach to anchor. The Germans wanted the American Captain to pretend there was engine trouble. This was not true. The American would not do it; if he had, within the law, the status of the ship would have been such that the Norwegians could not take off the German crew. As it was, it was legal. So the *Olav Trygvason* quietly sent a boarding party of thirty officers and men on in the middle of the night to remove the German artillery, wake the Germans up and fetch them ashore. Captain Gainard was still grinning as he told us.

The Captain and Admiral Tank-Nielsen, Commandant of the Bergen area, certainly "spoke the same language" in more ways than one, and, as I watched the Admiral, I remembered the phrase in one of President Roosevelt's letters to me. The Norwegians are "among the world's finest seamen, born with salt in their veins." I had already heard many stories about the Admiral and his busman's holidays. When off duty, he used to disguise himself as a fisherman and spend his nights on fishing craft and trawlers up and down and in and out the fjords, ferreting out belligerent craft who had no business in neutral waters. As soon as we had all had lunch we set out to visit the ship, where we found a restless crew. They had one question they wanted to ask; and I had many. They wanted to know when they could go ashore and did I know they'd been aboard and not a foot on land for weeks? I felt sorry for them, but I had to do my best to make them understand that, while negotiations were still pending between governments, a careless or chance word to the Press might precipitate all kinds of trouble. Like children kept in school, they felt as if Teacher was to blame, and side-glowered at the Captain; at me, too, no doubt, as soon as it was clear I had no means to ease the discipline.

Most enlightened people are convinced, of course, that seamen's unions are necessary, but, as I looked at the men aboard the *City of Flint,* I was puzzled again as to why the American seamen's union should proscribe some kind of neat uniform garb for their members. Why should there be a stigma attached to wearing a sailor's costume? If there is. I have always thought them the most attractive clothes that any man could wear. The contrast between our men and the appearance of the British and Norwegian merchant sailors was shocking. The fact that the men needed shaves and haircuts didn't enhance their looks, either; but that they knew, because when I asked them what I could send them, they shouted in chorus, "A barber."

About the time we were in Bergen, a number of British destroyers were sighted skirting the West Coast in territorial waters. Norwegian ships drew alongside and kept edging the visitors towards the open sea. The British Admiral, in command, called out to the Norwegian Commanding officer, as they separated, "All right, but mind you give my love to my cousin, the Crown Prince of Norway." It must have been Captain-Lord Louis Mountbatten. When I heard the story, I thought again how every European war, in some measure, is a civil war, with families sundered, everywhere, by nationalisms that divide not only families, but mankind.

What a week! We had to send for a vice consul from Oslo to help out, for the Bergen consulate is not heavily staffed. Even so, we all often worked until midnight or one a.m., for the case, being fairly important in itself, was very important indeed as a test case involving international marine law. We worked as if each detail might one day settle some point at a faraway peace conference. Or, at least, I did. Many dull and difficult things happened in Bergen, but I remember it all now in a kind of rosy glow—a rare week in a diplomatic life—and always to the tune of that old Navy song, which I heard hummed so often.

> "Bell bottom trousers
> And coat of Navy blue,
> He'll climb the rigging
> As his daddy used to do."

The *City of Flint* perhaps got more than her share of press comment. It is a press phenomenon, that in dull seasons (and that period of the war was dull) the spotlight will, suddenly, settle on one corner of the world, and one particular event will be followed in the utmost detail. In the succeeding months, when great events were stirring, we still got editorials from faraway countries. *The New York Times* and the London *Times,* as always, recording history pretty much as the final record will show it; but for our entertainment, we all preferred a clipping in German, from a German paper called *Der Bund* (NR 535 November 15, 1939) presented to me with great solemnity by the Swiss Consul General in Oslo. Foreign Minister Koht and I enjoyed it equally. It became a joke between us that lightened our more serious discussions.

I showed it once to a visiting American journalist, who exclaimed, "Good Lord deliver me, I wonder if I've ever pulled as many boners when the editor threw me a ten word telegram and said, 'Give me half a column.'" Here is the clipping:

"The Ambassadress of the United States of America

"The affair of the American merchant vessel *City of Flint* has turned the eyes of the world on Mrs. Harriman, the Minister of the United States in Oslo, and on her opponent Kollontai, the Russian Ambassadress in Stockholm. Both women, the only female diplomats in the world, are fighting each other for the political orientation of the Scandinavian countries.

"In front of the entrance to the Norwegian Foreign Office, a rather large building with the classical lines of the Empire style, a light gray automobile with a yellow insignia of the diplomatic corp, a slender lady with white hair and a small brief case, stepped out. Her dress is inconspicuous, only a double strand of pearls around her neck betrays luxury and riches.

"This lady is Mrs. Eugene J. Harriman, 'envoy extraordinary and Minister Plenipotentiary,' as it says in diplomatic langauge, of President Roosevelt to the Court of His Majesty King Haakon of Norway. Her visit was to the Norwegian Foreign Minister Koht, a huge man beside whom the delicate lady looks like a doll. The reason for her visit was to give the Minister a personally signed copy of her autobiography 'From the Pianoforte to Politics.'

" 'From the Pianoforte to Politics' is the entire remarkable career of this woman who in her home country, America, is called the first woman politician. As a young pianist she married the great and respected financier Jim Harriman, one of the lords of the American Railroad Industry. Her husband initiated her into the mysteries of his business, something which is very rare in American upper class circles. 'When I am no longer there you must carry on my work. I have not worked all my life to let strangers carry it on when I am dead,' was his reason.

"In the year 1912, the great Jim Harriman became ill and died. True to his wish, his wife, formerly well known as a pianist, took over the management of his affairs. In 1913 she entered the United States Industrial Commission, a kind of central Chamber of Commerce, of which her husband had been Vice-President. For three years she was engaged in that work, as the only woman. That started her reputation in her country. Her importance increased when the United States entered the World War. The Democratic Party, which was in power, called her to head the Women's Industrial Commission, which among other things controls the management of the American Red Cross. She was appointed Head and Manager of the Sanitary Service of the American cavalry. Immediately after the War she became President of the Democratic Women's Club, and a member of the Executive Committee of the Democratic Party. When in 1932 the Democratic Party came into power for the first time since Wilson, with the first election of President Roosevelt, she again entered active politics. Roosevelt summoned two women co-workers, Miss Perkins, to whom he entrusted the Department of Labour, and Mrs. Harriman, whom he placed in the Diplomatic Service. She is the first female Ambassador of the United States, after the Russian Kollontai, the second in the world. Shortly before the arrival of her colleague, Madame Kollontai was transferred from Oslo to Stockholm.

"Both diplomats worked feverishly. Madame Kollontai endeavoured to bring the Northern Countries into the Moscow sphere of influence. In her work of undermining she came upon quiet, simply dressed, white-haired Mrs. Harriman, who in plain, calm words preached the Principles of Neutrality. Madame Kollontai gives receptions, hurries from Ministers to Journalists, talks, shines, attempts to persuade and to impress. Mrs. Harriman plays selections from Chopin, Liszt and Mozart, her favourite composers, on the piano for Foreign Minister Koht, and throws in here and there a few short political remarks. That is sufficient for the remarks stick.

"Then comes the affair of the *City of Flint*. America wished that the control of the ship be given back to her American crew, according to International Law. That was not done in the Russian harbour of Murmansk. The ship sailed for Germany, keeping within Norwegian territorial waters. The decision lay in the hands of the Norwegian government. All America looked to Mrs. Harriman! From Stockholm Madame Kollontai attempted to interfere so that the Murmansk manoeuvre would not be canceled. In vain! The *City of Flint* went into a Norwegian harbour, the harbour authorities interned the German prize crew, the American captain again took over the command. All America breathed again, the newspapers are full of praise for the correct attitude of the Oslo government.

"Mrs. Harriman, America's representative in Norway, has won a signal victory. As if nothing had happened, she continues about her business, quiet, simple, making no fuss, modest, spending every free moment at the piano. The first woman politician of America has not disappointed the trust of her Chief, Roosevelt.

"M. P.

"Der Bund, NR 535 November 15, 1939
"Bern, Switzerland."

I decided to frame it and to play the piano, and take the nonsense of this world in my stride.

CHAPTER XVII

The Nazis Come

Hindsight we all seem to have. But it is fantastic that none of the things which happened in the week preceding the fatal daybreak of April 9th awakened us to danger. A hundred incidents should have prepared us. Instead we were transfixed, still watching the war in Finland. Early in January the ten-million-dollar loan to Norway for purchase of foodstuffs in America was arranged. In the middle of January, the King opened parliament, calling for a policy of strict neutrality and for greater defense appropriations. Princess Märtha went about quietly laying plans for the taking over of men's work by women in case of war.

Even the *Altmark* incident, with all its political implications, excited us less as a portent that war was already in our own fjords than as some grotesque medieval story of rescue from dragons. Norwegian neutrality had been violated, but by whom? That was the important question. The Nazi ship had come down through Norwegian territorial waters, its ship's paper having been examined at Bergen, but the ship's hold not having been investigated. But the British had reason to believe that she carried British prisoners from ships sunk in the Atlantic by the *Graf Spee*. The very name of the British destroyer which discovered and pursued the *Altmark* up the narrow Jossing Fjord, H.M.S. *Cossack*, turned the incident into headline and legend. The fighting with cutlasses, the discovering of the prisoners, the rescue itself, of men who had been below hatches for weeks, were so dramatic that the legal consequences were overlooked by ordinary people. And a curious and equally startling incident in the aftermath was entirely unreported in the Press —unreported certainly, hushed up, more likely.

One afternoon in February, a Nazi plane landed, without warning, at Fornebo airport just outside Oslo. Without a by-your-leave, thirty passengers were disgorged who scattered over the field with cameras, taking photographs, making sights and memoranda. Asked for papers, the Pilot officer showed a permit to investigate the *Altmark*, some forty miles away. The effrontery of the incident was a warning, but the quite sincere, pro-British official of the company operating the field, when questioned by the British Legation, explained that the Germans were planning a commercial airline between Germany and Norway. One of his juniors, however, with no taste for easy explanations, was dining with me that night; he returned again and again to the subject with foreboding. But not even he had a glimmering that within two months, Nazi planes would be landing troops from Denmark on Fornebo Field as regularly as any ferry service. Squadrons of ten planes, each with mechanical precision depositing fifty soldiers with equipment, and returning to Sylt for more. But I go too fast.

On Friday, April 5th, all the officials of the Norwegian Foreign Office received invitations to see a peace film. The engraved cards from the German Minister indicated an occasion. They read "full dress and orders to be worn." The invitation arriving at such short notice, the Foreign Minister and the more important personages were previously engaged. But all the Bureau chiefs and a number of minor officials, in white ties and with mild curiosity, accepted and went. What they were treated to was a film, terrifyingly documentary and horrible, of the bombing of Warsaw. The German Minister explained—the entertainment did require explanation—that the pictures were peace propaganda, because they proved to all observers what happened to any country which resisted Nazi attempts to "defend it from England." The audience was shocked, and—this seems strange now—still puzzled, as to why the film had been shown to *them,* to Norwegians.

The Foreign Minister and Mrs. Koht did not see the film. They were, as a matter of fact, dining with me. My party was for the new French Minister and Countess de Dampierre. The Foreign Minister, who arrived half an hour late, explained briefly that the day had been the most nerve-racking of his official life. I had had an interview with him at midday, and he went on to say that after I had left, the German Minister, Dr. Bräuer, had visited him, and that the British and French Ministers had occupied him until half past seven. His face was drawn, and I sensed that the day really had been more tense than usual, but for months he had been between these fires, and the evening passed without anyone's awareness that we were on the eve of tragedy.

Early the next day, Dr. Bräuer called me personally on the telephone. Would I dine at his Legation on April 19th?

He was inviting also the Foreign Minister and Fru Koht, and the Danish and Swedish Ministers and their wives. He threw in cozily that it would be his own wife's first appearance after her return from the hospital, and would I excuse her if she retired at half past ten. As I think I have said, dinner parties in Oslo used to run on to well past midnight in candid talk, sometimes with dancing, and often with cards. Frau Bräuer was a great favorite with all the corps. A small, pretty woman, looking far more French than German, she had just borne her first child, after twelve years of marriage. The Minister went on: "The baby's name is to be Dorothea. Do you know what that means?"

"The Gift of God."

"Right," he said, perhaps a little surprised at my knowing, "and that is why we call her that." I could not help smiling at my end of the phone.

The next day, Sunday the 7th, came the formal engraved invitation for the dinner with "*pour memoire*" written in the corner. By April 19th no "*Aide-memoire*" was necessary to remind me of Nazi notions of hospitality. For days and days, by then, I had been dodging their bombs on the outskirts of a good many towns, and finding it hard to get shelter anywhere.

On the morning of April 8th, news came to the Legation that the British had laid bombs at Narvik, the harbor fjord in the north, terminal of the railroad from Sweden and port for the great iron mines of the north. In the course of the morning, a telephone call from the United States Legation in Copenhagen apprised us briefly that a large body of the German fleet was passing through the Great Belt. The call did not tell us how many ships. "A great many. Details will be cabled you." I put on my hat and set off as fast as I could for the Foreign Office. The Minister was at a meeting of the Storting, the Norwegian parliament. I gave my news to Mr. Bull, whose job is like that of our Undersecretary of State. Neither he nor his Government had any definite information to give me as to the Nazi fleet's destination. As I look back, my impression still is that neither Mr. Bull nor his associates considered the likelihood that the destination was the Oslo Fjord, and I cannot recall a single diplomat that day who even suggested that we ourselves were in the line of the coming battle. Most people surmised that the fleet was on its way to engage the Royal Navy in the North Sea. The British must have based all their plans upon this one expectation of a North Sea battle, because certainly—notwithstanding that they had promised to patrol the mines which they had laid—when the Nazi attack came, all British ships were discovered to have been withdrawn from Norwegian waters.

Just before dinner, a coded cable from Copenhagen came to me, giving the number and classes of the ships which had passed through the Kattegat, and reported great activity all day at Sylt, the air field on the coast of Denmark. The message closed "we fear retaliations." This we construed to mean retaliations against England for her minelaying.

At half past eleven that night, Oslo sounded the air raid alarm, but as the street lights were not turned off for some time, we, at the Legation, did not take it very seriously. Members of the staff telephoned in to ask if I thought they ought to come round and take shelter in our new bomb-proof room in the basement. It had been finished only three days before and we had joked about it, saying, "Now the Finnish War is over, our bomb shelter is finished, too." I told everyone cheerfully that I was going to bed and advised them to do the same. Presently, both house and street lights went off, and we ran around in the dark in search of matches and candles. And still we thought it was just another of the occasional practice air raid alarms we had been having all through the winter. Only, never before had the city authorities failed to give warning of one beforehand. Ray and Margaret Cox had been dining with an official of the Foreign Office and had kindly stopped in to ask if I were frightened. What did I think it was, they asked. It seems incredible now that not one of us connected that alarm with the proximity of the German ships; the idea of their attacking Norway still seemed so remote a possibility. I have since been told that the Crown Princess, with a woman's intuition, had sensed danger, and had commenced packing Monday afternoon.

After the "all clear" the Coxes went home, and everyone went to bed. It has never been explained why that alarm was given. Perhaps it was that some reconnoitring planes had been sighted.

At 3:00 A.M. the telephone made me jump out of bed. Sir Cecil Dormer asked if I would take over the British Legation, as German warships were coming up the fjord. Generally, such a thing is not done without permission from Washington. In the emergency it was impossible to delay. The answer was "yes."

I ran downstairs, and put in a call for Dr. Koht at the Foreign Office. He told me ships were approaching, but that the weather was so thick they had not yet been positively identified as German, although, "of course," he added, "we are sure that they are." Twenty minutes later, he telephoned to say there was now no doubt of their nationality. He would let me know, shortly, the plans of his Government.

In the meantime, Ray Cox and one of the clerks had arrived, and we got off a cable to the Department of State. It was not possible to reach Washington by telephone. We suddenly became aware that the voice of the Oslo telegraph operator, who was saying that perhaps our message would not get through to Washington, was an unfamiliar one. More German, we thought, than Norwegian accent. We put in a call for the U. S. Legation at Stockholm. Minister Sterling, we knew, might not be there, as he was en route from a short, much-needed rest, after his strenuous duties throughout the Finnish campaign. Mr. Greene, Secretary of Legation, answered the phone, and agreed to forward our message to Washington both by telephone, if possible, and by cable. I could hear him catch his breath, and his tone change, as I dictated our cable and he caught the full significance of the news.

Within the hour, the French Minister made the same request of me as Sir Cecil Dormer, to take over his Legation. We called our consuls and they hurried over, leaving their families to dress, pack and follow them. Commercial Secretary Klath went to seal the French Legation and Vice Consul Kelsey went to the British, and got from the Ministers their requests to me in writing. Again I spoke to Dr. Koht. He said the Court and Government were going by special train to Hamar, and he hoped that I would accompany them. When, at twenty minutes to seven, the Foreign

Office called to say that the train to evacuate us would leave at seven o'clock, twenty minutes was too little time and I could not be ready. Wives and children of the Staff had been arriving so thick and fast that between five and six o'clock, twenty-five of us had sat down to breakfast. We made several trips to the bomb-proof room before, during, and after the meal. German bombers whirred overhead, circling the city. We could hear the little Norwegian planes pursuing and the fire of anti-aircraft guns.

It was decided that Margaret Cox, her boy Alan, and the Consulate wives and children should go to Sjusjöen, one of the mountain resorts above Lillehammer. My own instructions being to "follow the Government," I would stop off at Hamar, some few miles nearer Oslo, and join them. It had been planned that in case of a Russian invasion during the Finnish War, evacuation should take place in the direction of Lillehammer, through the Gudbrandsdal Valley. As it turned out that was quite the worst place we could have gone. But who could foresee that?

By 9:45 we were all in our cars—I was proud of the speed and calm of our mobilization—and joined the procession that was steadily streaming out of town. In my trusty Ford were more suitcases than seemed possible. The chauffeur, one of the clerks, a maid, a typewriter, me, and the code book. As we approached Lilleström, on the outskirts of Oslo, we could hear the snap, snap, snap of machine-guns overhead. A small Norwegian plane was giving chase to a Heinkel—we craned to watch. Drivers pressed forward, not exactly frightened, but we all breathed easier, as we moved out from under those dark outlines in the sky. Only one car, the third ahead of us, was struck by falling shrapnel.

No one was hurt, but dents and scraped paint were sharp reminders of how narrow the escapes were.

As I had been in bed only one hour and had had breakfast between five and six, I was beginning to feel the strain. Though all around us was one of those lovely northern spring days which made you feel as if the whole world were young again, I was aware only of the contrasts between the earth itself and the ill will and crimes among men.

As we passed Kjeller Airfield—the field from which I had made my flight over the glacier that first summer in Oslo—we saw that it had been bombed and that the hangars were still burning. Stunned and silent groups stood on the street corners of the little settlements we passed, dumb before the rush of events. Men in uniforms and grim lads with muskets, alone, or in small companies of a dozen or so, hurried past us, apparently on their way to answer the order for general mobilization.

Behind us the Nazis had occupied Oslo. From all reports they had simply moved in. Someone, describing it, kept repeating, "They let the Nazis in with smiles on their faces, frozen smiles." There has been a great deal written about how the easy occupation of Oslo was due to treachery. What we have to call the "fifth column" had indeed been busy; the Nazis were indefatigable in an infinite variety of ways, from defamation of the British, to a thousand minor tricks and courtesies of propaganda, in an effort to make the Norwegians German-friendly. There was trade acceleration. There was interchange of tourists and students. But not a bit of real evidence has been adduced, aside from Major Quisling and his small group who moved swiftly to obtain possession of telephones, telegraph and radio, that the Norwegian people, for a single moment, welcomed the invasion. Everything in the Norwegian Democracy was opposed to Nazi brutality. If the "frozen smile" was upon the faces of any of those who saw the German troops march in, it was from shock at the Gorgon's visit. As for Quisling, many people had for a long time regarded him as of unsound mind.

The seizure by him and the Germans of the instruments of communication spread havoc. Orders would come through to officers of the Army and Navy to report ready for battle, only to be followed by orders, "Offer no resistance to the Germans." It was a dark day in history. Only the invasion seemed to go as planned.

The unexpected sinking of the battleship *Blücher* and disabling of the *Gneisenau* in Oslo Fjord were the Germans' only major set-back and delayed their plans by a full eight hours. If all had gone as schemed, the King himself and the Government would have been surrounded before there was time to evacuate. Minister Bräuer paced the quay expectantly. But Oslo was not taken from the sea. The new warfare from the air made the coup.

A single man, a retired naval officer (I wish I knew his name), is hero of the strange delay. To him, in his house on the mainland near the island on which stands Fort Oscarsborg, came news that German ships were bearing up the fjord. He came to the shore. No sign of life in the fort; no sign yet of the oncoming ships. He untied his boat and rowed himself across to where the fort's two old guns, affectionately treated as museum pieces, turned their muzzles to the sea. One of them, because it had fallen into the water when being hoisted into place back in 1900, had long been known as "Moses," its fellow, therefore, as Aaron. Inside the fort he rallied the younger officers, gave the orders to them to man the guns. As the *Blücher* came leisurely within five hundred feet of the fort, old Moses belched, carrying the ship's bridge and top hamper clean off into the water, and with it, the General in Command of the expeditionary force, the Admiral and high officers of the Gestapo who stood beside them. Then Aaron followed suit. The *Blücher* and her crew, the German financial experts, laden with plans for a new fiscal system for the country, and Heaven knows what other papers, went down in Oslo Fjord. The Germans in that day of their "famous victory" must have lost upwards of twenty thousand men by drowning alone. The British official communique for April 10th, speaks briefly of troop ships sunk in the North Sea.

The last official version given me is that "the old fort at Oscarsborg was really manned and had its commanding officers on the spot. Whether the old guns or the more modern guns did sink the *Blücher* is not known." But the first story has already settled into legend. It is the one that people tell, and the one I like to believe. Anyway, after the sinking of the *Blücher,* Nazi officers went to Horten and demanded sketches of her.

The Norwegian officers answered, "We never have had any."

"But you must have, because the *Blücher* had only one weak spot, and you hit her there."

Meanwhile, the little Norwegian gunboat, the *Olav Trygvason,* who had convoyed the *City of Flint* in November, was actively defending the naval station of Horten, where she had been reconditioning. She crippled the *Emden* so badly that she was put out of action. Now she serves with the Royal Navy in the North Sea. The German cruiser, *Karlsruhe,* was also sunk outside Kristiansand the same day. When the war is over, there will be many gallant stories to be told of the tiny, outmoded Norwegian Navy manned by seamen second to none; and of the coastal forts, only one of which fell without resistance.

That the citizens of Oslo were petrified in those first days is explicable. The blitzkrieg seemed to be over before it had begun. But there was no such lethargy amongst the country people, far from airports, to whom the rumor came of menace. The peasant youth rallied. They literally sprang to arms, with hunters' guns and tools faithful to their Norwegian colors. But that is not the right way to express it; they opposed the danger, willing to lay down their lives, but the suddenness of the attack and the breakdown of communications made concerted action in the beginning impossible. Rumors flew about that the British were coming to help.

It took us six hours that lovely April day to make our steady but uncertain way, in our heavily laden car to Hamar. The roads were not only crowded, but everybody we met stricken—not afraid, but uncertain as to direction. Nobody could tell what was happening, and when we reached Hamar we found not only every hotel, but every inch of space, under every roof, "full up" with members of the Government, so we trekked on to Hösbjör. Here, we found that the family of the Crown Prince and members of the French and British Legations had preceded us. While we were dining, Sir Cecil Dormer came to my table and whispered that he had just heard that the Germans in their armored cars were expected at Hamar in half an hour. The French and he were going on to Elverum, and didn't I think I had better join them. I inquired where the Government intended to go, and when I heard they were leaving Hamar at once for Elverum, I, of course, agreed to follow. Just before we had entered the dining room, a member of the Foreign Office, standing outside the hotel in Hösbjör, had looked at the tinderbox of a building and shaking his head at me said, "Yes, the enemy must know the British and French are here. They will surely bomb this place tonight. It will take ten minutes, no more, for it to be destroyed completely." Recalling this cheerful bit of information, it was a pleasure for me, though I was tired, to move along to Elverum.

It was now dark and the scene in front of the inn was a shambles. Everyone, and that includes most of the British Legation staff which, swelling and swelling after Great Britain declared war, was now numbered at forty, scurried to salvage what little luggage they had brought. People were politely but firmly shoved aside; suitcases grazed shins on the crowded staircases. And I think we all must have looked like intent runners in a foot race, stretching for the tape. I don't in the least intend to imply that there was any panic, just that our manners were a little grim. The French, with great agility, were well on their way ahead of all of us. In the blackout, it was risky to leave one's bags and boxes and go back for more, and all the motors looked alike. I carried the code book which I had been warned not to let out of my sight day or night; and someone lugged a typewriter, which in the end we never used. Without analyzing the situation, I think we all, subconsciously, expected to settle down comfortably, as the Belgian Government had done in 1914, and send out "Despatches as usual." This was 1940, not 1914. We were not yet ready to imagine that King and Government would be hunted like wild animals. With me was one of the clerks from the Legation to do the typing and coding, and my maid who, being a British subject, would be made prisoner, I had feared, if left behind in Oslo. In the confusion of getting away from Hösbjör, the clerk lost her small trunk and all the new wardrobe she had acquired six weeks before, when she was evacuated from Helsinki. And my maid also had lost a bag.

But there was no way of turning back to look for missing things, if we were to hold our place in the long creeping line of cars winding their way through the night, from the Gudbrandsdal to the Österdal Valley. Outside Elverum, we came on a squad of ghostly soldiers, in white suits, familiar to us from the Finnish war, preparing to erect a barricade as soon as the King and the Royal Family passed by. They did their work so well that when the pursuers came along, two hundred of the Germans were killed, and their quarry got away. When the news came through that the Nazi air attaché was among the fatalities, it was the only death that afforded any satisfaction. He had been at the German Legation in Oslo, had accepted hospitality and courtesies from the Norwegians, and now he had led the attempt to capture or kill their King. At Elverum we drew up with a sigh before a commodious hotel. The proprietress shook her head. "There is not one bed in Elverum tonight." Darkness was black over the town except for the schoolhouse, which was a blaze of light. There the Storting was sitting, a veritable beacon for the Germans, but proof enough of the naïveté of the Government, neutral until then, and unused to stratagems. A hundred years of peace had bred in them kindness, hospitality, and decency. One does not learn suspicion in a day, nor how to meet the wiles of war. As we stood in the April night wondering which direction to take, His Majesty and the Royal Family passed by in motors, bound, we later learned, for Trysil, some seventy miles further north. Meantime, someone directed both the British delegation and our car to a farm on the fringe of Elverum, and towards this our snake-like cavalcade proceeded. They gave us rooms in a primitive guest house. We were busy allotting the sleeping quarters when the British Minister received word from the police that the Germans had left Hamar on their way to Elverum. We could not know then how effective the barricade they had been building would prove.

At once, Sir Cecil and Lady Mary and their numerous retinue gathered their luggage to go further afield. As a neutral, I felt it unnecessary for me to continue the trek. The fact that I had had only one hour's sleep in the last thirty-eight may have had something to do with my decision. They all went. Suddenly, we found ourselves alone in the house. Then every sound made us jump. Suppose the Germans had traced the British that far and entered to catechize us as to their whereabouts! Fortunately, the barricade had held. We slept until 5:30 A.M. Then the first contingent of German planes came roaring over us toward Elverum. From then on, there was little cessation for them or us. The war had caught up with us.

The telephone wires in some directions were still unbroken. I was able shortly, that afternoon, to talk to Dr.

Koht in Elverum, and to our Minister in Stockholm. It was impossible to connect with Oslo. An air alarm in the evening sent us all scurrying to the wood near the house. The snow lay still, white and deep. Some carried their bags with them, trying to use them to rest on. A crowd of business people had arrived from Oslo that morning, and the "guest house" was a hive of refugees. The lady who owned the farm said firmly that we would have to feed ourselves. So we bought eggs, sardines and biscuits at a little country store. There was a stove of sorts in the basement of our cottage but, as twenty-seven people were trying to use it at the same time, we were lucky to find space to boil an egg apiece.

Next day the Foreign Minister communicated the news that the Government was moving into Nybergsund. There they might remain for two days before going westward, meaning, I supposed, the Gudbrandsdal Valley. He asked if I would come over to see him as soon as possible.

I quickly got my car, but when we tried to take the road, we suddenly realized we were in a trap. Every available road, even the short one into Elverum, was barricaded; and how well! Wooden ship masts were laid criss-cross on each other to a height of eight or ten feet, and fifteen to twenty feet in depth, with barbed wire threaded through them. At one of these barriers a young Captain came forward and told us to go back at once, as ten Nazi armored cars were due at any moment. I gazed in dismay at the twenty-five young country boys with their rifles, and two Red Cross nurses and a doctor, in a sedan, standing quietly by.

"How can such a mere handful of you," I asked, "hope to defend yourselves against so many Germans?" He took me by the arm. He led me to the edge of the road and said

"Look." There, on the thick wooded hillside, completely concealed from anyone approaching the barrier, I could spot scattered machine-gun nests. By such guerilla warfare alone was the attack made so costly that twenty Germans were killed to every one Norwegian. The Germans getting out of their cars would walk openly up a road from the woods, and a fusillade would come that mowed them down like ninepins. I often wonder what did happen that particular afternoon, and if the charming young Captain is alive today.

There is a code in the Norwegian countryside, that no man may make a blind attack on another, no matter what the feud. The enemy must have warning first. A Captain later told me the story of how his company was drawn up in ambush, ready to open fire on an approaching Nazi detachment, when he heard one of the boys say to the others, "It isn't fair to take them by surprise, we must fire into the air first, then they'll know that we are here." The Captain shivered as he told me the story. "I stopped them just in time, and explained later that in war one dare give no quarter."

Someone else told me that on the first day he had passed two hundred Germans going north and presently he met sixty Norwegian soldiers, going south. He stopped to tell them that they were marching into a trap, and must turn back. They assured him that it would be all right, as they were only going to the mobilization post. "We will talk to the Germans and explain everything," they assured him, "and it will be all right." Stupid, of course, and they were all made prisoners as soon as they were met and were less than no use in the defense. These incidents are trivial, but they show how honest, how fair, and how unfitted for a war with Nazis Norway was. Yet after the first shock, though weapons and training were inadequate, and officers few and unprepared for the new tactics, the young Norwegians took their places in the lines and stood firm.

The story of the bus drivers has been told before in America. It has become a modern saga. A group of bus drivers was under orders to convey a detachment of German reinforcements to a given point. They left notes for their families. "If we are forced to make this trip," they wrote, "you will not see us again ever." So much they told and no more. There were three bus loads. They came to a steep hill with a sharp turning at the bottom. Instead of putting on the brakes, prepared to turn gently, as they had so many times before with home folk on the journey, they drove with brakes off headlong into a deep ravine. Three Norwegian patriots and a hundred Germans fought no more.

In the wood where we sought shelter from bombs, on the night of the twelfth, there were strange noises. It seems the Cadet school at Elverum had turned their horses loose to save them from confiscation, but the next day, being observed, the beasts were machine-gunned from the air. I think of those horses still, comrades in our misery, more frightened perhaps than we at the Heinkels overhead.

At half past three on Thursday I was in touch with Dr. Koht again. This time at Nybergsund. A half hour later the hotel was bombed and the King forced to run to the woods for his life. Dr. Koht still said he thought it a good idea if I could be nearer the Government, and I determined to make one more effort to reach them. There is a certain sort of satisfaction in moving, and it seemed no more risky than halting for cover, so wayward and unpredictable was the bombing. All day planes had been flying low over our heads in the direction of Elverum. Suddenly the dropping of incendiary bombs was observed, and we could see that the whole town was being enveloped in a thick cloud of yellow smoke. Wicked tongues of fire presently began to lick through the poisonous smoke screen. Someone tried to telephone. The wires were cut. The road north now being absolutely closed, I decided to experiment. I would try going south and detouring. The main road was closed, of course; the snow was impassable on the ways through the forest. Still, there must be some way. Eventually we gave up in despair. Every road was blocked either by stockades or snowdrifts.

We caught sight of a comfortable-looking farmhouse and climbed out to knock. The sweet-faced mistress of the place opened the door and welcomed us. But there was no bedroom for us—besides her own eight children, she was already sheltering several mothers from Oslo and their babies; but the parlor was ours if we wanted to have it. We could still hear the rumble of planes flying low, but they were not overhead. We all relaxed as if we had suddenly come home, so simply did Mrs. Peterson offer us hospitality. Late as it was, and with only a little running water in her kitchen, she made us coffee and gave us cakes and boiled eggs. I shall never forget that Norwegian country parlor, the family portraits that looked down from the wall, telling I know not what story of better days; the linen sheets and pillowslips with their handmade lace insertion, the many little touches of grace in our welcome. Our beds were narrow sofas, and there were no blankets to spare from the babies; but we slept in our clothes gratefully, while the farmer and the chauffeur discussed roads to take us on our way. The farmer did his best, and before dawn went scouting on his skis through the neighboring forests, but snowdrifts barred every lead. He could, he finally offered, take us beyond the forest in a sledge, if we cared to leave the car behind until the war was over. "But on the other side of the forest, what shall we do without the car?" That was something he could not answer. He went off again in search of a clever neighbor. How to get the car over the forest? The neighbor had an idea. They would both try to get us by the barrier on the road to Elverum. The friend, arriving on his bicycle, took charge. If we hurried, between air raids, the soldiers at the barrier would devise us something. The sink being in use, I was at the pump in the yard, breaking icicles for my tooth brush, when I heard the news.

I called out that we would come at once. Only the clerk saw no hope and crumpled up. She clung to the idea that we ought to get a safe conduct from the Germans. Out of patience, I told her to choose quickly, to come along, or to stay on the farm until the war was over. I confess that I, too, felt that the Germans flying at low altitude were almost in my hair. The deafening roar was terrifying. But so intent were they on laying waste any town in which the King might be, that it was not until several days later that their shrapnel began to rake the roads.

All in the car at last, with the farmer and his friend clinging to the runningboards, we sped down the road to the barricades. The soldiers saluted warmly and set to work at once. I felt like something from an old picture-book of rescues in the Alps. The blockade and barbed wire ran from the steep hillside on the right to the precipitous bank of the River Glomma. Each of us was passed from one soldier to another and squeezed round the end of the entanglement; while the car itself, held in check by six or eight of the soldiers, was let slide slowly down onto the ice of the river's rim. "Lucky for you," spoke up someone, "there's no sun today to melt the ice on the river edge." Several more men went down with poles, "to fish out the car if it breaks through." Five hundred yards further upstream the men found an incline, steep but not impassable, and shouldered the car up onto the dirt road again. There was no way at all to thank our rescuers for letting us out of bondage. We could only give them change to get cigarettes. And this we do: we remember them with gratitude.

Where Elverum had been, but a few hours before, only the church and the Red Cross hospital were still standing. In the hospital were many wounded Germans. We drove down the principal street which was littered with débris, past the wreck of the very hotel that had been "too full" to receive us less than a week before. The ashes were still steaming. Hardly a house but what had been razed to within four feet of the ground. There had been over three hundred casualties. The car stopped and we gazed around. There is something ghastly in a ruined city. And we who looked about us knew how pleasant and how vital the human life of Elverum had been.

We got out of the car while the chauffeur took off the chains, which had been necessary for the river escapade, and as we stood there, Captain Ibsen, grandson of the great poet, came up to speak to me. He wanted to know if I could get a message through to our Legation and through them to his wife, Lillebil, one of the best known Norwegian actresses. He wanted her to know where he was and that he was still alive. This I was afraid would not be possible until I crossed the border into Sweden. But I would try. Everyone along the way everywhere bombarded me with similar requests. The invasion had been so sudden, the mobilization so instantaneous, that none of the men knew where their families were and could only surmise what was happening in Oslo.

Captain Ibsen gave me warning that the long bridge this side of Nybergsund might be destroyed; he had heard bombings from that direction shortly before. Nothing for us to do, though, but to drive on, a long, cold drive, over the mountain pass with only one stop, for gas. We had biscuits and chocolate for lunch, and felt lucky to have them! Bus loads of soldiers passed us from time to time, moving probably to the Gudbrandsdal Valley where we thought fierce fighting was now going on.

As we approached the bridge, we slowed up. We found it intact, but there were very large craters at either end, showing that bombs had been dropped but missed their objective. On the far side, where Nybergsund should have been, there was nothing to be seen but smoking ruins. Not a wall was standing. Wiped out! The only two men left in the whole place were talking disconsolately together in the middle of the road. In spite of the American flag on the roof of our car, they were suspicious of us and avoided telling us anything. No, they "knew nothing" of the whereabouts of the Government, and the only information we could get from them was that there had been only one casualty. A little girl of four had been killed as she ran across the street.

Afterwards, I wondered if I had shown them my passport whether they would have been less reticent. They seemed so stunned.

After considering the matter from every point of view, I came to the conclusion that there was no use searching any further at that time. The members of the Government might have taken any one of three roads. Also, as it had not been possible for several days to communicate with our Minister in Stockholm, it seemed wise to go to the border where I could telephone him that we were still alive. One road, we were told, was not yet free enough of snow, so we took the other that skirted the River Glomma.

CHAPTER XVIII

On the Border

It was comforting to settle back in the car on a route that had so far escaped the Nazi bombers. We drove east and south through the Glomma Valley, the sun at times so bright and the sky so blue, the snow so quiet, that it seemed as if good dreams followed bad dreams. Nothing was real. For all the sun, it was freezing cold, and the way was long, until we reached the border. The young man at the Customs was not one to be lightly taken in. A woman the American Minister to Norway?—No, Madam, he would telephone to Headquarters before he let us pass. My English maid stood nervously about, uncertain what she, too, would have to face but, when my unlikely story had been verified, and I was welcomed across the border and had explained that she was one of my household, all went smoothly, and no one ever asked to look at her passport. Just as well, because I had hidden all her papers in the front of my dress when there seemed a chance of encountering German raiders. We had made great plans, too, as to what to do with the code book, far too large for eating, too bulky to be tossed unnoticed into the snow, not easily burnt in a hurry.

Swedish troops, plenty of them, apparently well organized and disciplined, manned the border. We saw artillery and armored cars on either side of the road, and the dream of the afternoon was gone. War, as yet only potential war, hemmed us round again. My business was clear—to get in touch with Freddie Sterling and be guided by whatever information was (or so I hoped) pouring into Sweden, and my orders from Washington. The ABC of blitzkrieg is the seizure of communications. No one who has not been through it can readily understand what that first week of the Norwegian War was like. And everywhere these blows effect the same phenomena. The whole outside world is shut out, orders are interrupted, falsified and every hysterical personality tends to float rumors, give frightened orders and multiply the fog. I understand what happened in June in France the better for the period of running and waiting in Norway. For a week, from hour to hour, we did not know what was happening. Everybody I came in contact with behaved well. A certain stolidity in the Norwegian character saved us from panic, but could not prevent a general bewilderment.

I think I never had a clear picture of the many directions from which the attack came until long afterward I saw some graphic maps in the German propaganda magazine (printed in English for distribution in Africa and Latin America) showing how planned and how complete the attack from the air and all along the long coast had been. My own duty was simply to collect all possible information, whether I could collate what I saw and heard or not, to find the Norwegian Government, and to keep in touch with Stockholm.

The Customs officer waved us through, and we were directed to a small pension at Holjes. The little inn proved most comfortable. Its modern plumbing fixtures delighted us, but there was no hot water and only a little trickle of cold. A local drought turned the bath I had dreamed of into a mirage again. But I could take off my clothes. The bed was real! My first act was to telephone our Legation at Stockholm, for it had been three days since I had been able to report, and I knew that Washington was probably anxious to know that we were still alive. The Minister's first news for me was that Mr. Hull had instructed him to send a military attaché to join us and that I might expect Captain Losey would reach the border somewhere around midnight.

It was so reassuring to be talking to Freddie Sterling, and I suppose here is as good a place as any to set down for the record what I think of him. I know no better example of the career diplomat. Trained in the intricacies of professional diplomacy, he yet keeps an open mind, for he knows that only those traditional practices endure which add and grow and change as new occasions require new precedents. Continuity need not be static. His patience is amazing. His naturally sensitive nervous system is under complete control. I should be able to judge, for in the two months which followed I was in and out of his office at the Legation at Stockholm, a most trying interruption for any official and I knew it, but not once did I detect the slightest irritation. It is not too much to say that all his staff adored him; his devotion to his job was felt by all of them. Many more than I were grateful to have him *en poste* during those trying times. I called him constantly for advice, while I was on the border and in Sweden, and as I look back now, I realize afresh that he never erred in his judgment where I was concerned.

My room at the inn was in an adjoining cottage. Just as I was tidying for dinner, the clerk rushed over and, tapping at the door, announced breathlessly, "There are newspaper men arriving. But I have warned them you will not want to give a statement. They are lying in wait for you now. They are insisting."

Even the Press could not keep me from warm food; besides the Press might have far more to tell me than I could tell them. As I went to my table, the two men sprang up and introduced themselves as Arthur Menken of New York and M. Valeri of *Paris Soir*. The usual fencing began. I compromised by saying I would telephone my mentor in Stockholm and abide by his decision. Fred Sterling's answer was simple, just to tell my story objectively as I had told it to him earlier. People at home, he thought, had for a week been getting almost no news of Norway. So I fetched down the notes I had been jotting as I traveled and, for almost two hours and a half, gave the tale of our flight, filling in details here or there, to the two men opposite me. At two a.m. Mr. Menken rang up Stockholm and read them what he had written to be cabled to America. I heard him spelling "H for Horace, S for sugar, C for Charles, M for Mary, etc." I began to get some idea of the tedious chore of newspaper work. And months afterward I was to appreciate the craftsmanship in the Menken story, when I saw it in the American papers. Only the most trivial mistakes in it; printed and read a day after I had given my account on the Swedish border. There was a sequel to the interview, however, not so gratifying. Some days later I received a cable from the State Department questioning the wisdom of giving the U.P. an exclusive story. I had not even inquired what American paper Menken represented. I was quite distressed until the wife of an old newspaper hand laughed at me. "Oh, so you have missed the Thirty Years' War at home between the Press Associations—why, men have died, and been fired, which is worse, for being three minutes late with a story and, as for letting the rival association get a two column beat! The Department tries to be a Hague Tribunal for the competitive newspaper business. It's better for the public, they think."

Menken had finished telephoning; I was suddenly aware of my accumulated weariness, and too tired to stay up to greet Captain Losey, but both journalists hailed his arrival. He was an old friend, and they promised to find him a bed. I never asked which of the three had finally to sleep on the stairs.

Five minutes later I was in bed; and five minutes later than that, or so it seemed, I was up, so soundly had I slept. I ran into Captain Losey on the way to breakfast. I find I have noted in my diary, "The new military attaché is a nice, spare young man in a flying corps uniform, and seems in every way acceptable."

Directly after breakfast, we had a council of war. It was decided to let the clerk go on to Stockholm. There was no way for me to send out any code cables, and as there was no work for her, her seat in the car had better be made available for the Captain. So we packed all the cumbersome luggage for her to take with her, and in the two cars, with the two newspaper men, went to the station at Malung with her, waved goodbye and set off for the north.

On and on we drove over the frigid mountains and through the snowy woods, the lights in the cottage windows throwing fantastic gleams across the snow so that the whole journey seemed to go through some fairy tale of Hans Christian Andersen's. It was 9 P.M. before we came to Särna where Freddie Sterling had told us to go as he understood the British had established themselves there and would tell me where to find the Norwegian Government. Sure enough, both French and British were there, just finishing their dinners. The hotel, the size of a doll's house, was crowded, but we found a place about ten minutes' walk down the road, with a comfortable couch in the parlor for me and a cot in the dining room for Elizabeth. Captain Losey and the chauffeur were packed like sardines in a tiny bedroom. But shelter is shelter, roof, walls and floor. As I ate my dinner the British and French Ministers brought me up to date on their news.

"The Norwegian Government is again somewhere in the vicinity of Hamar." Messengers had been sent back to the foreign representatives, however, suggesting that the diplomatic cars trailing the Government only made it more difficult for them to escape unobserved. That explained the halt. The Court Chamberlain had passed through Särna and stopped a few hours the day before. Whispered rumor had it that the King had been smuggled in with him, and had been able to snatch a few hours' respite. Not true. His Majesty had never crossed the border. But the two newspaper men bombarded the British and French Ministers for interviews. "See what you have let us in for," chided my diplomatic colleagues. I disclaimed the journalists, but smiled quietly, for I knew they would get their information.

Sunday, April 14. As I ate my breakfast, I thought there was nothing to do but wait. But at luncheon Captain Losey was ready to press on to Lillehammer, back across the frontier, where the Norwegian General Staff was supposed to have headquarters. As I was anxious to have news of the welfare and whereabouts of Margaret and Alan Cox, and the Consulate wives and children who had set off from Oslo for a mountain resort beyond Lillehammer, I agreed to the Captain's leaving.

Menken and *Paris Soir* had disappeared on a news foraging expedition; and a heavy snowstorm blew over the little town and hemmed us in. I dined in solitary state, my loneliness punctuated by darting little visits from the Countess de Dampierre, who kept notes of everything she heard in a little red book. Gifted with languages, she hung onto the radio, whirling the dials, and catching "official" propaganda, and contradictions from all over Europe. Now she would stop to serve as interpreter for some member of a delegation who needed her. She hovers over that day in my memory, at once calming and exciting, always delightful. When King Haakon made his thrilling proclamation over the radio, it was she who had someone take it down in Norwegian; she then made the French translation, and I the English from her French. Nothing has been stranger in this war than the role of radio. What name the town had where the King had fled no longer mattered, he was with us in Särna, he was everywhere, speaking to his people:

"In this hour, the most difficult our country has ever

known for a hundred years, I send the most pressing appeal to each of you to do all in your power to save the liberty and independence of Norway. We have been the victims of a lightning attack from a nation with which we have always maintained friendly relations. That nation has not hesitated to bomb the civil population, who are suffering intensely.

"The situation is such that we cannot at present tell where we are. In effect, the German High Command has not hesitated to bombard the Royal Family and the Government at the moment when they were in an unprotected place. They have employed against us, and against the civil population, high explosives and incendiary bombs, and also machine-gunned us in the most savage fashion. The assailants can have had only one object, to exterminate those who were gathered together trying to find a solution as to what would be best for Norway.

"I thank all those who are today with me and the Government, and who are fighting at their posts of duty for the independence and preservation of Norway.

"I pray you all to treasure the memory of those who have already given their lives for this country.

"God protect Norway."

The King's voice—firm, though tired—did not break, and when the voices broke out singing the Norwegian National Anthem—always for me one of the most moving of the songs of a people—a new strength flowed through us all.

The little company, taking cheerfully this cross between being snowbound and shipwrecked, compared notes . . . almost all of us were making official reports. Some young

Britishers arrived who had been at Nybergsund when air raid alarms had come. With the King and Crown Prince and members of the Government they had all fled, many on skis, into the woods behind the inn. The British were safe when the bombs struck, but the King had literally to flee for his life and the hotel was reduced to ash and splinters. Admiral Boyes, attached to the British Legation, took upon himself the arrangement for our baths. The drought in all that part of Sweden had made for a sort of rationing of water.

The charming little house where we were lodged, and its story-book family, were symbols of peaceful Scandinavia. The handsome young father, still on crutches from a leg broken at skiing, a large blonde girl of ten, another seven, a curly-headed boy of two, and the gentle mother, plainly ready for her time once more, were all so pleasant with each other. The simple and tasteful furniture, the rows of book-shelves with modern titles and classics, fine bindings and shabby, well-worn editions, gave me a fresh sense of the deep culture of the country. The ground floor of the house was taken up with the store of which the father was proprietor. The mother waited on customers at the dry goods counter; the eldest girl assisted. Even with several other sales clerks, the little shop had an air of business and of interest in the needs of the community, but no bustle. My constant telephone calls to Stockholm neither excited nor bothered them, though I had to make them at the office desk. Everybody merely nodded and smiled at a Minister at work.

At luncheon the second day Sir Cecil came by my table and whispered, "You had better come, too!" I was puzzled —where? Why? Beneath all our calm was an undertone of confusion and expectation. I went to Lady Mary's room where she and the wife of Admiral Boyes told me that Lascelles, their First Secretary, had telephoned to Mrs. Boyes in Russian from Salen. They thought it must be Lascelles as he was the only one besides Mrs. Boyes who spoke that language. "Come at once, tomorrow may be too late!" Sir Cecil said he had no idea what was meant. They were going. He persuaded me not to stay on without my aide. It was mysterious, but reasonable . . . the bags were packed in twenty minutes; I hired a taxi as Captain Losey still had my car. The French Minister's motor car was already at Salen. He had gone along with Mr. Lascelles in search of news. Countess de Dampierre squeezed in as well and kept me roaring with laughter all the way, even when her dramatic imagination all but convinced us we were in the midst of a Warner Brothers movie. The poor taxi driver spoke nothing but Swedish. That was bad, she said . . . doubtless he was a Nazi in disguise, driving us to some rendezvous behind the German lines.

Once we passed some C.D. cars (Corps Diplomatique) going very fast. Perhaps one of them was French. She had forgotten the numbers. Our driver certainly was restless, and nervously insisted on passing everybody on the road. The British car was now far behind. But we did arrive at Salen only to find a call for me at the hotel. I was to tell Mme. de Dampierre that she must come at once to a place fifteen miles away as the members of their delegation were going to cross the frontier at that point. Mr. Lascelles was lukewarm about my coming, too; especially when he heard that I now had neither car nor money. So I decided to wait for Captain Losey. It wasn't easy to persuade Mme. de

Dampierre to go off with "that Nazi driver" alone. I had no cash to volunteer to go along and to pay for the drive back again. When the French Minister called, himself, I could only assure him on the phone that his wife had left and would join him shortly. Now and then a distracted Norwegian would appear, inquiring for his family. I felt helpless. I could request our Legation in Stockholm to ask those who were left in our Legation in Oslo to make inquiries, but would there be any result? There was really not much any of us could do for each other. Besides, I had just heard that all communication between Oslo and Stockholm was cut off.

Just then, going up the stairs, I saw the Crown Princess of Norway. Her behavior was wonderful. "Of course, I cannot help thinking," she said, and told me how the King had picked up fragments of the shells shot at him in the woods by mitrailleuse. They all felt keenly the sense of being personally pursued. The little Princesses came down to join their mother, and she smiled, saying that little Harald would soon come, too.

At dinner I saw three gentlemen of the Norwegian Foreign Office, and after piecing together their stories of the bombing—Mr. Aas had had two buildings bombed and fall around his head—I wrote my dispatch to Washington: "The German bombing of the open towns of Elverum and Nybergsund had no military significance and was in my opinion directed against the Royal Family, the Government and civilian populations." No other conclusion was possible. But the Royal Family was safe; and more than ever exalted in the hearts of their people.

After dinner, Princess Ingeborg of Sweden, mother of

the Crown Princess of Norway, came and asked me to sit beside her in the hall. "Do I look a hundred years older than I did when you saw me last spring?" she asked. "Think of me," she said, "with one brother being hunted like a wild animal, another who has lost his country, the country of my birth. My daughter, Marghareta, is married to a Dane and cannot write to me. One son-in-law is in constant danger; and my other son-in-law is who knows where." Her other son-in-law was Leopold of the Belgians. She spoke, not in pity for herself, but with a quiet enumeration of the mounting heap of disasters to be dealt with. Worn and tired she certainly looked; but lovely as ever. At dinner she had been gay with her grandchildren and calm; she was no less so with the rest of us.

I shall remember those days always, like days on a desert island; telephones ringing, Freddie Sterling helping me to plan how to get the American women out of Norway. There were rumors of more fighting. Minister Lie's wife and two girls were there and Mrs. Thorp, wife of the Minister of Finance, and her son, a splendid youth of seventeen, chafing to get out and fight.

Only afterward did I hear the story of the Gold Saga. Not one of us knew about it at the time, yet on the morning of April 9th someone of genius was on the job. The cleverest, quietest counter-blitz of the war was carried out by two or three—no one knows by how many or precisely by whom—on the staff of the Bank of Norway. Planes whined overhead, troops were landing. Consternation everywhere. But casual trucks loaded with furniture and driven by two most unofficial-looking drivers, took the road to Lillehammer, fleeing from Oslo. Refugees, like any others? Not at all.

They looked like other trucks going north but, beneath the bed and desks, the chairs and old trunks, lay the twenty-million-dollar gold reserve of the nation. At Lillehammer the trucks halted; and the better to avoid suspicion, there they stood unguarded on the side of the road. Only more abandoned vehicles, they seemed. No one had time to bother with them, not even to commandeer them for the battle going on all around. Somewhere some German may remember his own sardonic smile at those deserted lorries, loaded with the simple household goods of one more free man on the run.

How the gold was unloaded in the night and taken across country on sledges to the coast, and taken piecemeal to England on destroyers, will some day be told in a book by itself, one volume in this story of a contest of men and machines *and* money.

When I came downstairs on the morning of the 16th, I heard that the Crown Princess and her children had left for Stockholm. The Court Chamberlain, Mr. Wedel Jarlsberg, had arrived and was the more pleased to see me because he thought I was a late arrival from Oslo and might have news of his family, and especially of his son-in-law, Per Paus, who was fighting. I shook my head. I did not know. I had left Oslo about the same time he had.

Just before luncheon I looked out of the window and saw Captain Losey with Fröislie, the chauffeur, getting out of my car. He had certainly made a lightning trip. At Lillehammer he had found it impossible to get up the road to Sjursjöen for it was blocked with snow. He had left a note for our Naval Aide, Commander Hagen, telling him orders were to rescue "our wives." It was important to get them to

Sweden before operations cut them off. Captain Losey had seen Commander-in-Chief Hvinden Haug near Hamar. The General's son had just been killed that morning. He had gathered all the military information that he could. Lest even one telephone operator be either bought or stupid, it seemed better that Captain Losey go as quickly as possible to Stockholm and make his report in person. He went off in a hired car, accompanied by Major Lunberg, Aide to the Swedish Crown Prince, and they drove all night.

Their journey to Stockholm over fresh-fallen snow must have been long and tiring, but next morning Freddie Sterling called me, saying that the reports had been received and there was very valuable information in them about German and Norwegian troop movements and that these were the first that had come out of Norway. I was proud of our staff. Captain Losey would return the following night by train.

Then Freddie read me several cables. Anne Vanderbilt was dying. Two messages were from Secretary Hull. "I am greatly relieved to learn that you and your party are safe and in good health. I congratulate you on the courage, energy and efficiency with which you are performing your duties under such trying and dangerous conditions. It is in the best traditions of our diplomatic service." I quote it not alone out of pride, and because it gave us all new energy, but because it was so kind and so like Secretary Hull to be personally encouraging. The second cable I have spoken of already, and it was by no means so pleasant to receive. It dealt with my having given the U.P. what it claimed was an exclusive story of the occupation of Norway, and ended, "It is proposed that should you grant an interview to any other newspaper man that it be given out to the whole press of the United States and that it not be copyrighted as an exclusive account." Freddie came to bat for me and sent an explanation to the Department, took half the blame on himself for having advised me to talk, said that I had only given facts, and that Mr. Menken was the only correspondent on the spot. Good old Freddie. It was spilt milk and, as someone said, "already champagne to Mr. Menken."

Thursday, April 18th. Still we waited. That day, to my joy, many friends turned up. It was like watching a gangplank in a strange port. Baroness Beck-Fries with her boy, and Mme. Oxholm and her girls, one of whom had been at Lillehammer and had seen "our wives." Alan Cox had mumps. Poor Margaret. Mme. Oxholm then came to my room and passed on information from her husband who was very close to the Government, information which he had said could only be passed on to a Minister. All she and her husband had was probably lost in Denmark. She hardly spoke of it, but bore herself with courage and philosophy. Then Captain Losey turned up again in time for dinner and we at first planned to start off at once for Lillehammer to find our own refugees. But we decided to make a morning start instead, and spent another evening, calm and ordered enough on the surface, but each new arrival brought fresh stories, and an undercurrent of excitement flowed strong.

Countess Douglas had ordered a first aid kit for us as soon as she heard that ours was lost. She explained all about it to the Captain in her sweetly fetching, broken English. "What a charming woman!" he whispered to me. Mme. Paris had come from Stockholm; Mrs. Holst, wife of the famous surgeon, turned up near midnight on her way to Stockholm to get more medical supplies. Mrs. Lie bespoke the Captain's aid and mine in rescuing her nine-year-old child from Lillehammer.

Mr. Neumann, the Polish Minister to Norway, heard that we were going north and came to me and asked if we could squeeze him in. I was so sorry that we did not have an inch of room. He had told me the evening before that five thousand Polish troops were arriving in Norway, to help with the defense, and he hoped to go to meet them. I heard later that he finally went with the Finnish Chargé and at Rena had just escaped with his life when the town was bombed. So, by deciding at the last moment to cross the border into Norway further north, we had been prevented from witnessing the destruction of one more town.

I was very happy for Mr. Neumann—whose composure through the Polish debacle and the invasion of Norway had won everyone's admiration—when I heard that the Polish contingent had been the best fighters of any of the troops that came to Norway.

Countess Douglas and Baroness Beck-Fries were out on the steps to see us off. Captain Losey was very pleased that I had followed his advice and limited my luggage to one small bag and a dressing case. One change of frock—that was all. Elizabeth was sending all her things to Stockholm, and was in the village getting a ruck-sack. Not to be outdone, Captain Losey himself bought a ruck-sack and lightened our load of his own bags. Now we had room on the back seat, and a clean conscience toward the motor. We could ask speed of it. We were off. We discussed all along the way whether I should accompany him to Dombås, taking the northern route, as the road to Elverum was closed.

"You might be bombed," he argued; "the Germans are strafing the roads."

"But so might you," I said, "and that would be worse for you are young and have your life before you, while I have had a wonderful life and nearly all of it behind me."

"I certainly don't want to be killed," he would go on in a cheerful fashion, "but your death would be the more serious as it might involve our country in all kinds of trouble, whereas with a military attaché . . ."

He would explain that, in a moving car, it was almost impossible to hear the sound of a bomber overhead if it approached from the rear, which I already knew from experience. We argued about sounds. He gave me such precise details of the dangers we might encounter that I began to chaff him about being nervous. He laughed, but said he knew a lot more than I did about the kinds of danger so plentiful that morning. His final argument for my safety was that if he and the chauffeur went on alone, they could travel day and night without stopping. I was loath to listen but told him I would make up my mind after luncheon.

At three o'clock we found our hotel up north, and it was crowded with the members of the American-Scandinavian Field Hospital, originally designed for service in Finland. Arriving just after the Russian-Finnish armistice, they had now been ordered to Norway from Stockholm, and were not a little upset at the chance of being once again mobilized for service, yet prevented from working because the theatre of war was so unpredictable. There were fifteen nurses, an X-ray technician, ambulance drivers, thirteen American trucks lent them by the Norwegian Government, sufficient to move an entire field hospital of a hundred beds. The chief surgeon was Dr. Fishwick of Bellevue Hospital, who used to play on the Yale football team. Pretty Polly Peabody, only twenty-two, was in charge of the commissariat. Also, of the group, was Baron von Blixen, brother of Countess Clarence de Rosen, and two Norwegian girls, Karin Paulsson and Astrid Lange Aulie, a doctor. It is hard to be patient in war time, yet that is what war is, hideous spurts of destructive work, and waiting. Karin Paulsson was from Oslo, wife of a doctor, and memorable for her beautiful, soft voice. I listened to her, went for a long walk with Baron von Blixen, answered telephone calls.

At the lunch table I told Losey that I had decided to be unselfish and not go with him. He was pleased and said, "When you stay behind you gather so much information one way and another that it is as useful as what I get."

I find in my diary, "The Captain couldn't be nicer, he is so understanding and gentle. I am certainly in luck to have such an aide sent me."

I hated to see him go, but when he impressed on me that "our first job now must be getting those women out," I knew that he was right. So with the first aid kit, some chocolates and biscuits, he and the chauffeur fared forth. Again I see in my diary, "I will cheer when they return."

Mrs. Worm-Müller, wife of the Professor in Oslo, got through from Göteborg to ask if there was anything she could do—drive an ambulance, or what? I remember best my six o'clock engagement. I went to the public bath house and had a hot bath (they were only allowed on Fridays and Saturdays) for one kroner fifty. Food is something to be doubly grateful for in war time; and the beds one can really sleep in are rare; but I have talked to soldiers. In war-time dictionaries, champagne becomes loot. The definition of luxury is "hot bath."

On Sunday, April 21st, early in the morning, I had a telephone message from the Norwegian Minister of Justice, phoning from some unspecified point. He gave me warm greetings from Dr. Koht and wanted to know how I was. Then Mr. Meloney arrived, representative of the American Red Cross in Scandinavia; we discussed conditions, and talked on the telephone with Mr. Hambro, who advised his returning to Stockholm where reports were centering. I rather thought Mr. Meloney should make a trip through Norway and perhaps gather some fresh impression of what was needed, but he seemed to feel he would gain "impressions" only and decided to return to Stockholm. Another day of waiting. Toward evening, good news came from Commander Hagen somewhere farther north that he had rescued all "our wives and children" and brought them safely across the border. No news of Captain Losey and I jotted in my diary, "Uneasy. No report from the Captain."

The next day Freddie Sterling called me, at about eleven. He had cables to read me. Anne Vanderbilt had died of pneumonia. Suddenly all the past work in the last war, the awareness that she was gone now, and her generous life swept over me. But that life had been long and varied. I caught my breath and Freddie went on. "And now I have some terrible news. Captain Losey was killed yesterday by a German bomb." So generous a human being, too, so young, only thirty-two. Cut off—and for what? There were no particulars, not even whether my chauffeur had been killed, too. The news was a horrible shock. All day we had been expecting him. Our sense of loss in the world was centered in that one young American.

Bringing the body to the border, my motor became stuck in the snow and it was necessary to continue the journey by sled, leaving the car on the Norwegian side. Then we went on. The Scandinavians dealt with our loss movingly. The railway men lined a boxcar with branches of fir, and someone laid a touching little bunch of flowers on the American flag which covered the coffin. It was the same flag we had stretched on the roof of our car when we traveled in the combat zone, with some vague idea that it might deter a Nazi from dropping a bomb on us, or aiming machine guns at us as we sped along. Often people said things were done to neutrals purposely, though afterwards it was easy to explain it had been a mistake. There is no trust in war time.

I had the sad story from my chauffeur. An air raid had come when they were at Dombås. The car had just been loaded on a train. The passengers went into a railway tunnel to escape the bombs. Very soon an English officer said to my chauffeur, "You had better go to your Captain. He is badly hurt." Losey had been standing about thirty feet inside the tunnel, but not flattened against the wall, trying both to be protected and still to make observations. A splinter of shrapnel had gone through his heart. Mercifully his death must have been instantaneous. Five Britishers had been killed at the same time.

Arrived in Stockholm, I ate dinner with our senior military attaché, Colonel Hayne, and listened to his talk, for he and Captain Losey had been together in the Finnish War. The boy was dead, and suddenly one saw how every-

International News Photo

CAPTAIN LOSEY AND THE AUTHOR

The day before he was killed by bomb splinters at Dombås.

one who knew him had the same impression that I had. Menken and the correspondent from the *Paris Soir* were very much cut up. He had been so young, so disinterested, so thoughtful.

The next day, Freddie Sterling, his staff, representatives from the different legations, the military attaché and I followed the body from the station to the little chapel where the service was to take place. Many of the journalists and military attachés who had known Captain Losey in Finland—and each had had some special reason for remembering him—attended the services the next day. The bier was piled high with flowers. I saw many new and many familiar faces. King Gustav's nephew, Count Folke Bernadotte, and his American wife were there—she, Mr. H. Edward Manville's daughter. In her adopted country she has made a remarkable place for herself, at home there as few foreigners ever are, and yet no less an American.

I had known the young Captain only a few weeks, but the circumstances had been so full of danger and problems, that I felt I had known him a long time, for I saw what his character was, and as taps were sounded, it seemed as if I had lost a son. All our hearts ached for the young wife in California who must go on without him. She would be hearing Menken on the radio to America, telling of the service; she would read the beautiful tributes to him in the American press; she would not have the picture of the friends of his last winter, who mourned him in the north.

CHAPTER XIX

MARKING TIME IN SWEDEN

THERE WERE NO fresh instructions awaiting me in Stockholm, so I took it for granted that I would soon go north to join the Norwegian King and Government when they were permanently settled. With that end in view, I questioned everyone coming in from that direction. It was still necessary, I found out, to make quite long trips on skis, and some told of having to lie flat in the snow at times to escape an occasional bomb. The trip under the best of circumstances would take four or five days and had to be made by rail, motor-bus and fishing smack. Men kept arriving at the hotel in their ski clothes, utterly worn out after days of travel across the mountains. So it seemed wise for me to defer my going until the weather broke.

Staying at the Grand Hotel was like being at the Ritz in Paris in 1919, when the nations and the interests making the Peace Treaty eddied and swirled like rapids. In Stockholm in 1940 there were refugees from all quarters of the globe, the richest of them, and correspondents resting from their hard winter in Finland, and sending off cables to the Americas, to Tokyo, to whatever countries in Europe still could afford foreign news, and not the Nazi version. Tolischus and Callendar of *The New York Times,* Leland Stowe of the *Chicago Daily News,* and Stevens of *The Christian Science Monitor* were among old acquaintances.

I was a possible news source and was plied with all sorts of questions. One hated to be quoted at all, the rumors were so thick, there was no chance to check reports and official orders were just to "stand by." So I decided to leave town for a time. It was not until I was well away in the country that I realized that, if the correspondents did ask me too many questions, I had myself grown frightfully dependent on their answers to mine. There is something highly spiced and habit-forming about the give and take of still unprinted "stories"; and the breed of witty, shrewd, hard-working, cynical, experienced, international newspaper men comprises one of the inner circles of the modern world.

Mr. Hambro, President of the Storting, was in Stockholm. We had a long and interesting talk before I left. He told me he proposed to treat with me as Dr. Koht always had, in complete confidence. His hope was that I would remain within reach, for there were sure to be occasions when I might do what Freddie Sterling could not perhaps do, since he was accredited to Sweden but not to Norway. Together we looked over the German papers and he gave me translations of the scurrilous things the Nazis printed about me in particular . . . "British agent" . . . "Norwegian agent" . . . now and again I would recognize some phrase I had used in talking over the telephone to Freddie Sterling. Somebody, somewhere, some "German agent" or some little listening machine, must have been in on every wire, even when we were at Elverum. There were quotes, too, made up out of whole cloth. Plenty of them.

I was near enough to come into town by train, and I would visit Mr. Hambro every few days at one of his six or seven hideouts. The Germans were anxious to force him out, so he tried to be as inconspicuous as possible. With all he had on his hands, he seemed to have time for everything and everybody. His memory for small matters, as well as large, is phenomenal. When I asked him anything, I knew that, if he had not the answer at hand at that moment, it would be forthcoming almost immediately. He never forgot anything.

Through him I had the news that the King and the Government, after a narrow escape from Molde, on the West Coast, had been taken north on a destroyer, and were settled somewhere near Tromsö. Then one day, Count Douglas, the Swedish Secretary of Legation, ran after me in the street, and said that he had just come down from Tromsö to report to his government. The Swedish Minister, Baron Beck-Fries, and the Italian were the only heads of Missions remaining in Oslo and they, too, were asked soon after by the Nazis to leave. The one Minister who had been able to remain with the King and Government all the time was the Danish, Mr. Oxholm. Douglas had made much of his journey south on skis, and expected to retrace his steps in a few days.

A little later, Mr. Zorifopol, the Roumanian Chargé in Norway, appeared with his wife. They had a sickening tale to tell of Molde. They had finally caught up with the Government there, having left Oslo some days after the rest of us. The poor British and French, they reported, were at

Molde, too. The two Missions had traveled directly across Norway when they parted with me at Salen. Molde was so full that they had only been able to find lodgings in the grounds of an insane asylum, and their nerves had been much shaken by this added experience. He described the midnight on which the King and Government left for the north, and the French and English embarked on a warship for England. The bombardment was so terrific that they had lain flat on their stomachs for hours to avoid being hit by a bomb fragment. The bombing continued all the way over the North Sea until the party was within about fifty miles of the British coast. Madame Zorifopol decided to remain in Sweden, while her husband went to Bucharest for a short stay.

Two weeks later, when the invasion of the Low Countries shoved Norway onto a back page, I returned to the Grand Hotel. While I remained there I was bound to see nearly every day someone from Norway. A few people, on forty-eight-hour permits, would arrive, having convinced the Germans that they had necessary business in Stockholm. The lobby of the hotel became a clearing-house for aching Norwegian hearts, behind their brave and calm fronts. News from the north and from the south came in broken bits, and we all tried to get our bearings in the mêlée.

Neither the newspapers nor rumor gave any coherent picture of what was happening to the British or to the Norwegian forces. We did not know just where the Germans were attacking. Only now can one know that this and this happened at such a time.

North of Narvik the defense was, so people said, better organized than elsewhere. General Fleisher's Norwegian command had stood guard over the Finnish-Norwegian frontier during the Russian-Finnish War, and were to that extent "seasoned troops." The Germans, however, had succeeded in the first onslaught on Narvik because the land defenses there had not held up. They had entrenched themselves in the town and seized the Elvegården training ground to the north and several arsenals.

We got stories of the little detachment of cadets who had established a line from Kolbeinskaret by Gratangen, fifty miles north of Narvik, and had held an immensely larger German force for two days, long enough for mobilization to be completed.

With all of South Norway in German hands, it was perhaps too much to hope for something which would turn defeat to victory. Still, French troops had arrived at Narvik on April 30th; the Germans had been encircled and the town recaptured. Two companies of Scots Guards, French Chasseurs-Alpins, Foreign Legionnaires and Polish mountain detachments would have special talent for such fighting as the north demanded. Among the Legionnaires were Spaniards, veterans of their own Civil War; and one of the saddest stories of the war is that of twelve hundred lives lost at Narvik, eight hundred of them were Spanish.

The Germans were entrenched in the mountains. Constant reinforcements arrived by air. But north of Narvik the Germans were on the defensive and in retreat. The Norwegians pressed constantly, living in snow caves, as did the enemy.

The Norwegian, French and Polish troops chosen for the attack on Narvik had advanced to the embarkation places on the north shore of Rombak Fjord on Sunday evening,

May 26th. Simultaneously, the British warships advanced up the Ofoten Fjord and formed a semicircle north of the peninsula on which Narvik stood. The warships opened fire on all the points where German batteries had been spotted and where it was believed the German forces lay. Allied shore batteries from the north side of Rombak Fjord joined in. In the air, the R.A.F. engaged in reconnaissance. Other troops attacked from the south.

At midnight the first troops were shipped across the fjord in small boats. Polish and French troops were sent ahead to establish the necessary bridgeheads. They got across without meeting any strong opposition, but soon after the German batteries opened a fierce fire on the troops still waiting to be ferried across. The fire was answered from the warships. Then the German guns were silenced.

After the French and Polish troops had established themselves as bridgeheads, Norwegian troops followed and attacked the mountains east of Narvik from where the town was to be forced. Armored French cars were to have taken part but they got stuck in the soft sand of the beach and could not be moved.

The first attack seems to have taken the Germans by surprise, but reinforcements reached them quickly and there was severe fighting before the allied forces overcame them on the steep mountainside by Ornesset. Six big German bombing planes appeared and began a bombardment. None scored upon the British warships. When the planes left, the formidable part of German resistance was over, and after a twelve-hour battle, Narvik had been again in Norwegian hands—all that was left of Narvik, for many houses had been burned. The news of the victory acted in Sweden like the greatest stimulant. The numbing news from southern Norway was completely counterbalanced. For the moment it seemed as if surprises could work powerfully either way.

The often turbulent milling in the lobby was left behind in the glassed-in restaurant of the Grand Hotel. It looks out on an inlet from the sea, like a canal. The Venice of the North, to my eyes, is even more beautiful than Venetia. Balm to all our spirits were evenings over tables there, half terrace, half deck, while the deepening blue of twilight and the night enveloped the Palace across the water or dimmed the masted ships lying along the quay. Sometimes a moon would rise behind the Palace; always there was a marvel of the light in the summer night, that miracle of every summer in the north, like no other in the world.

On the 17th of May, we all foregathered in one of the largest Swedish churches, we who had lived in Norway, to hold a sacred service on the Norwegian National Independence Day. No gathering I ever attended made a greater impression on me. Deep and quiet feeling flowed among us all. When the Norwegian National anthem was sung, and the flag carried down from the chancel, there were tears in all eyes. Behind the placid faces of the north lie unplumbed depths of feeling. Like all still waters, someone said. I found myself remembering the year before. I had been touched at the way the Norwegians normally celebrate the patriotic holiday. Not with firecrackers and oratory, but with the singing of children. Thousands and thousands of them with their flags and flowers march to the Palace grounds to sing to the King. Like crocuses and bluebells, they spring up on the Palace Hill and their treble singing becomes an anthem not alone to the founding of modern Norway but to its future.

In Stockholm we missed the children. But the children are still there; and the future is still unwritten. And often when some Norwegian boy was telling his story of hair-breadth escape, and a fine outwitting of the enemy, I forgot to be sad, and said to myself, "Wait and see." There was the day the Mayor of Narvik turned up with his thriller. We were ready to hear the story of Narvik all over again. His was a story of how the Germans had been served by those fifth columnists who, either for pay or for enticement by the Germans, welcomed the invasion. When the Germans seized the town, they went directly to the only secret arsenal, which was in the neighborhood of the house of a Nazi named Müller. He was in Narvik ostensibly to check the iron content of the ore that was destined for Germany. He drew his pay from Krupp. The Mayor described the behavior of one Norwegian Colonel, a friend of Quisling, the arch-Nazi sympathizer in Oslo. He gave the order to his men not to shoot, and surrendered the city to the Germans. He later joined Quisling in the capital.

Mr. Broch, the Mayor, told how he tried to run the town under the Germans, how British warships appeared and attacked the town. In three days they succeeded in sinking all nine German destroyers in the harbor. He gave a vivid account of how the German sailors struggled ashore and made for the mountains behind Narvik. There were not many Germans left now and the men in the mountains were prevented from getting supplies by the Norwegian army, abetted by several hundred young men who stole out of Narvik at night to join their countrymen.

One evening the British Intelligence got in touch with the Mayor to ask about the British Consul and his staff, who had fled to the mountains and taken refuge in a road-mender's tool shed. As the Germans were scouring the mountains for Norwegian troops, it was thought safer to bring Mr. Gibbs and his men back to Narvik, even though the town was in enemy hands. The Consul and his staff, therefore, were wrapped in tarpaulins and put in the back of a truck like so many corpses. And indeed, more dead than alive, they had been driven into town and carried into a vacant house next door to one in which several German officers were quartered. The Nazis forebore to search the house, as a rumor was spread that it was quarantined because of some contagious disease.

Over the famous Swedish smörgåsbord at the Grand Hotel, the Mayor told me how hard it was to feed the British—"salted fish was all we had left in Narvik." But the very day the canned food ran out, a piece of luck befell the Norwegians who were befriending the British. A British shell blew up a German field telephone headquarters in the annex of the Royal Hotel. It was in the ruins that Mayor Broch found the sack of white grouse. The delicacy had evidently been intended for the table of the Nazi Command General, Dietl, and all the more delicious, therefore, to Consul Gibbs and Mayor Broch and a staff who were more than tired of salt fish.

From day to day the Nazis' grip on Narvik seemed to slip. By the end of May the situation became desperate. The Allies launched their final attack the evening of May 27th. There was fierce fighting on the outskirts for an hour and then the Germans withdrew first from the city and then along the railway line towards Sweden. The Germans who had crossed over from Sweden, disguised as Red Cross workers, began dynamiting factories, supply depots, piers, railroad tracks, and locomotive stalls before they left. Fierce fires raged and one burnt all of Narvik's supply of coal for the following winter.

The Mayor described how the Norwegians, French, English and Poles paraded through the streets and the British Consul came to view again.

Although after this Narvik was Norwegian again, the life did not perceptibly improve. Daily visits from German bombers, sometimes as many as twenty at a time, marred the sense of deliverance. The Allies had few anti-aircraft guns other than heavy machine-guns. The Nazi bombers were in control. What had not been destroyed by British shells and German dynamite was now being destroyed by German bombs. Only a few churches and suburban homes withstood the pounding.

The morale stood strong, however, until the rumor leaked out on June 3rd that the Allies were planning to leave on June 7th. The worst of it was the rumor proved true. Two battalions of French Legionnaires, some British troops and 2,000 or 3,000 Polish chasseurs embarked on waiting warships and transports. Then the Norwegians evacuated the town and Mayor Broch went down the coast to Harstad.

The Germans were left in supreme command of all of Norway, but we know now they had paid for their aggression with 70,000 German lives.

The Mayor now worked in an evacuation office, trying to organize Narvik's scattered population. Suddenly, on June 15th, he was arrested by the Germans. A radio broadcast, picked up by some Nazi listening post, had let it out to General Dietl how much the British Consul and the Mayor had enjoyed the General's white grouse.

"So that made me guess," said the Mayor, "that my own 'grouse was cooked.'"

Under guard at the local hotel at the time, he overheard the German adjutant discussing which prison to send him to. We looked around at the other diners and wondered about their stories.

"I noticed a little staircase near the kitchen which led down into the cellar," went on the Mayor. "A few minutes later my guards turned the other way and I raced into the kitchen and down the stairs. At the far end of the cellar a door led to the back yard. I ran and jumped onto a passing car. I yelled to the driver to speed. In a few minutes we screeched to a stop before the house where I had been staying. With my wife and child and a few belongings, I chartered a small fishing boat manned by two Norwegians and set sail from Harstad. Thank God for the heavy mist that cloaked our movements and hid us from Nazi eyes.

"With a friend of mine on an island we passed, we left some documents for safekeeping. We slept out that night on deck a safe distance from shore. Then down the coast we landed the next day at one of the wildest and most mountainous parts of the whole Norwegian shore. We wanted to get to the home of a friend, but there were Germans in the neighborhood and so we walked on. At an isolated farmhouse we got food and I arranged to have my wife and little girl stay there until they could reach my friend. Then, with a Lapp boy to guide me, I set out over the mountains towards Sweden. We plodded through snow that came up to

International News Photo

THE "NEW ORDER" COMES TO NORWAY

The city of Kristiansund after a three-day bombing by Nazi planes.

our waists at times and across icy streams. We had no skis and no snowshoes."

It must have been a terrible trip, and the sight of the Swedish soldiers on the frontier was something he will never forget. As I listened I thought how many hundreds of thousands of stories of escape were being told all over Europe—of escape and of "no escape."

Mr. Broch's plan was to continue his work at Harstad, to go right on getting relief for his people and, as soon as arrangements were made for his American visa, he set out across Siberia for San Francisco, with the blessings of the Norwegians who were in Stockholm.

"Nobody counts in war time," General Kuhn used to say to me in the Great War. "We are all only grains of sand on the seashore."

Who or what is important in war time?

There was the sad case of Mr. Thompson, rector of the English church Queen Maud attended in Oslo. He had escaped from the British Legation grounds by sliding down a drain pipe that ran from the garden into the sunken side street, just as the Nazi guards entered the gates. He had gone with the British to Elverum and, when we arrived in Stockholm, he was already there, without a sixpence and in very shabby clothes, and a letter from his Bishop in England saying the five pounds he enclosed were all and the most that could be sent him ever. Doubtless he was only one of the many clergymen of the Church of England who were uprooted by the Nazi tornado in one occupied country after another. Mrs. Mallet, the British Minister's wife, found him an overcoat and other necessities. It is not as easy as you think to shop in friendly attics for an outfit; and we all hoped the scholarly man, whose excellent extemporaneous sermons we had all enjoyed and whose prodigious memory could fish up endless passages of English prose or poetry, could be fitted into some schoolroom for "duration."

My old friends from Washington, Victor and Peggy Mallet, were wonderful, stretching the days to get their many duties done. There were British wounded and prisoners of war to trace and look after, political developments to watch, yet they still had time, invented time, to see their refugee friends. I watched her, though, grow paler and thinner every day. She never said anything, but I laid it to the fact that her own three children were in England and she seldom heard from them.

The Swedish Foreign Minister was now Mr. Gunther, whom I had met first when he was the Swedish Minister to Norway. I was constantly indebted to him for many courtesies both official and unofficial. His way of doing things made you aware that he was still the poet he had been in his youth. His face, illusive, gentle, with a withdrawn expression that seemed to be seeing other times and places, always reminded me that the statesman was still a poet. The official residence of the Foreign Minister is a museum piece. It was built in the seventeenth century and was one of the most spacious and charming houses I have ever known. It is all very well for decorators to deal in indirect lighting, but there is an air of "great occasion" only to be lit by crystal chandeliers, and Utrikesministerhotellet had wonderful ones. Fru Gunther was famous in Stockholm for her fine needlework and knowledge of line and materials. She is probably the only Foreign Minister's wife in the world whose hobby is making her own clothes.

Lunch I had often with the Sterlings and there met again one of the most charming good-will envoys our country has anywhere, the Countess Folke Bernadotte. She, as president of the American Woman's Club, not unlike our club in Oslo, asked me to make a speech on my experiences on April 9 and after, and in trying to give a coherent chronological story, I saw again how one's personal experience is nearly always just in scattered bits. Then, as in the many times I have spoken since, I have realized why the history of wars takes years to write.

Besides the Countess Bernadotte, another member of the Royal Family who was a familiar face at Legation occasions was the Prince Eugene, artist brother of King Gustav and the one who participated most in the building of the Stockholm Town Hall, which is, I think, a sort of lay cathedral in which are expressed not only the traditions of the north but their aspirations for the future.

Everywhere I went I was asked for news of Nancy and Leland Harrison. He had been American Minister in Stockholm from 1927 to 1929, but by the warmth of the inquiries, it is my guess that our present Minister in Berne and his wife were the most popular Americans who ever went to Sweden.

More and more as war raged south on the continent, Sweden, for all the refugees, and its minute-to-minute press, became, as the summer nights grew whiter, a pleasant place. Informal lunches and dinners went on, often at the prettiest and most attractive outdoor restaurant in Europe, Hasselbacken, and I often met and enjoyed the company of Mr. and Mrs. Axel Johnson. He is one of the great financiers of modern Sweden, and both of them are famous for their thoughtfulness to foreign visitors.

So we were all marking time when Mr. Hambro suddenly went north to Tromsö to confer with the King and his Government. He wrote me from Rovaniemi in Finland a short note to the effect that he was finding conditions in the country he was traveling through so adverse that he hoped I would delay my own journey to Tromsö a little longer. But other reports less discouraging came from returning soldiers. After all, I needed no special comforts, whatever Mr. Hambro might have wished for women diplomats, and Colonel Hayne, our military aide, agreed with me. Plans for my departure were quite in order when a message from the Swedish Foreign Minister, asking me to call, confused them. He told me that, for reasons which he was not at liberty to disclose, he would like to ask me to defer my journey once more. I waited. Several days later I saw him again and he told me in confidence that the British withdrawal from Norway was under way, and that King Haakon and his Government had decided to remove themselves to London. The secret was so well kept that no mishaps occurred. The evacuation was marvelously carried out. The Polish Minister and his wife, who had started north via Finland, before the step was agreed upon, alone reached Tromsö in time to go along.

I was disappointed that I had been unable to complete my mission and accompany the Norwegian Government to the British Isles, but I dare say I was of more real use in staying by the relief work for refugees in Stockholm than I would have been elsewhere. At least Mr. Oxholm, the Danish Minister, encouraged me to think so when he stopped on his way from Tromsö to Copenhagen.

"There was very little to do up there," he said, "and all communications are certainly better here in Sweden."

And I was completely reconciled when I received the confidential request from the Crown Prince of Norway, through our Embassy in London, that I accompany Princess Märtha and their children to the United States. They had been invited to come as guests of the President. Meantime, instructions had come from the Department of State directing my return home via Siberia and the Far East. The weather was very hot, and accounts of poor food and discomfort on the Trans-Siberian railway were not encouraging. The Crown Princess hesitated to take the children on so long and hard a trip. So we kept putting off naming a date to leave. Then Washington cabled, asking to be advised as to my plans. I answered, explaining the delay. Three days later came the news that the President had ordered a transport sent to Petsamo to fetch the Royalties, Mrs. Sterling and family, myself and such American citizens "and their spouses" as still remained in that part of Europe.

Telegrams flew to all Legations and Embassies within reach asking a report on how many applicants each had. The returns ran over a thousand. The captain of the transport, then en route to Petsamo, radioed the capacity of his ship and a halt was called on passengers at 895. We should rather have asked him how many women and children he could put up comfortably. He had replied in terms of doughboys, 910, and the point about army passengers is that they can take a lot of rigor, and the very word regimentation comes from regiment.

Nearly a thousand people of all ages and sizes and experience and inexperience to take over uncertain mileage to

Petsamo! It was not a simple problem, but once again I began to feel proud of Americans. One of the General Motors officials came to bat, got in a Travel Bureau, mobilized bus service, arranged for food along the road; and as always, there was Freddie Sterling, a sagacious general, remembering everybody, and smoothing all sorts of passport snarls and ticket troubles.

CHAPTER XX

THE "AMERICAN LEGION"

THERE WERE TIMES in Stockholm when America seemed a dream, only the strange sense of shipwreck and commotion in Europe seemed real; but, as plans were settled and the journey to America was routed and dated, it was the world about me that seemed dreamlike. The summer nights, ever longer, ever whiter, had begun to steal upon us. Goodbyes that wrenched were being said. Then one night we were off, my motor put on the train for Haparanda. I listened to the stories of the old days of the last war, and before it when there had been no rail connection between Sweden and the Empire of the Czars, and the Grand Duchy of Finland, and of how the twenty-five kilometres between the two countries was made by passengers in sledges and droshkies. By so much as rails meeting, Sweden and Finland were united now.

The overnight trip was a slow one. We got out at Haparanda at half past three the next afternoon, and spent the night in the only uncomfortable and not too clean hotel I ever saw in either Norway or Sweden. Here we had our first glimpse of our ship's company. A large contingent of mothers and children, the children already tired, began to arrive at the junction, and we saw them rounding up at the hotel for supper. I felt sorry for the mothers who I knew had another night on trains before them and twenty hours by bus before they came to Petsamo. My own journey, because of the Ford, was going to be wearying but would be quiet and give me a snatch of intimate glimpses of Finland. Our first stop was at Rovaniemi. Salute to the Finns! At tea time in that northern waste, for the country was lonely and full of scrub Arctic pine, we came upon a large, modern hotel, the very flower of modern construction. The hotel had been partially destroyed by the Russians less than six months before, but the Finns have brought the zeal to reconstruction that they brought to war. At tea in the pleasant rooms, with simple, beautifully made furniture and hand-woven curtains and tablecloths, I laid the foundations for a hope that, when this war is over, man's energy will really make a better world to replace what is being destroyed. We can make material structures over again; but who will bring back the dead?

A fleet of buses was being loaded with luggage and with people. I was to take the same road to Ivalo first, through the forests of small trees, stunted like gnomes. All night we drove under the opal sky, for it was never dark, and the desolate country laid some weird spell upon us. One could not sleep. Hour by hour through the wild emptiness we sped on the Arctic Highway. Now an antlered deer or a whole herd of the beautiful creatures would rush across the road ahead of us. Then abruptly we came upon Ivalo, people, noise, busloads of Americans Petsamo-bound, and supper! It was half past two in the morning. Colonel Waddell, the

United States Military Attaché in Sweden, was there superintending the transportation of our refugees, and we exchanged greetings over the very welcome hot food. Then we pushed on to Inari, a fishing lodge where Fred Sterling and I had heard there was marvelous trout fishing. One more trout, I said, before I leave the north. The little inn lay on the river bank closed in by forest. It was still under repair—the Finns had used it as a hospital—but it was spotless. The water rushed and tumbled over the stones like a medley of lullabies, so that sleep came easily, tired as we were, and with the music of such waters.

The next day Freddie Sterling and his family caught up with us, still resting at Inari. Had it not been for a sudden rumor that, after five months of no hostilities, the Russians were about to start things again, perhaps I should have caught my trout. But the Finnish men were swiftly mobilized again and not a gaffer was to be had; and as amateur fishermen, we had all the wrong hunches. The fish were certainly running elsewhere. One of the younger Sterling boys caught one tiny trout; but we will all always swear that Inari is a fisherman's paradise and worth traveling far to wind a reel in.

August 11th. I laugh now as I look at my diary. Nothing there but that we were setting out at 8 A.M. The drive, I remember, was long and tedious, but as we traveled we had to imagine what its loneliness had been in winter, for here some of the fiercest fighting in the Finnish-Russian War took place. Acres of forest had been felled. We could see the huts and round houses built by the Russians just as they had left them. We stopped and walked around them and into them. Perhaps Russians do not mind cold and discomfort.

They must have had their fill of them. One encampment ran a mile long on either side the road, with camouflaged shelters and block houses still standing in the deserted scene.

There was still evidence of dead horses. Dead Russians, too, for in the snow at the time the Russians left, the dead must have been hidden in the bush. And now, there was more to do in Finland than assist wind and weather to eliminate traces of man and beast. No monument has yet been built on the site where seven hundred and fifty Finns stood off 20,000 to 30,000 Russians from November to March, but the legend halts all travelers and is already strong as granite.

All along the road we came on small encampments of Finnish soldiers, veterans still contending, determined not to live under Russian domination. "We had rather fight to the last man!"

I remembered the American on her way to and from Finland who used to call at the Legation in Oslo.

"Geography is the master of us all. When the Finns and the Russians finally see that peace can be made with as much violence and energy as war, that will be the beginning of the new life in Europe. And the devil take the Germans in the north."

How the Finns work! We saw an old woman building herself a house out of crates and odds and ends. It was a house! We saw a burned farm where we had heard, in a Russian broadcast the winter before, that a "city had been taken." It was at least all the city that there was. We continued on through the military zone, and passed many huts where whole families of Finns were biding whose farms had been destroyed. The bombing of the road had been pretty awful, for much of it was still under construction and repair, and we passed several wrecked trucks which had slid onto the soft shoulders as they turned out to let others pass. One thousand trucks ply on the Arctic Highway between Haparanda and Petsamo. It is now the only trade artery to the Scandinavian countries except through Siberia.

Now and again the road leads not far from the Norwegian border, only a narrow stretch of water lies between. My heart ached as I looked across at the land I might never see again; and if I was homesick, how must the Crown Princess have turned her eyes to the last glimpses of her adopted land, when she followed that same road to Petsamo. For she and her children were coming with us to the safety of America.

At long last we passed a little Russian church with its onion cupolas. The harbor and docks of Petsamo were just beyond.

Petsamo! For centuries it has been a cold stone of contention among Finns, Swedes, Norwegians and Russians, the stretch of Arctic coast changing hands many times. Sometimes it was held in common by two or three; but in the fighting and contending, honest husbandry was often forgotten.

I am afraid that more than one of the homeward-bounds felt like retreating, for not even the *American Legion,* as it lay out in the stream, seemed very inviting. And as the dreary business of getting eight hundred and ninety-five passengers and their luggage from shore aboard her went on, and those who arrived first found fault with their accommodations, clamored for better places, more than one of us thought regretfully of the Trans-Siberian as possibly the more attractive way out. The ship was just a transport normally equipped to carry nine hundred troops. The Commanding General's quarters were luxurious enough, and these of course were allotted to the Royal Party. The hundred first-class and fifty second-class cabins were not too uncomfortable. The orders from Washington were that these should be saved for very old people, invalids, and women with small children. As we had three hundred children amongst our refugees, the so-called good quarters were soon filled; and there was no other way of transporting those who would be safe but by simply allotting the refugees fifty to a hatch, men and women separated. In the hatches, the hammocks were hung two side by side, three tiers of them. There were no closets; clothes had to be hung at the head and foot of the beds. And the result was awful, I suppose, unless of course you had an eye and a sense of humor and felt that God was good that you were moving home at all. Then you merely looked and laughed, because it all seemed like a floating Klein's store, and as exciting as Union Square. Many American wives of Swedes and Norwegians spent twelve and fourteen hours a day in these below-hatch jungles, and they simply took it in their stride.

Give me a first-rate crisis and I can tell you what people are. It is easy to be mannerly and kind when things run smooth. Lieutenant-Colonel Burns, army officer in command, never lost his poise and good temper. When things would wind up in some sort of threatened hectic outburst, he would simply smile and say:

"Oh, no, I'm the one who took so many loads of Gold Star mothers to Europe and back, and we had few casualties. I can't be floored by *this.*" Nor could he. Hundreds of requests for better accommodations and better weather always found him somehow so pleasant that there were those who felt that things really *had* improved, so tactful was he even about seasickness. Diplomatically he soothed us all.

I told him the story of the American woman who was on the Bergen-Newcastle boat on one of my crossings. There is an unusually heavy ground swell off the Norwegian coast. It happened to come that time just as we were all at lunch, with a tremendous shattering of crockery.

"Steward," she called, "this is ridiculous. Send for the Captain. He must have it stopped at once."

The two days we waited for orders in Petsamo harbor were dark and gloomy. Everybody thought everybody else was under foot; somebody of course must have remained over foot, said one of the older youngsters. To add to the confusion, all who had not been vaccinated were told to roll up the sleeve, according to Immigration law, and then for good measure they each had an anti-typhoid shot. And the after effect of all these precautions was, shall we say, a lowered amiability.

But to offset this, our captain was the best navigator in the Transport Service, chosen especially for this delicate and dangerous job through hazardous seas. And it was always interesting to see how the ship's crew managed to make us comfortable at all. The individual tables had had to be removed from the first-class dining room, and planks on trestles put in their places. At that, three servings were necessary. The Mexican Minister to Sweden and the other officials ate in the smaller second-class dining room with the ship's officers.

Our bad start, waiting for orders in Petsamo harbor from the Navy Department in Washington, sawed on the nerves of many. The rumors flew thick and fast—"We sail in an hour"—"Here we lie for three or four days." At 2 A.M. Saturday, August 16, the order having come, we sailed, our course presumably down the coast of Norway, across the North Sea, through the passage between the Shetland Islands and the north of Scotland.

We could not quite understand this route. "Sticking our necks out, we are," said one of the officers. He did not tell us the British had refused to guarantee our safety over the northern route. Perhaps he did not know. Petsamo harbor had been thickly sown with mines; we seemed to be edging out by a very narrow path off shore. All that first night and the next day we moved through the mine field, and for those who knew anything about the last war or this one, it was an anxious time. With your voice and manner you could seem to have banished the thought, but underneath you simply could not help remembering photographs and stories of how one minute all was well "and then the ship struck a mine!" But we came through to a Sunday of such fine sailing weather that the whole ship's company relaxed and there was a pleasant air of peacetime North Cape cruise about us. Monday and the day after, mines again, as we passed within sight of the Shetlands, the lifeboats swung out and eight men on watch. Our last night in those waters my heart was wrung for the Captain, responsible for so many lives. In the high wind and rough water I doubt if a third of our three hundred children could have been saved. But there was no panic, and with a few exceptions none of the passengers showed what was passing in their minds by so much as taking their life preservers to their deck chairs.

Princess Märtha seldom moved about the deck, but the

little princesses and Prince Harald, in all weathers, played their games without even one faint shadow of seasickness. "The little Vikings" might have been born afloat. I was touched by the final scene before sailing when all the sailors from the Norwegian ships in the Petsamo harbor gathered on the dock and sang the national anthem in farewell to their Crown Princess and her children:

"Yes, we love this land that towers
Where the ocean foams;
Rugged, storm-swept, it embowers
Many thousand homes."

And also as the coast of Norway dropped away, and I saw her say goodbye to both her native and adopted lands, and face the four thousand miles of war-swept sea with her family. The children's father and grandfather were in England. Her own mother, Princess Ingeborg, was in Sweden.

Dorothy Sterling excited my admiration. She, too, was traveling with her three children, leaving their father behind, and she bore herself so cheerfully that she was a help to everyone. She and I had made a trip together in 1917, through submarine-infested waters, and all across the Atlantic wove our memories of the last war into our discussion of this one.

Two elderly women, who had been ill before leaving, one from Denmark and one from Sweden, died on board from heart trouble. One left an only daughter, quite young, who seemed very much alone in the world. It was pitiful to see her efforts to be brave, as indeed she was, when her mother, one midnight, was buried at sea.

Twelve days after our departure, we were met, still twenty-four hours from the home shore, by two destroyers, a guard of welcome and honor for Princess Märtha. A thrill ran over the whole boat; the sun came out in the high blue sky, and it was bright and calm as only the American eastern seaboard can be in August. The days of fog and dampness gave way and in jubilation we, who had heard the news, told the others about the night in mid-ocean when the German radio had falsely announced our sinking with a loss of six hundred passengers. Luckily this report had not reached the United States. War of nerves indeed!

Suddenly the whole trip seemed an omen of the future. We had had many nationalities aboard—Swedes, Finns, Norwegians, Danes, Estonians, Lithuanians, Dutch, Mexicans, French. What would remain always with us were the evenings when the Lithuanians, in native costume, lifted their fresh, young voices in the ancient songs of their people, and gave them to us. Not the discomfort, the odd little games of bridge, the fears; but the Lithuanian peasant songs, and the games on deck of the Norwegian royal children; and the sight of the New York skyline through a gray mist.

The next morning, in the pouring rain, we arrived at Quarantine. There the Royalties were met by the Norwegian Minister and a representative of the Department of State, and taken on a tug to the Battery. Also, at least twenty reporters with cameras came on board, and two Naval officers and an Army officer assigned to me as aides for the day. The officers were most welcome as they seemed to have had wide experience in handling news men. It was a comfort to have them tell me just how much and how little was necessary in the way of giving interviews.

The harbor of New York, the skyscrapers that had been

invented and built in my own lifetime, never looked so welcoming and wonderful as on the 28th of August, 1940. Behind me I had seen destruction of forts and homes and buildings, which might or might not be as nothing compared with the destruction of old ideas and old ways of living.

CHAPTER XXI

Some Observations of a Non-Career Diplomat

In my joy at seeing Ethel, the excitement of interviews and my official report to Secretary Hull and to the President, there was only pleasure and warmth. It was August. But always around the corner since my return there is, not chill fear, but constant speculation. For, no matter how much faith one has in the enduring values that were in the old life, one knows that change is upon us—in small intangible ways, in new questions asked, in new things taken for granted. It was interesting to me to find that questions that were agitating everyone when I left, that then seemed of lifelong importance, were now nearly forgotten. Entirely different ones had come to the fore and were causing the same agitation.

I know quite well that I have less chance than ever to "settle down." How do I know if another skyscraper will ever be built in New York; people talk of decentralization. Not merely because of hemisphere defense, but because already ten times as many of my friends have been to Rio de Janeiro as ever went before, I find myself meaning two continents instead of one when I speak of America.

After an absence of only three and a half years, it was apparent to me that America was moving into a period of fresh interest in international affairs. We begin to understand the relation between foreign and domestic politics; and are divided into two schools, those who put domestic issues first, and those who see no possible isolation in the new orientation of races and classes.

More than once since my appointment, and since my return from a post in the American Foreign Service, I have heard discussions of our system of choosing representatives to other nations. Those who plan to give their whole lives to the service and who work through all its branches, and study the history of the "science," the "art" and the "craft" of diplomacy are called Career Men; the others, the non-career appointments, are chosen either for distinguished service to the nation as a whole or to the party in power. The service may, say the critics, all too often be merely contribution to campaign funds. Even the severest are aware how many of our finest representatives from the very beginning of our nation have brought not riches but experience of the United States at large to the business of dealing with other countries. Benjamin Franklin was one of our first and best. When in doubt about anything, a Philadelphia friend of mine always says, try to recall some chapter in the life of the old printer.

As a non-career diplomat, my conclusion is that our system of mixed appointments is a good one. I have to stand up for my own inexperience, of course, since it gave me so often a fresh point of view and a special zest for my job. I found that, in times of crisis, I could improvise action, without stopping to think too much of the usual red tape or protocol. But the career diplomats are always the enduring bones of the service. I cannot be grateful enough that my first Secretary of Legation, Jefferson Patterson, was one of them. How indefatigable, loyal and patient he was in helping me to supplement the instructions given me in Washington about the duties of my office. How well he knew the service history; the practices of other countries; the precise meaning of every technical word. I needed him. His diplomacy was ingrained, too; he accepted women as citizens, and me as his chief, with a grace that was gratifying to me personally, and which made an excellent impression on the Norwegian statesmen we dealt with.

H. G. Wells, I think, has commented more times than one on the fact that foreign ministers, ambassadors and diplomatic methods came into existence in the days of personal monarchy in the seventeenth century, to promote dynastic interests and mutual aggressions of the various kings and princes of Europe. The common people barely existed then as a factor in international affairs. They were passive, and often passive victims in the European game. Though the world has begun to change with horrendous rapidity, diplomatic methods remain, for the most part, what they were. Though the machinery of communication makes it necessary for diplomats to compete with newspapers, travelers and pressure groups, they still cling to the old ways. Neither career nor non-career diplomats, as my own experience in Norway taught me, are as important as once they seemed.

I blush now to remember that, years ago, when my husband was considering accepting a minor post in the Service, my instant notion was that it would just be lots of fun, gay parties, and meeting people at Court, traveling to "strange and foreign places."

In those long ago days, before two wars, and the whole break-up of Europe of the nineteenth century, it may have been natural to think of the Foreign Service in such amiable but frivolous terms. Not now. Not ever any more, for it seems to me that the business of the American Foreign Service is to make a great contribution to the eventual democratization of all diplomacy. Our mission everywhere is to convince people of the benefits of our own democracy, to make our connections when we go abroad, not merely with the sovereign, the Government and privileged society, but with the democratic elements wherever we may find them.

The essence of democracy lies not only in the form of any government but also in the care with which the Government benefits all classes and all persons in such a way that the humblest feels himself a part of and in communication with whatever community he lives in. This freedom and this sociability make the post of diplomat from abroad harder but richer in experience. It is no longer enough that the duties of diplomatic office should begin and end with occasional calls at the Foreign Office, and dining out in society. Yet the notion persists in many minds that this is so, and that all diplomats are snobs. Only the other day a well-known man argued with me:

"My son wants to go into the diplomatic service, but I won't have it. The young cubs I have met abroad with condescending manners as if they were made of finer stuff than the rest of their countrymen are no part of the life I want for him."

I told him that, plainly, much of the name for snobbery

in the service was utterly undeserved; and was a charge brought against serious government servants who knew quite well that their jobs did not begin and end with entertaining the hundreds of thousands of traveling Americans who wanted "lunch at the Embassy" or an introduction at Court. Perhaps there does seem to be a "better than thou" attitude in a few members of the Diplomatic Corps, but that is a question of individual failing, more than anything else. The discerning man realizes that there is nothing more stupid than being a snob. Snobs, in cutting people off from themselves, are cutting themselves off from people, and this, from a purely selfish standpoint, is foolish because nowadays one never knows who will come to the top and have one's number, so to speak. As a matter of fact, a snob has no place in the Diplomatic Service today, nor anywhere else, for that matter.

If, by and large, those who could afford to take posts in the Foreign Service had to be rich, it was because the upkeep of an Embassy was something not everyone could take on. Ex-Ambassador Hugh Gibson, in a magazine article, made it plain that the low pay in the service had proved an enormous hardship for many junior members without private means, especially when in the absence of his Chief in Legation or Embassy the younger man was obliged to continue the official entertaining.

The Department of State has never fared as well in appropriations as the Army and Navy, and the Diplomatic Service has become a little sensitive, a sort of stepchild of Congress, though no Americans traveling abroad are so exigent, or expect as much of our Foreign Missions, as our Senators and

Representatives, and their sisters and their cousins and their aunts, and their friends besides!

Happily, in Oslo, there was no rent for the Minister to pay, for 28 Nobelsgate is owned by the United States Government and there is a small allowance for its upkeep. But, in general, ministerial salaries in the U. S. Foreign Service are by no means as adequate as those of many other nations. Once in Norway, the French Minister, making a report for the Quai d'Orsay, sent around a questionnaire to all Legations asking about the salaries paid to the staff. We politely filled in ours promptly and completely; and were very amused when it was returned with a note saying that surely we had made a mistake. He wanted the Minister's salary, not just that of the Secretaries of Legation.

If there are complaints that often posts in the Foreign Service are the perquisites of the favored classes, this matter of emolument may have something to do with it. But again, some of the best of our non-career diplomats have been men of learning and of modest means—Claude Bowers, now in Chile, for example, and Nelson Johnson in China. And, regardless of money, career diplomats like Ambassadors Grew in Japan, William Phillips in Rome, Norman Armour in the Argentine and Fred Sterling in Stockholm, as well as Ex-Ambassador Henry Fletcher and others now retired, have been hard workers and have given distinguished service that has made history.

One thing more. It has not always lately been easy to be an American Minister abroad. How often when discussing the mistakes of Europe's statesmen, sadly as the alarums preceding this new war were heard—now faint to the east, now loud to the south—some government personage would look at me, representative of a safe and remote continent that once was a solution for many of Europe's problems of overpopulation and political and economic discontent, and say, with thinly veiled bitterness in his voice, "But your hands are not clean either."

And a wave of regret for this whole last quarter of a century would pour over me. For I think that most of us must see now that Woodrow Wilson was right. The United States should have been a party to the League of Nations. We should at least have given it a trial, for it remains, even now, the only form of collective international effort that has yet been suggested. We brushed the League aside. It never really lived because the United States withdrew. This I believe. Advocates of the League in America and England used to warn its opponents that, when chaos broke loose again, theirs would be a share in the blame. The Sin of Omission, the sin of the selfish, marches with the Sin of Commission, the sin of the brutal.

How truly Ernest Hemingway quoted John Donne at the beginning of his novel about Spain:

> "No man is an *Iland* intire of it selfe; every man is a peece of the continent, a part of the *maine;* if a *clod* bee washed away by the *Sea,* Europe is the lesse as well as if a Promontorie were, as well as if a mannor of thy friends or of thine owne were; any man's death diminishes me, because I am involved in Mankinde, and therefore never send to know for whom the bell tolls. It tolls for *thee.*"

And for myself, as the months of this new war pile agony on agony, and the tale of the winter of 1941 is written, I want to repeat the prayer of the sixteenth century Queen Elizabeth of England:

"Thou, O Lord, provideth enough for all men with thy most liberal and bounteous hand, but whereas thy gifts are, in respect to thy goodness and free favor, made common to all men, we, through our naughtiness, niggardships, and distrust, do make them private and peculiar. Correct thou the thing which our iniquity hath put out of order, and let thy goodness supply that which our niggardliness hath plucked away."

There is no future for a Christian world but in truly and generously respecting the dignity of all men, and in working relentlessly (I choose this word) that some equality of opportunity be common to all races and classes. It is plain that the "under-privileged" define themselves in no such blurred word. They feel themselves "restrained from rights." In Norway I found joyful assurance that a Christian world is practical and that sharing creates abundance. From my privileged experience as a non-career diplomat, I draw fresh reading of Queen Elizabeth's prayer. There must come a sharing of all food, and of all culture. Democracy at home and abroad offers us on liberal terms a vista of endless possibilities.

INDEX

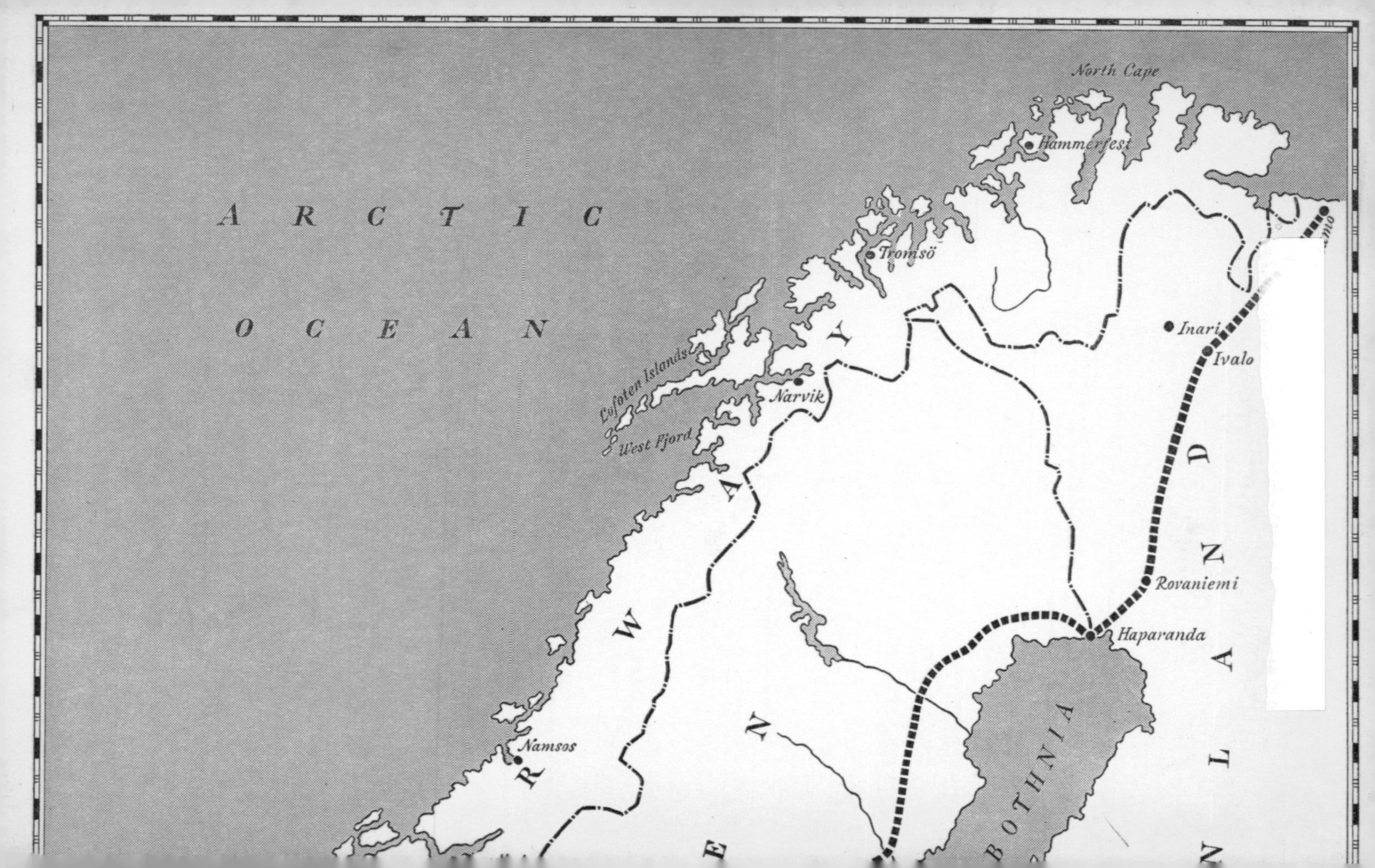
ARCTIC
OCEAN
North Cape
Hammerfest
Tromsö
Lofoten Islands
West Fjord
Narvik
Inari
Ivalo
Rovaniemi
Haparanda
Namsos
BOTHNIA